"Can it really be, a journalist's memoir that is funny, charming, and immensely literate? The answer is yes. Jack Germond has written a wonderful, engaging book about covering American politics in an era when journalists and politicians still talked to each other and the game was still fun."
—David Halberstam

"For political junkies, Jack Germond's *Fat Man in a Middle Seat* is a high treat. Germond is a total professional and a decent human who has covered it all for 40 years and can still laugh about it."
—Molly Ivins

"Reading *Fat Man in a Middle Seat* is like sitting in a bar with Germond long after midnight. . . . Read this book to discover how a great reporter operated—and had fun doing it."
—*National Review*

"[A] colorful reporter's memoir . . . Germond has built up a bank of tales as substantial as his waist line. . . . Candid and often hilarious."
—*Newsday*

"Germond . . . has traded toasts with many of the nation's leading postwar pols. And the book is at its most engaging when he delivers his personal critiques of those figures. . . . Marbled throughout *Fat Man in a Middle Seat* are clear examples of how the politics/journalism equation has changed. . . . Germond is clearly no devotee of the introspective, self-flagellating brand of journalism. And it's refreshing to read a book about the media that doesn't lecture on how to restore faltering public trust in the fourth estate."
—*The Atlanta Journal-Constitution*

"When Jack Germond covers a campaign, he attracts as much interest as the candidates he writes about. People across the country seem genuinely glad to see this modern Falstaff, a balding oracle of wisdom and humor in a field of blow-dried, superserious talking heads. With scores of inside sources, political knowledge has always been his specialty."
—*George* magazine

"Its smooth blend of self-needling irony and unapologetic embrace of modest expectations is representative of this outstanding reporter's memoir. . . . Throughout a long career as a political correspondent and columnist . . . he has been a reporter's reporter. . . . Germond doesn't like to make himself the issue, but his consistent voice infuses the book with his character. Rumpled, cantankerous and blessed with a sense of humor as dry as the best martini, Germond tells great political stories and tells them expertly."
    —*Publishers Weekly* (starred review)

"Engaging memoir by a veteran columnist, reporter, and pundit. Germond is a reporter's reporter. . . . Germond takes politics and reporting, though not himself, seriously, and still believes some good may come from both. His optimistic cynicism is refreshing."
    —*Kirkus Reviews*

"Germond raking a deserving politician over the coals makes for good fun even if you don't know one politician from the other. His prose is witty, his anecdotes are amusing . . . his points are well taken, and overall, he's as hard on himself as he is on anyone else."
    —*Booklist*

"Such fun to read."
    —*Baltimore* magazine

JACK GERMOND has been the political columnist for the *Baltimore Sun,* Gannett bureau chief in Washington, and a columnist and editor for the now-defunct *Washington Star*. He first appeared on *Meet the Press* in 1972 and was a regular on the *Today* show, CNN, and *The McLaughlin Group*. He now serves as a panelist on *Inside Washington* and as a commentator for National Public Radio. He lives in Charles Town, West Virginia.

FAT MAN
IN A
MIDDLE
SEAT

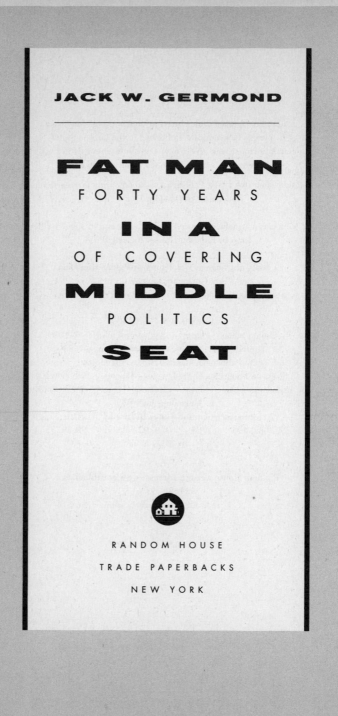

JACK W. GERMOND

FAT MAN
FORTY YEARS
IN A
OF COVERING
MIDDLE
POLITICS
SEAT

RANDOM HOUSE
TRADE PAPERBACKS
NEW YORK

RANDOM HOUSE TRADE PAPERBACKS and colophon are registered
trademarks of Random House, Inc.

This work was originally published in hardcover and in slightly different
form by Random House, Inc., in 1999.

Library of Congress Cataloging-in-Publication Data
Germond, Jack W.
Fat man in a middle seat: forty years of covering politics / by Jack W. Germond.
p.   cm.
ISBN 0-375-75867-4
1. United States—Politics and government—1945–1989.
2. United States—Politics and government—1989–
3. Politicians—United States Anecdotes.
4. Press and politics—United States—History—20th century.
5. Presidents—United States—Election—History—20th century.
6. Germond, Jack W.
7. Journalists—United States Biography.   I. Title.
E839.5.G395   1999   070′.92—dc21   99-29753
[B]

Random House website address: www.atrandom.com
24689753
First Trade Paperback Edition

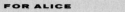

FOR ALICE

In 1959 Nelson Rockefeller offered me a job on his staff. He had just been elected governor of New York and he clearly intended to run for president of the United States. He looked like a good prospect, and I liked him. By any conventional measure, the offer was a handsome one. The salary would be twice what I was making as a thirty-one-year-old political reporter for the Gannett Newspapers and, I was told by the intermediary who made the offer, perhaps significantly higher if that was the only sticking point. There would be perquisites—a lavish expense allowance, walking-around money, the use of a car and driver (particularly attractive if you live in New York, as I did then), and a staff of my own choice. If Rockefeller abandoned politics or if I tired of it after a few years, there would be a place for me working on one of the intellectually interesting and altruistic projects of the Rockefeller Brothers Fund.

I turned it down without a moment's hesitation. It was not a difficult decision. I was a reporter just getting his first opportunity to cover national politics, so why would I want to become a flack, even for a Nelson Rockefeller? The rules were clear then. If you once crossed the line from journalism into partisan politics, you could not return. They were them and we were us.

I wouldn't suggest, however, that my decision was founded on some dedication to journalistic principle. I didn't become a reporter because I felt a commitment to public service. I had no illusions about changing the world and no particular interest in doing so. I didn't go around wringing my hands about the people's right to know. I was a reporter because it was fun. I liked being paid to satisfy my curiosity. I liked the fact that I didn't have to sell anything or butter up the boss. I liked the idea of being judged by what you did every day. When you screwed up, there was always another chance tomorrow. I enjoyed writing. I relished picking up the newspaper and reading my own byline—by Jack W. Germond. (I began using the middle initial to avoid any confusion when I heard of another Jack Germond, who was a banker in Adrian, Michigan, and, perish the thought, an active member of the Junior Chamber of Commerce.) I always read my stories through to the end to see what some wretched deskman had done to my copy. I still do.

Like so many of my generation, I had started as a sportswriter, only to discover very quickly that it is boring work even if you love sports. I had covered city hall and labor for a small daily in Michigan, and I had done some investigative reporting for Gannett Newspapers in cities in which the Mafia's influence was particularly conspicuous or the city officials particularly corrupt. But my indignation threshold was too high to sustain me as an investigative reporter. I couldn't get worked up about the mayor getting his driveway paved with public asphalt.

I gravitated to political writing early. Reporters usually end up covering the stories they enjoy the most, and they find their own level within a few years. I loved politics and, I confess, I enjoyed politicians immensely. They can be craven, exploitative, and sometimes dishonest. But they are good company, and you can always figure their motives. They want the next higher office within reach and greater power and influence. And, believe it or not, most of them want to accomplish some purpose that, by their lights, is worthwhile. You might not agree with either their goals or their methods, but most of them are serious people with serious aims they would like to fulfill. Moreover, they have the nerve to put themselves on the line. Watching a politician waiting for the returns election night is an engrossing experience because you know that he—or she—believes he deserves 100 percent of the vote and takes every ballot counted for the other guy as a personal affront.

After more than forty years I still enjoy covering politics. But the business has deteriorated in many ways. There are fewer colorful or interesting politicians; there is too much pressure on them to be politically correct. There are too many young men and women whose aims are harsh and negative, people who come into politics while excoriating it to reflect—and, of course, to exploit—the alienation in the electorate. There are too many politicians who mistake their public roles with a license to hand down decrees on morality under the rubric of family values.

Meanwhile, press coverage has become too controlled by the lowest common denominator. The television networks set the national agenda even as they devote fewer and fewer resources to covering politics. The power of television has nothing to do with its quality, as I have discovered in almost twenty years as one of the talking heads, first on NBC's *Today* show, then on *The McLaughlin Group* and Cable News Network, and now as a regular panelist on *Inside Washington* and occasionally on *Meet the Press* and *Washington Week in Review.* Some of my writing colleagues sniffed at my joining the dispensers of instant wisdom on camera, but I don't apologize. It has allowed me to continue reporting and writing for newspapers while making a decent living rather than becoming an editor sitting in an office juggling travel budgets and listening to other reporters whine about how the copydesk has screwed up their stories once again.

That is what this book is about—forty years of politics and reporting on it. When people ask me how long I intend to go on covering campaigns, I always reply that I'll do it until they get it right. I no longer expect that to happen.

ACKNOWLEDGMENTS

I know that it is customary for an author to acknowledge the assistance of enough people to suggest that writing the book was a project roughly equivalent to building another pyramid. In my case, it was largely painless thanks to three people: My agent, David Black, who nagged me into writing it; my editor at Random House, Ian Jackman, who was consistently relaxed and good-humored and has the added virtue of being a baseball fan; and my wife, Alice, who has an ear for false notes among her many virtues. My daughter Jessica has listened patiently to many of these journalistic war stories several times over the years. My stepdaughter, Abigail, helped me gain a proper focus on Bill Clinton. And my stepson, David, and his wife, Yukari, have helped me solve some of the mysteries of computer technology.

The people who most deserve my thanks are the hundreds, perhaps thousands, of politicians and newspapermen with whom I have spent my life. I am especially grateful to two reporters I considered myself privileged to count as friends because of their personal qualities and willingness to tolerate mine, Bill Ringle and Tom Ottenad. Both set standards of professional performance unexcelled in my experience. And, of course, I owe an everlasting debt to my partner, Jules Witcover, who set an example any political reporter would be proud to replicate.

Finally, I am indebted to competitors and colleagues in the political reporting dodge with whom I shared so many laughs over the last forty years: Dan Balz, the late Bruce Biossat, Ken Bode, David Broder, Hal Bruno, Don Campbell, Jim Dickenson, Jim Doyle, the late Leo Egan, Tom Edsall, John Farmer, Pat Furgurson, Ed Hale, Bob Healy, Herb Kaplow, the late Peter Lisagor, Jon Margolis, John Mashek, Walter Mears, Loye Miller, Jim Naughton, Martin Nolan, Bob Novak, David Nyhan, the late Emmet N. O'Brien, Jim Perry, Richard Valeriani, the late Warren Weaver, Jr., Paul West, Curtis Wilkie, and David Yepsen. Good company.

CONTENTS

FAT MAN

IN A

MIDDLE

SEAT

CHAPTER 1

—

A DETACHED LIFE

I never worried about politics while I was growing up; I don't remember politics or world affairs ever being discussed at home. I have read about those families who sat around the dinner table talking about the Great Books or the news of the day, but we were not one of them. My father was an engineer preoccupied with his work. My mother listened to the soaps and gossiped endlessly but harmlessly with her friends about her other friends. If she had any interests beyond her own life, she kept them well hidden from her only child. Nor was I the kind of kid who had a precocious interest in serious matters. My life revolved almost totally around sports and, once I reached the proper age, shooting pool and trying to get girls into the backseat of the car, an enterprise at which I was not notoriously successful.

The family came from New England. The Germonds were French Huguenots; according to family legend, my forebears sailed on whaling ships out of the Hudson River ports. My mother's family was Scottish. There were some Indians on my father's side, although he was a little uncomfortable about admitting it, even until the day he died at ninety-two. But I remember a picture of a great-grandmother who looked like a squaw in a Tom Mix western, and my father's mother, whom I met only two or three times as a small child, had straight black hair and prominent cheekbones often seen in Indians. But we were a family largely isolated from relatives. My father had a brother, but I have no memory of ever meeting Uncle Arthur. There was also a half sister, Aunt Edith, whom I met a few times but never came to know. We never saw my mother's brothers and sisters after her parents died while I was a youngster. There were several cousins on both sides with whom I played a few times as a child. Later I wouldn't have known them if I had met them on the street.

We were striving middle class. My father never went to college, a failure that weighed heavily on him for his entire life, but he had taken night courses to qualify as a mechanical engineer and later as an electrical engineer and as a specialist in heating and air-conditioning. Late in life, when he was living in Maine, he developed a special interest in the use of solar energy in cold climates, a topic on which he could deliver a forty-five-minute lecture at the drop of a question. He worked in housing for years, and the family fortunes seem to rise and fall with his different jobs. On more than one occasion I had the impression things went sour on the job because my mother didn't get along with the other company wives. At times we seemed to be scraping along, at others we had some household help, a cook perhaps and, for one glorious interlude in Trenton, a young live-in maid named Maria who came from somewhere in eastern Europe and cheerfully gave me introductory lessons in the mysteries of life that obsess twelve-year-old boys. When we were flush, my mother, who had grown up a Methodist, would suddenly become an Episcopalian. At one point she even had me confirmed, whatever that meant, at a very uptown Episcopal church in Trenton.

When I look back on those days from a distance of several decades, I am struck by how detached we were from family and the community around us. I wonder if growing up as a peripatetic outsider was one of the reasons I gravitated toward the newspaper business, where a healthy detachment is an essential quality of a reporter's success. I was born in Boston. We moved every two or three years—so often that I attended ten different schools in my elementary and secondary years. We lived in and around Boston until I was ten, then spent three years in Trenton before moving on to Mississippi and Louisiana, where I finished high school in Baton

Rouge just as World War II was coming to an end. I was always the new kid in school, which sometimes intrigued the girls but seemed to require fistfights with the boys whose turf I was invading.

The South was particularly traumatic for a Yankee in those days. Southerners seemed remarkably defensive and prickly, quick to take offense. If you called someone a son of a bitch, he would take it literally as a judgment on his mother rather than as a passing comment. The result was often a fight and, on my end, a torn ear or a fat lip or both. The boys most admired were those known as battlers, but I never qualified. I spent one fall semester at Ocean Springs, Mississippi, High School, while my father was working for a company building prefabricated rafts for the Navy. We lived in a run-down resort hotel, which marked me as different. And my hard-soled shoes and hand-knitted sleeveless sweaters, a specialty of my mother's, confirmed that I was an alien presence, one with unhealthy designs on Dixie Ann Weider—to the severe discomfort of her brother and several classmates with similar designs on her who felt obliged to punch me out. I lived long enough in Baton Rouge, however, to get past those initial hostilities and to make some friendships that have endured in one or two cases for fifty years.

Race was a complicating factor for a Yankee moving into the South during World War II. I had gone to junior high school with a few colored kids, as they were called there, but never thought much about it one way or another. The most memorable encounter was with a Hispanic, a black-haired, golden-skinned kid the rest of us thought was some kind of Indian. We were taking boxing in physical education class and reached a point at which someone was going to have to fight the Indian kid, although we were all terrified because he looked so implacably tough. When our reluctance grew embarrassing, I finally volunteered, since I was the right size for the matchup. I was scared to death. I will never forget the relief I felt when tears welled in his eyes after I hit him on the nose with a left jab. He was, after all, just like me. A punch in the nose and the tears pop out.

There was not such easy epiphany involving blacks. In the South in those days there was no debate about race relations or equal rights of which I was aware. They were just the "niggers" who cooked our food, washed our clothes, cut our grass, and kept out of our way on the streets. Some of the sons of even the "best families" in Baton Rouge would spend an occasional Friday or Saturday night "nigger knocking"—driving through the black section of the city and setting upon black men at random. They didn't all do it, but the ones who did always seemed to resent my unwillingness to join them. I wish I could say I was making a statement of principle, but it would be more accurate to say I was just puzzled. One of the things I discovered as a reporter years later was that racial attitudes were remarkably and enduringly harsh in Louisiana, for reasons that were never clear to me.

At Baton Rouge High School during World War II, however, we never argued about race or, for that matter, anything else that might have been called public affairs. I was accepted enough to become a member, even an officer, of the leading high school fraternity. My athletic career, never promising, had been ended on the football field by a fractured shoulder that eventually required three operations over a year and a half and left me with a badly atrophied deltoid muscle in my left shoulder. But I was a good student and coeditor of both the high school newspaper and yearbook. I found it easy to make good enough grades to be in the top 10 percent of my class but not marked as a grind. I was particularly strong in mathematics, where I profited from the attentions of an extraordinary teacher, Judith Pillow. To my father's delight, I was good enough to be offered a scholarship to study math at Rice Institute in Houston. To my father's dismay, I turned it down and followed the conventional course of enrolling at Louisiana State University and becoming a Sigma Chi pledge. Although I was a good student, I still had no intellectual interests, and I wasn't caught up in college life. I had some vague notion I wanted to be a newspaperman, but I was essentially just going along with the crowd. When you finished high school, you took advantage of the free college education at LSU and then went on to get a job and pursue a "real life."

It wasn't an exciting prospect, and I was restless. I had missed fighting in the war but felt there must be something more adventurous than what I was doing, someplace to go where there weren't the same people every day. It was a restlessness I had felt all through my adolescence, a feeling that there was something more out there that was at least different and perhaps better. I spent the first half of my last two high school summers working and saving my money so I could spend the second month or so hitchhiking around the country—once just around the South, once to the west as far as New Mexico and Arizona. It was educational in its way. I met my first homosexuals, drivers who picked me up along the road. I met some women more worldly than my high school girlfriends. I drank a lot of beer and once spent a night in a small-town jail in Arizona while the police department determined that I was not responsible for a rape that had occurred a couple of days earlier.

I always went back to Baton Rouge, but I never thought of it as any more than the place we happened to be living. So in 1945, after a semester at LSU, I decided to join the Army, although I could have avoided the draft with a student deferment. My friend Buddy Souter had agreed to enlist with me after the recruiting sergeant assured us we could take basic training together. When the day came, however, Buddy couldn't bring himself to leave home and family, so I left alone for Camp Chaffee, Arkansas, and life in what was then called the Army Air Corps. It was a marvelous, transforming experience that made me a lifelong advocate of universal military training immediately after high school, not because of the military part but because it helps to just get thrown into the pond at that age.

Basic training was quite different from life at the Sigma Chi house in Baton Rouge. My fellow trainees at the San Antonio Air Cadet Center—known as Sack Field—were mostly unlettered country boys from the rural South and Southwest. There was a man named Mysinger from Oklahoma who believed the world was square because he had heard about "the four corners of the earth" and could not be persuaded otherwise by my diagrams of the solar system. "If it's round, where do we get the corners? Answer me that," he would insist. There was a hillbilly from east Tennessee who showed a sweet piety and asked me to write his letters to his girlfriend back home, always including a paragraph about how much he missed her performing fellatio on him after church every Sunday. He signed off the letters, "Yours in the service of God."

After basic training I was sent off to a school for finance clerks at Lowry Field in Denver, an obvious recognition of my superior intellect that permitted me to learn how to type and fill out the endless forms involved in paying the troops. Once I had mastered those skills, I was sent off to the Air Transport Command and spent a winter in Iceland, where it was perpetually dark and usually raining or snowing, then a spring and summer in Greenland, where it was light enough to read a book on fire watch at midnight. I worked for a finance officer who taught me the tricks of getting a little but important edge in the world of the military. Although I was only a corporal, I was designated to be the base auditor because we didn't have a qualified commissioned officer on the base. That duty gave me leverage I had never before enjoyed but quickly learned to exploit. When a particularly obnoxious first sergeant kept giving me extra duty on kitchen police (KP)—he didn't have much use for "college boys" playing soldier—I spilled ink on his name on the payroll so he had to wait for a supplemental roll ten days later, as the regulations required. When the KP continued, damned if the ink didn't spill again until old Russ got the idea. I was putting through his allotments to his wife and I was paying his insurance, but he wasn't getting any cash for his beer and cigarettes until the KP stopped. When pilots flew from Greenland to Gander, Newfoundland, or Goose Bay, Labrador, and spent a night in what were much more civilized surroundings than we enjoyed in Greenland, I had some discretion about how quickly to approve their per diem payments. After a while they learned the process moved faster if they brought back a steak or a couple of lobsters or maybe some fresh milk for the boys in the finance office. I had a part-time job on the side keeping the books for the officers' club, although I had no idea how to do it as the Army regulations required. So when a team from the inspector general arrived for an audit, I found that a case of Scotch did wonders in passing their inspection. My behavior wasn't something I would recommend to my children, but it made my stint in the Air Corps a lot more comfortable than it might have been.

Borderline criminal behavior was not the principal lesson of my military career, however. Despite spending the time under military discipline, I learned to make my own decisions without the guidance of my parents, which had been rarely offered anyway, and free from any pressure to conform to the standards of my friends in Baton Rouge. The result was that I came out of the service enjoying a kind of independence I could never have enjoyed without those eighteen months on my own. My parents had moved back to

Boston, and I had no reason to return to Baton Rouge. So I decided to use my GI Bill at the University of Missouri, where I took one degree in journalism and another in history and enjoyed my new freedom. In those years immediately after the war, the MU campus in Columbia attracted hundreds of ex-GIs like me from the eastern seaboard cities simply because places were available if you could find your own housing. Although we spent our required share of time drinking beer at Collins Tavern, we were reasonably serious about our work and in my case and many others not impressed by some of the conventions that had seemed so important a few years earlier. I went to dinner at the Sigma Chi house as the first step in becoming a member but decided I didn't care about fraternities any longer. After all, I had the VFW Club, which had two pool tables and was one of only two places in town—the other was the American Legion—that served liquor by the drink. When the brothers at Sigma Chi tried to impress upon me how I ultimately might profit from the contacts I would make through fraternity life, I didn't believe it. I qualified for an English honors program but quit halfway through a semester when I discovered it required enduring a course in Roman architecture. When my academic adviser insisted I would regret passing up the honors degree in "later life," I didn't believe that either. When I was elected to Phi Beta Kappa, I joined because I was sort of puffed up at the idea and thought it would please my parents—but I never bought a key. It was sort of like someone smoking pot and never inhaling.

That was the wonder of those two years in the Army Air Corps when I was eighteen and nineteen. For whatever reason I came out of the service as a thoroughgoing skeptic. I had already decided religion made no sense, and I had learned firsthand that the authority of the military, although it had to be accepted by a soldier, was hollow and mindless. Now I felt the same way about the university. I was obliged to meet its standards to get a degree and a job, but I didn't have to accept its conventional wisdom about what was necessary to get ahead. It was, of course, an attitude of mind that equipped me peculiarly for the newspaper business, although I don't recall ever reflecting on that point at the time. I wanted to be a reporter because I enjoyed writing and reporting seemed like a good way to make a living, not as much fun as playing baseball but the best option available for someone with a weak arm who couldn't run.

Despite my blasé attitude, I found some aspects of university life were rewarding. I took a two-semester course in Shakespeare taught by a leading scholar, Hardin Craig. I studied economics with Harry Gunnison Brown, one of the few Keynesians teaching in those days. And I took a course in dialectical materialism taught by Morris Eames, a class I was convinced was allowed because no one on the State Board of Regents had any idea dialectical materialism was another way of saying Marxism. I met a wonderful old man, an epic poet named John G. Neihardt, who taught a course in writing the critical essay and, more to the point, taught all his students what it was for a man to grow old totally comfortable with himself and what he had done with his life.

I supplemented my GI Bill benefits with various jobs, as a bartender at Collins, as an instructor teaching a lab section on statistical method in the department of psychology, as a graduate assistant teaching copyreading in the journalism school. At one point I graded papers for Donovan Rhynsburger, who taught courses in theater and ran the workshop theater at Missouri—a job worth mentioning only because it allowed me to overhear a fellow journalism student named George C. Scott read for his first role as an actor. As a student reporter I covered the football team, and this allowed me to moonlight by covering the games for International News Service, which paid me a penny a word for three hundred and fifty words at halftime and the same again after the game. Seven bucks was a fortune. You could take one of the rich girls from Stephens College up to the VFW and have enough, at a quarter a drink, to convince her you were sincere.

When I finished school in 1951 I was in an ideal position to get a good starting job in the newspaper business. I had made good grades, and because of my prior service I was exempt from the draft for the Korean War. So I took what was probably the worst job offered, as sports editor of the *Jefferson City Post-Tribune,* only thirty-five miles from the campus. It paid fifty dollars a week, and its prime virtue was that I could start even before graduation, which was important because my GI benefits had expired and I was broke. I also needed some cash to pay Nelson Royalty, the proprietor of

Tut's Café, fifty dollars for meals I had eaten on the arm. His wife, the formidable Lena, was afraid I was going to skip town without paying and she was leaning hard on old Tut. But, as much as I loved sports, I found covering it and writing about it tedious. Whatever your pretensions as a writer, and mine were fairly extravagant, there are only so many ways you can report a baseball game.

After only three months, however, I was saved. I had fallen in love with a fellow student at Missouri, Barbara Wippler, who was working as a copy editor for *The Monroe* (Michigan) *Evening News,* a daily of just under twenty thousand circulation. When we became engaged the *News* offered me a reporting job rather than lose Barbara, and my career as the next Red Smith came to an end. I was suddenly out of the sandbox and doing grown-up work covering city hall and labor.

Working for *The Evening News* was an almost entirely misleading experience. The owner and publisher of the paper—JS Gray, no periods after the initials—belonged in a newspaper textbook. He was totally professional and so was his newspaper, not in the sense that it was a polished and sophisticated product but in the sense that it understood its place in the community. It was there to print the news, no more and no less. There was no boosterism, no political agenda, no favorites to be coddled. JS backed his reporters to the hilt. When a city commissioner who owned a department store threatened to withhold his advertising because of a story I was writing, JS told him the advertising would not be accepted until he apologized for the threat. When one of his regular golf partners refused to deal with me about a strike he had caused at a local plant, JS told him he would deal with me or no one.

One day I heard that someone was measuring the height of the masts of the small fishing boats that used a channel from the River Raisin into Lake Erie. The only inference could be that someone was planning to build a bridge on a tract of marshland that, I soon discovered, was mostly owned by the Detroit Edison Co., the huge utility that served most of eastern Michigan. This was particularly intriguing because Detroit Edison was involved in a long and contentious process of trying to get a license to build a nuclear power plant. But the company had never revealed where it intended to build. When I called Detroit Edison, I was promptly invited to lunch at the Detroit Club with Walker Cisler, the chairman of the company. For a twenty-four-year-old reporter on a small daily, this was pretty heady stuff. I had never been to a club like this one, all dark paneling and red leather. Nor, for that matter, had I met anyone as charming and personally forceful as Walker Cisler. The burden of his message was that I had stumbled into their plans and he wanted the story held up for a week or two so they could get their ducks in a row, which sounded like another way of saying until they could buy up the rest of the land at bargain prices. To refuse the request, Cisler said, would be "an unfriendly act." I drove the forty miles back to Monroe, head spinning, and reported the conversation to JS. He promptly called Cisler and told him we were "sometimes unintelligent but never unfriendly" at *The Evening News* and in any case were going to print the story, which we did the following day. The sky, it turned out, did not fall. It never does. That's one of the things you learn in the newspaper business.

JS Gray also taught me a lesson in restraint, although I was slow to learn it. At one point he suggested I write an occasional editorial on local issues. And being a twenty-four-year-old know-it-all, I quickly proposed several critiques of the obvious inadequacies of the city commission. But JS stayed my hand. The voters, he told me, get about the level of competence that they are willing to pay for, so we shouldn't be nipping at the heels of the commissioners about every little thing. I was skeptical, suspecting my publisher of timidity, until the day Roy Fisher, a member of the commission, bought the bus company. The city charter, I pointed out, prohibited any commissioner from holding office if he operated a business licensed by the city. Although the bus company had a franchise rather than a license, it was clear to me that the spirit of the charter was being violated and that Fisher was no longer eligible. JS agreed and told me to write a brief editorial making that point, which we printed that day. About three hours after the paper came out, Fisher called me to read a statement of resignation from the commission. When I asked why, he replied, "It was that editorial. I don't have any choice." The lesson to me was clear: If you don't nip at their heels, you retain some influence.

The two years in Monroe were a special experience, but it had always been understood that I would want to move on to a larger pond. That was the conventional route then for a beginner in the business—two or three years on a small paper learning the mechanics and, not incidentally, building your confidence as a reporter by covering a wide variety of stories under the pressure of tight deadlines. Covering city hall and labor in Monroe, I sometimes wrote five or six stories a day and was always obliged to confront those about whom I wrote the next day. The labor beat was a particular learning experience. I covered twenty-six strikes, most of them wildcat walkouts that required dealing with union leaders, most often from the United Auto Workers, who made up in aggressive toughness what they lacked in sophistication. Once you learned to deal with Carlos Gastambide, the business agent for the largest UAW local at the Monroe Auto Equipment Company, you would not likely be intimidated again by any source at any level, up to and including the White House.

The first job was a training experience. Then you moved on to a larger newspaper that would offer bigger stories to cover for more readers and the chance to compete against more experienced reporters. There are exceptions, reporters and editors who spend their entire careers on a small newspaper because they like living in a community where everyone knows everyone else or because they like the hunting and fishing or, sometimes, because they aren't good enough to move up. But I wasn't one of them. So after two years I quit. JS Gray gave me best wishes. Barbara and I packed our belongings into a two-wheel trailer and drove east.

CHAPTER 2

"DON'T BLAME

THE BRIDGE"

There was no great demand for my services when I decided to leave Monroe in 1953. Barbara and I set off in our aging Plymouth brashly confident that there would be many editors out there who would recognize my talents. But *The New York Times* and *The Washington Post* brushed me off, and even *The Detroit News,* for whom I had been a highly successful stringer in Monroe, was not impressed. Some of the editors to whom I had written were considerate and encouraging; others didn't even reply. The managing editor of a Charleston, West Virginia, newspaper responded tartly that anyone making ninety dollars a week at my age "should reconsider" his situation. It apparently didn't occur to him, I thought with the arrogance of youth, that there might be a reason I was worth ninety bucks, which may help explain why he was still pushing copy in Charleston. The whole experience of hunting a job without a job was tense enough to be memorable. When, years later, I was the one doing the hiring, no letter of application went unanswered.

As it turned out, the choices weren't great. There was a job available in Kokomo, Indiana, but that didn't seem like much of a step up life's ladder. There was another, better job in Burlington, Vermont, covering the state capital in Montpelier for *The Burlington*

Free Press and the *Rutland Herald,* the only two morning newspapers in the state. But in those days before jet planes, Vermont
seemed a long way from Yankee Stadium. The best I could do was a
job as a general assignment reporter for the Rochester, New York,
Times-Union, an afternoon paper of 125,000 circulation that was
then the flagship of the Gannett Newspapers. They offered Newspaper Guild scale, seventy-seven dollars a week, and I snapped it
up, confident I could make up the lost fifteen a week in merit raises.
At least it was a paper big enough to put out several editions a day,
and it competed fiercely with the morning *Democrat & Chronicle,*
also a Gannett paper but published separately in its own building
two blocks from the *T-U.*

It was, as they say, a learning experience. What I learned most of
all was that working for JS Gray and *The Monroe Evening News* had
given me a totally mistaken notion of the way newspapers function
in the real world. Not all publishers or all newspapers have the same
devotion to giving their readers a picture of events uncolored by
their own prejudices, politics, and personality quirks. The *Times-
Union* was not a bad newspaper. It covered Rochester and Monroe
County with reasonable thoroughness and enjoyed the benefits of
reports from the Gannett bureaus covering Washington and the
state capital in Albany. It carried enough national and foreign news
to satisfy most readers; the others could buy the Sunday edition of
The New York Times if they felt the need.

The city staff I joined included some excellent reporters who, like
me, had moved up from smaller dailies elsewhere and thought of
themselves as basically transients. Bill Ringle, formerly of the
Rome, New York, *Daily Sentinel,* was a general assignment reporter
of extraordinary talent. After working with him in one situation or
another for the next twenty years, I never found his equal. He could
be dropped into any situation and be relied upon to figure it out and
file. The science writer, Harry Schmeck, late of the Danville, Illinois, *Commercial-News,* had a genius for translating complex material for newspaper readers without sacrificing accuracy or nuance, a
talent he later displayed in a long career with *The New York Times.*
There were several others with special skills, not all of whom stayed
in the business. The political writer, Kermit Hill, ended up as a political operative. Bert Reisman, a good-humored bear of a man from

Brooklyn with a flair for flamboyant writing, produced one good story after another but believed, correctly, that he was denied merit raises because he was a Jew. He moved on to public relations and became a vice president of IBM. Among the reporters themselves, the acknowledged star was a rewriteman and local columnist, Del Ray, who combined a poet's touch as a writer with an eye for the anomalies that make great newspaper feature stories. As Ringle often put it, "We walk down the street looking at the women's legs, but Del is looking for a story."

There were some excellent editors at the line level. John Dougherty, the telegraph editor and later city editor, was a thoughtful man with a wide range of knowledge that he brought to his editing. Gene Gribbroek, also a telegraph editor, who later came to Washington to work for me as the news editor of the Gannett bureau there, had a genius for improving the copy of those whose writing skills were still unpolished. Abe Miller, the news editor, was something out of *The Front Page,* a small, intense man with a pencil mustache who was extremely combative in competing with our morning opposition. He was the one the young reporters most wanted to please.

There was one clear division in the reporting staff. On the one hand, there were those—like Ringle, Schmeck, and me—who had come to Rochester only because it was where we could find a job, and, on the other hand, there were those for whom it was home. These were not only local people but in most cases people from the right side of the tracks—meaning that they lived on the east side of the city or in suburbs such as Brighton and Pittsford. Some of them even belonged to Oak Hill Country Club and played golf there regularly. They were, not to put too fine a point on it, part of the establishment and people with apparently limitless futures with the paper and Gannett. Most of us transients were convinced, for example, that Calvin Mayne, the fair-haired and hardworking city hall reporter, was destined to be publisher of the *Times-Union* at the least and probably the president of Gannett before it was over. The salient point was that this group included the publisher, Paul Miller; the managing editor, Vern Croop; and the city editor, Howard Hosmer. They might have come from somewhere else—Miller was an Oklahoman who had become president of Gannett as well as *T-U* publisher after a long career with the Associated Press— were now thoroughgoing Rochesterians. As such, they we cially concerned with how their friends and golfing partners respond over lunch at the Genesee Valley Club or on the first Oak Hill.

The problem for the aggressive young reporters like me was t we tended to look at stories in terms of their intrinsic news value a perhaps too often, our own ambitions, while our bosses viewed those same stories through the prism of their associations. For them it wasn't just a question of whether a story might be good but how it would be viewed by their friends or how it might affect the image of this notoriously smug and culturally conservative city. For Vern Croop, the pressures were particularly intense, because he felt constrained to worry about both the community leadership in general and publisher Miller in particular. In Rochester at that time, these concerns led to some ridiculous things.

At one point Ringle and I proposed to do a series of stories about how Hanover Houses, the city's only public housing project, was faring after its first year of operation. Conservative, affluent Rochester had resisted public housing until it was the last city in upstate New York to build such a project, and then only after considerable grumbling about whether it was necessary. So a fresh look made sense, and Ringle and I pressed for the time to do it. Croop knew our arguments made sense, but he was uneasy about the prospect of what two young and probably liberal reporters would find. The last thing Rochester needed, he kept saying, was any more controversy about more projects or improving Hanover Houses or anything to do with it. But finally, when we persisted, he approved the project. As we left his office, he called out after us. "Don't make it look too good for the niggers," he said. "They'll all be coming up here from Georgia."

Ringle and I rolled with it, more amused by the notion of the *T-U* causing some mass exodus from Atlanta than outraged by Croop. That was something you had to live with.

It is easy to say that sort of thing wouldn't happen in a newspaper office today, because it obviously wouldn't. It would be a mistake, nonetheless, to believe that news organizations these days are not influenced by the prejudices of their editors and publishers, however benign and politically correct they might be. They move in circles quite different from those of most of their readers. They don't like to invite controversy, and they worry about having to put so much trust in reporters, who also come from a different world. They are notoriously ambivalent about the power of a newspaper story or television broadcast. They fear damaging someone or some institution unfairly, although they also relish the influence they enjoy.

That influence is often less than they imagine, but publishers can get carried away. There was a classic upstate New York story in those days about G. B. Williams, owner and publisher of the *Geneva Times*, a small daily in a community thirty-five miles east of Rochester. He arrived at the office one morning and informed his editorial writer that boys in his neighborhood were shooting at birds with their BB guns. The editorial writer quickly produced a piece decrying the practice. But the following day Williams complained accusingly, "Those boys are still shooting at birds." There was a little of G. B. Williams in Paul Miller in those days, the notion that the paper could simply change the world with a single stroke.

One of the major annual events in Rochester during the early 1950s was a meeting at the University of Rochester of nuclear physicists from all over the world. These were scientists, mostly young men, engaged in a field so complex and remote that it seemed too arcane and esoteric for a newspaper to cover intelligently. The temptation, to which we yielded every year, was to assign some feature writer to do a piece making fun of these oddballs and the abstruse material with which they were dealing in their meetings. Just printing the list of topics was good for a laugh. But Harry Schmeck actually understood the substance, so the *T-U* was blessed with, in addition to the dumb features, intelligent and understandable reports on the scientific meaning of what the physicists were discussing. Schmeck's talent was so rare that the acknowledged leader among the physicists, J. Robert Oppenheimer, wrote an unsolicited letter to *The New York Times* suggesting they might want to hire Harry.

Harry had a problem, however. Miller, conservative and Republican in his thinking, viewed Oppenheimer with the same suspicion that was directed toward him by the communist-hunters in Washington in those days. So he decreed that anytime Oppenheimer was mentioned in a story in the *T-U,* we had to point out that he had been denied security clearance by the Atomic Energy Commission. After making the obligatory complaint to the city desk to no avail, Harry became locked in a kind of tug-of-war over the Oppenheimer mention. He would make it the final sentence in his story only to find that city editor Hosmer had moved it up to the fourth paragraph. Harry would reclaim the story from the news desk, explaining that it needed some revision because of a late development. He would move the Oppenheimer sentence up a few paragraphs but still effectively buried. Then the editors would have another crack at it, trying to find a place "higher up" in the story that wouldn't halt the flow of Harry's account of the meeting. In the end the Oppenheimer sentence would stick out like a sore thumb, as Miller wanted, but nothing happened as a result. The boys were still shooting at birds, and J. Robert Oppenheimer was still teaching physics.

The stories that made the editors uneasy weren't always political. There was, for instance, the infamous case of the Troup-Howell Bridge.

Downtown Rochester is bisected by the Genesee River, and the paper campaigned for several years for another bridge across it, connecting Troup and Howell streets. It was necessary, the *T-U* argued editorially, to reduce rush-hour congestion downtown. We did not make a point of the fact that the bridge would be only a block from the paper and thus a great boon in getting circulation trucks out of the plant and out of downtown more expeditiously, an important consideration for an afternoon paper. Finally the city and state engineers all agreed, and the bridge was built. But winter set in before the blacktop pavement could be laid, leaving the concrete underneath exposed to the elements. The engineers announced the bridge would have to remain closed until spring. Without the blacktop, they said, there was too much danger it would ice up and become too dangerous to drive on. But the paper kept complaining that this was a senseless delay, until the city finally caved in and opened the bridge.

A few weeks later I was sitting in for Del Ray as the rewriteman, a regular Monday assignment I enjoyed, when Tom Connally, the police reporter, called in a few minutes before the deadline for our main home-delivered edition. Sleet was falling, the Troup-Howell

Bridge had iced up, and there had been one hell of an accident involving an ambulance carrying a man with a heart attack and eight cars, one of them driven by the heart attack victim's wife. The cars were strewn all over the bridge, and more ambulances were coming from every direction. The cops were going crazy trying to sort it all out.

I told Abe Miller, the news editor, what had happened, and he decided the story would go at the top of Page One. I should give it to him two or three paragraphs at a time because the deadline was upon us. Just as I began to write, Vern Croop came scurrying out of his office.

"What's the speed limit on the bridge?" he demanded.

"Twenty," I said.

"Get that in the lead," he directed, meaning in the first paragraph.

I protested. "I've got an ambulance, eight cars, a guy with a heart attack, his wife, and a whole bunch of other people hurt. I can't get that in the lead. It'll stop the story dead."

Croop kept insisting, I kept resisting, and the excitable Miller kept repeating he needed the copy *now,* we were out of time. Finally, Croop turned on his heel to return to his office, pausing halfway to call back to me. "I don't care what you do," he said, "but don't blame the bridge."

That became the watchword for the rest of my time in Rochester—whatever you do, don't blame the bridge.

It was never a question of Croop or Hosmer or other editors not knowing what should be done. They understood the beautiful simplicity of the news business at its best—find out what happened and put it in the paper—but it was ruined for them by all these other considerations. What would PM think of it? Who would be hurt? Who would be angry? Would it be "good for the city"?

Early one winter I got a tip that a prominent real estate broker had been using his position as a consultant advising the city to make a few bucks for himself. I went over to the courthouse and began tracing transactions, using the tax stamps on the deeds to figure the prices and found that, sure enough, old Tom was doing very well. Using his position as an adviser to the city council, he had inside information on several parcels they intended to buy six months to a year down the road. He bought them, then turned them over to the city when the time came at a neat profit. The losers were the people who sold to him without knowing the land would be worth more later.

The prospect of all this being spelled out in the newspaper sent Tom through the roof. He called me and then he called Vern Croop. Here Christmas was coming, and we were going to spoil it for his wife and kids and, besides, his mother had a heart condition and might die from the embarrassment. Croop was clearly conflicted. He knew it was a legitimate story that we had to publish, but it was going to cause a few waves. And, after all, Tom was a decent guy, a community leader, even the president of the Rochester Real Estate Board, for God's sake. He finally approved the story but ordered it published on an inside local page, where it wouldn't get much attention. It was a story that couldn't be buried, of course, and soon the political opposition was demanding that the council remedy the situation. So Tom gave most of the profit back by cutting his price to allow for only a legitimate fee for assembling the package. We ran another story, also appropriately buried. Tom's mother didn't die; they never do.

Then Croop announced that I had been given an unprecedented recognition, a bonus for my work on the story. It was only twenty-five dollars, but the gesture elated the entire staff. Reporters are like that. We talk tough, but tell us you appreciate a story and we'll follow you anywhere, wagging our tails behind us. The trouble with working in Rochester was that you had to keep finding reasons to wag your tail.

Despite all the griping, which is endemic in all news organizations at all levels, we had a good time. The ambience of the newsroom was a throwback even for its time. We used typewriters, mostly Underwoods and L. C. Smiths, passed on from the business office when the clerks there were through with them. We had one telephone for each two reporters, and you had to get permission from the city desk for any toll call, even to the next county. You could get a new copy pencil only by giving the managing editor's secretary the stub of an old one. Almost everyone smoked, and there were no ashtrays other than the metal cups from the ends of rolls of newsprint. But, what the hell, using the floor was acceptable. Carpeting was unheard of in newsrooms in those days. We played golf on our days off and drank a few beers together after work. Our wives were friendly enough to one another so we played bridge and cooked dinners back and forth. On New Year's Eve we all got drunk at the Ringles', called up Hosmer, and quit our jobs.

There was only one woman, the church editor, on the city staff at that time, and only a handful of other women assigned to what were still called the social pages and to feature sections about food and home economics. So if there was any significant illicit staff sex going on—other than perhaps some erotic after-deadline daydreams about the strawberry-blond Sally Miles—I missed it. The high point for most of us came about three every afternoon when Francine, a stunning and provocatively dressed secretary from the advertising department, would deliver the dummy pages for the next day's paper to the city desk. The city room would fall totally silent, all attention focused on Francine as she made her way across it and then back out again. When I was minding the desk—an after-deadline assignment that rotated among several of us—I would wait until Francine had reached the door, then call out after her as if there were a question about the dummies. She would saunter back to desk, then smile and blush fetchingly when I told her I had just called her back as a public service. Today that would be called sexist behavior, but the term hadn't even been invented then.

When not leering and prancing like juvenile goats, we also plotted to get good stories into the paper despite the best efforts of the editors to reduce everything to a bland mush. We particularly enjoyed finding ways to beat the *Democrat & Chronicle,* our corporate brother a few blocks up Main Street. A year or so after Ringle and I had first written about Hanover Houses, I heard one Thursday night that the *D&C* had prepared a series of articles on things that had gone wrong in the project. It was to run, in six parts, beginning in the Sunday paper. I called our city editor, Howard Hosmer, and got permission to try to take the edge off it the next day. So shortly after seven that morning, with three or four hours at our disposal, Bert Reisman and I arrived at the Baden Street Settlement House, a social agency that served the project and was run by a saint named Irving Kriegsfeld, whom I had come to know reasonably well as a volunteer adviser to the settlement house newspaper. I was guessing that he had been a prime source for the *D&C* reporters, and I demanded that he show us "everything you showed those guys." Kriegsfeld protested that they had been working on the story for weeks and it was too late for us to catch up. But finally he agreed to show us some of the "worst case" examples of the way the project had been allowed to fall into serious disrepair. By late morning Reisman and I returned to the office convinced we had found the juicy stuff, and we quickly cranked out two columns of type for a Page One story that stole the heart out of the *D&C* series—to the point that it had to be cut back and toned down. It was not the kind of thoughtful journalism to which readers are probably entitled. But in the *T-U* newsroom, we enjoyed it immensely. And I enjoyed it most fully when one of the *D&C* reporters, a golf-playing buddy, called me and began the conversation, "You miserable son of a bitch." Inevitably, some years later the Gannett managers decided that kind of thing was wasteful, moved the papers into the same building, combined the business and advertising operations, and scuttled the *T-U* when, like that of most afternoon newspapers, its circulation eroded dramatically.

After two years on the paper I was still a general assignment reporter, although beginning to edge my way toward government and politics. I helped Kermit Hill cover the local elections, and I was given Cal Mayne's leavings on the city hall beat, topics like slum clearance that didn't interest him as much as the surefire Page One stories about the new War Memorial auditorium being built across the street from the paper. But I began to develop a relationship with Joe Farbo, a member of the city council representing a section of the city with a large Italian-American population, including many tailors who worked in Rochester's men's clothing industry, to which the paper paid scant attention. Farbo was a short, chesty man given to black suits and dazzlingly white shirts. He gave the impression he was carrying a chip on his shoulder because he was so aggressive in protecting his core constituency. He was not part of the establishment, by any means, and neither was I. So when I complained mildly but pointedly to him that our patrician mayor, Peter Barry, wouldn't tell me if my coat was on fire, I found a sympathetic ear. The council did most of its business in closed session, and then Barry or the city manager, Bob Aex, would provide a laundered version of the discussion and the results. I discovered, however, that Farbo took extensive notes in those meetings and would share them with me over the telephone the next morning. It was one of those symbiotic relationships that often develop between reporters and sources, in this case based on the common condition of being out-siders. Neither one of us ever remarked on it, but Farbo's notes gave me a few stories I would not otherwise have written, and my stories in turn gave Farbo's views an exposure they might not have been given. But people can be too appreciative. At a Christmas party one of Farbo's cronies sidled up to me and stuffed a fifty-dollar bill into my pocket to thank me for "looking out for Joe." I was both startled and horrified, but I managed to give it back without causing offense, only puzzlement.

For a young reporter the lesson of Joe Farbo was that there are al-ways people in politics with their own priorities that may make them willing to be helpful. It is a lesson that applies as much to the White House or Congress as it does to city hall.

Late in 1955 I got a break—a chance to go down to Albany as the extra man in the Gannett bureau there for the 1956 session of the legislature. In my three years in Rochester I had written a wide range of stories. I had covered the major strikes. I had written sev-eral series of articles on subjects as various as abuses of migrant labor (an old standby for all northern newspapers) and the hidden costs of charitable fund-raising. At one time, when the editors de-cided we could reduce the murder rate by writing more graphically about the killings that did occur, I was assigned to report all the in-teresting murders—an assignment cut short when a story I dictated while I straddled the body of a victim in an East Side neighborhood turned out to be more graphic than they had in mind. But I had moved inexorably toward government and politics. That's the way it worked in the newspaper business then and, to a large degree, still works today. Reporters eventually find their way into the assign-ments that fit them best. Covering the legislature would take me a long way toward just such a fit.

CHAPTER 3

LEARNING THE

TRADE

Covering a state capital is one of the great assignments for any political reporter. You may not want to make a career of it, because after a few years you tend to find the same stories keep coming around. But for a reporter learning the trade, it is a prime beat. The dimensions are manageable. You're covering a governor and a legislature and, every even-numbered year, a campaign. Because the universe is small and well defined, you come to know the players well, and that allows you to report accurately and confidently.

Albany in the late 1950s was a marvelous place for someone as green as I. We had two governors, Democrat W. Averell Harriman and then Republican Nelson A. Rockefeller, who were trying to use the office to run for president, as New York governors other than Mario Cuomo tend to do. The legislature, controlled by the Republicans, was full of colorful and interesting people involved in all sorts of political intrigue they loved to tell you about, even if the story in the papers the next day might prove embarrassing. In those days the legislative sessions lasted just three months every year, ending about April 1. Then there would be a thirty-day bill-signing period, in which the governor decided which bills to approve and which to veto. The thirty or forty reporters who covered the legislature would spend the three or four months living in the DeWitt Clinton, a charmless, frayed-at-the-edges hotel a block from the capitol. At the time they were almost all men working for newspapers and wire services. Every once in a while someone from radio or television would show up, but we ignored him. The broadcast people weren't even eligible to belong to the Legislative Correspondents Association, whose sole function was a dinner roasting the politicians with song parodies late in the session. We worked long hours, ate the club steak at Yezzi's night after night, played rummy and poker in the pressroom, and drank after hours in seedy bars in a neighborhood known as the Gut that the Baptist Rockefeller later wiped out to make room for a huge state office complex. It was like being at summer camp, away from the daily supervision of our bosses and our wives.

The city itself was totally controlled for a half century by what was known as the O'Connell Machine, headed by one Daniel J. O'Connell, known to one and all as Uncle Dan. The machine won elections seven or eight to one and retained its power by spreading the public's money around as widely as possible. When, for example, they needed to cut the grass in Washington Park, an expanse of perhaps sixteen square blocks a half mile from the capitol, the city would send dozens of men with hand lawn mowers. The theory was that if you had ten thousand dollars to spend, ten guys each got one thousand dollars rather than two getting five thousand dollars each. They could count.

Uncle Dan's businesses also were paid some deference. He was reputed to be an investor in Hedrick's beer, a local product, so when closing time arrived at those bars in the Gut, two things happened: a shade was drawn over the front window, and all those drinking beer were obliged to buy Hedrick's as they drank on illegally. The bars had to close on time only on Saturday nights because, the local ethic said, Uncle Dan wanted the B-girls and bartenders to get some sleep so they wouldn't miss Mass the next morning.

Uncle Dan also had an interest of some kind in the Yellow Cab company, which caused an interesting situation every Monday during the legislative session. Two trains would arrive at the station about noon or shortly thereafter, one northbound from New York City, the other eastbound from Buffalo, Rochester, and Syracuse.

Both were packed with legislators who needed cabs to take them to the two downtown hotels, Democrats to the DeWitt, Republicans to the slightly classier Ten Eyck. But only Yellow Cabs were allowed into the station loading platform, so the legislators would have to wait for them to make several trips. Moreover, if they walked out of the station hoping to hail an independent taxi, they would find city policemen stationed for two or three blocks in each direction and waving off the independents until the Yellows took all the fares.

Uncle Dan, a Democrat, had some old-fashioned ideas about politics, too. On election nights he would be found awaiting the results at his cabin in the "mountains"—meaning some unimpressive hills called the Helderbergs a few miles out of town. Ward leaders, almost all of them on the state or city payroll, would arrive and personally report on their performance to earn a few words of approval from the old man. The results were almost always pleasing, but there was a rare exception when New York switched from a convention system to a primary system for making up the state ticket. For decades the rule for Democrats had been that "the three-I league" would be controlling and the ticket would include one Jew (Israel) and at least one Irish American and one Italian American. The other place might be given to the Protestants as a gesture to upstate, although that wasn't essential. But in the first Democratic primary the voters produced a ticket made up of three Jews and a black man, Basil Paterson of Manhattan, for lieutenant governor. Uncle Dan, the ward leaders reported, was not happy. "Look at that damned ticket," he was reported to have said. "There's only one white man on it, and he's a nigger."

When I was assigned to Albany, Harriman, the heir to a railroad fortune who had earned an inflated reputation as a diplomat, and was also among the first to recognize the menace of Soviet communism, was governor. Already in his sixties and hard of hearing, Harriman was hoping for one more chance at a Democratic presidential nomination in 1960, although no one else considered him a serious contender. The one thing that was most obvious about Harriman was that he had little or no interest in doing the job of governor. Although he had a highly skilled staff that included the young Daniel Patrick Moynihan as assistant secretary to the governor, Harriman's entire purpose seemed to be reaching out every day to one or another of the Democratic Party's many constituencies. Warren Weaver, the resident correspondent for *The New York Times,* and I once fashioned a letterhead for the organization that would most appeal to Harriman: Aged Afro-American Consumers Union for Democratic Action. Nor did the governor ever show even a touch of intellectual curiosity. Visiting the state College of Ceramics at Alfred, for example, he walked out on the director's description of the school's curriculum when he spotted two black kitchen workers whose hands he had to seize that very moment. Shaking hands on the campaign trail, he was always looking beyond the person he was greeting in the transparent hope of spotting some bigger fish. He seemed to make a point of not remembering names.

On foreign policy, however, he would discourse at length. Weaver and I were the only two reporters who regularly traveled around the state with the governor in noncampaign periods, which sometimes entailed a long late-night ride back to Albany in the governor's limousine. We soon learned that if we asked him what he thought about a situation in, let's say, the Middle East, he would launch into an exposition lengthy enough for us, seated on the jump seats, to catch a good nap. He didn't notice and never asked us anything because he didn't give a damn what we thought and didn't feel any need to hide the fact. He wore a hearing aid but turned it on only when he was talking.

Harriman's preoccupation with foreign policy could be a problem. He would give a speech on Soviet Jewry, for instance, in an obvious attempt to polish his political credentials as a national figure. But as governor he lacked a foreign affairs portfolio, which often meant that the *Times* would not run anything about the speech even if Weaver led his story with it. When Harriman discovered the next morning that he had not made the *Times,* the only newspaper that mattered to him, he would give the speech again—and again and again. I would plead with Weaver to get the damned thing into the paper so he'd shut up about it, which was exactly what would happen if they finally printed even a few paragraphs.

Campaigning against Rockefeller early in 1958, Harriman was leading in the polls and being advised to reject his challenger's demand for televised debates. But one night, eating dinner with me and Weaver at Rocco Canale's restaurant in Watertown while on a campaign trip through the North Country, Harriman kept leaving the table to take phone calls from his Manhattan office. When we inquired whether there was some kind of emergency, the governor replied that he was trying to negotiate a debate with Rockefeller, but, he added, it would be limited to foreign affairs. "I'll demolish him on foreign policy," he said, thumping the table for emphasis. When I made so bold as to ask him what foreign policy had to do with a gubernatorial campaign, he ignored the question. "I'll demolish him," he said again. To no one's surprise, the debate was never held.

Harriman was also famously frugal for a man with a personal fortune then estimated at about $75 million. Weaver and I used to needle him about the lack of a stewardess (a word still politically correct in those days) who could serve us a Scotch or two on one of the late-night flights we frequently made across the state on an ancient and slow National Guard plane. So we were pleasantly surprised when we boarded in Buffalo one midnight to learn that Harriman had dispatched his press secretary, Walter Mordaunt, to buy a bottle of Dewar's for the cross-state ride home. We were to fly to New York to drop the governor, then back up to Albany, a trip of three or four hours. Weaver and I also had bought some Scotch and shown the foresight to appropriate four glasses from the dinner at which Harriman had spoken. But we kept our bottle out of sight in a raincoat pocket so as not to trump the governor's hospitality. Harriman and Mordaunt were sitting together, Weaver and I played gin rummy in the two seats immediately ahead of them, and as we lumbered across the state we passed the bottle back and forth. When we landed in New York, Harriman began packing up his briefcase.

"Have I got everything?" he asked Mordaunt.

"I think so, Governor," said the press secretary.

"Have I got *everything*?" Harriman repeated with more emphasis.

Weaver caught on. "No, Governor," he said, "here it is." And he passed the fifth of Dewar's, perhaps two-thirds empty, back over his head. Harriman took it, corked it, stowed it in the briefcase, bade us good night, and got off the airplane with his $75 million and a third of a bottle of Scotch.

Whatever hope Harriman nourished of winning that 1960 nomination dissolved in 1958, when Nelson Rockefeller appeared out of some distant political left field—his entire public career had been in second-tier appointive posts in the Eisenhower administration—and defeated him for reelection by a half million votes. In the early stages of his political career, Rockefeller was one of those rare candidates who enjoy a celebrity status that transcends a résumé. He was an heir to this legendary fortune, but he was also the "Rocky" who joked unself-consciously about his wealth—"I grew up playing with blocks," he would say, "Fifty-fourth Street and Fifty-fifth Street"—and seemed genuinely interested in what he was learning as a politician. It was all new to him. On his first day of political handshaking that summer, he was taken to the Wayne County Potato Festival just east of Rochester, where he spent almost fifteen minutes talking with one farmer about the problem of a state requirement that manure spreaders be equipped with turn signals if they were driven from field to field on a state road. But even as he learned how to move it along, Rockefeller managed to project the image of a political candidate who was enjoying himself.

In that first campaign Rockefeller was refreshingly candid. Early in the game several of us cornered him in the Syracuse airport one day and asked if he intended to raise taxes if elected. We were expecting the usual blather about how he could see no reason for a tax increase and had no intention of promulgating one. But Rockefeller refused to play the game. It was possible, he said, it would depend on what the deficit proved to be. The budget was going to have to be balanced, one way or the other, and he didn't want to kid anyone. His forthrightness stunned the reporters covering the campaign, because it seemed to invite Harriman to accuse his challenger of plotting higher taxes. But Harriman knew some increases were probably inevitable, so he took the high road and withheld any criticism. He was ahead in the opinion polls that had been taken for his campaign, and he didn't want to make any waves.

That early lead was flimsy, however, and we saw more and more signs of the Harriman temper as things went sour. On one occasion I put myself in a position that seemed certain to invite his wrath. I had just spent several days with Rockefeller campaigning along the Southern Tier of upstate New York, meaning the counties that border Pennsylvania, and then a similar period in the same area with Harriman. We ended the day in Elmira, checked into the Mark

Twain Hotel, then stopped in the bar to have a drink before going off to dinner at a steak house run by Art Sykes, a onetime heavyweight contender.

Gannett owned the newspapers in Elmira, and several members of the staff came to the hotel to have a drink with us. I was holding forth about the comparison of the popular reaction to the two campaigns, the point being that, counter to the conventional wisdom at the moment, I thought Rockefeller was going to bury Harriman. It was just barroom talk, not something I felt confident enough about to write for my papers. But when I came downstairs for breakfast early the next morning, there was a story in the Elmira *Star-Gazette* about how I was predicting that Rockefeller would bury Harriman. The local reporter had written the story not out of malice but instead out of simple naïveté. But I knew that if Harriman saw it I would be a dead man with him for the rest of the campaign. I bought all the copies of the paper in the hotel newsstand, then called the press secretary traveling with the governor. He had seen the story, he said, but the governor had not and he would try to keep it that way. I owe you one, I told him. You owe me a big one, he replied.

I was saved by two fortuitous developments. The first was that we were scheduled to move on to Binghamton even before the first event of the day, so when Harriman demanded the local paper he was given a different one. The second, vastly more important, was that this was the day *The New York Times* chose to publish its editorial endorsing Rockefeller over Harriman—in the governor's eyes a treacherous and calamitous deed beyond the understanding of any rational man. Once the revered *Times* had stabbed him in the back, Harriman wouldn't worry about some shabby reporter from some, ugh, upstate chain.

As it turned out, the *Times* and I were both right. Rockefeller did win easily, and he was a better governor than Harriman had been.

Despite his easy rapport with his constituents, Rockefeller had a lot to learn about their lives. Both reporters and some members of his staff were surprised at some of the gaps in his knowledge of the culture. He couldn't pronounce *bar mitzvah,* an oddity for a New York politician. Sometimes his lack of background was more striking. At a meeting with his advisers immediately after the election, the governor-elect was told there might be "a problem" with a promise he had made during the campaign to raise the salaries of state employees. Now it was becoming clear that the state was in serious financial straits that would require a tax increase. Raising salaries while raising taxes was not politically prudent, Rockefeller agreed. Then someone came up with a solution. The state had agreed earlier to allow state employees to participate in the Social Security system as well as the state pension plan. Now the state would pick up both the employer and employee share of Social Security taxes, thus giving the workers an increase in their take-home pay. To which a puzzled Rockefeller asked: "What's take-home pay?"

Unlike Harriman, Rockefeller was intrigued by the governor's job, even if he did view it as a stepping-stone. He took office full of enthusiasm and, not incidentally, a few wild ideas. In his first year, for example, he proposed that every household in the state be required to equip itself with a nuclear fallout shelter—a notion that sent the legislature into hysterical laughter. Some of his other innovative ideas made more sense, even if they were too unorthodox to be politically feasible. At one point, for instance, Rockefeller learned that much of New York's costly and chronic welfare problem was caused by migrant workers who left specific communities in the South and then, when the work ran out, settled in Rochester or Syracuse because welfare benefit payments were so much higher than at home. Rockefeller's idea was to use New York State development funds to, for example, finance food-processing plants in those home communities in the South. The theory was that the cost of creating jobs there would be far lower than that of providing welfare benefits. He had the figures to support his case, but the plan was too different to be politically marketable.

Rockefeller finally served three and a half terms before moving on to Washington as President Gerald R. Ford's vice president, and he left many memorials, the most impressive of which was a radical upgrading of the state university system, in which he converted backwater teachers' colleges into liberal arts schools that gave New Yorkers of modest means the same kind of opportunity land-grant universities offered elsewhere.

Meanwhile, his quest for the presidency failed spectacularly, in large measure because he lacked the political judgment he had never had time to acquire. His best opportunity came only a year after he became governor, when he made a series of trips to the Midwest and Far West to determine whether there was a market for the progressive Republicanism he was selling. The popular response to his celebrity was matched only once in the forty-odd years I have covered politics, in that evoked by Robert F. Kennedy a decade later. As had been the case with New Yorkers, voters in places as diverse as California and Wisconsin turned out in huge numbers to see this new phenomenon, lining his route three and four deep to scream, "Rocky, Rocky, Rocky," as he passed, crowding into meeting halls to hear him talk.

The Republican regulars were, of course, another dish of tea entirely. Most of them were committed to Vice President Richard Nixon, and they considered Rockefeller the quintessential candidate of the eastern establishment that sought to force the party into more liberal positions on issues such as civil rights and welfare. So they went to great lengths to limit Rockefeller's exposure as he passed through their communities, setting up events such as a Milwaukee luncheon limited to patronage employees of the county that the candidate himself later described wryly as "a very correct occasion." Rockefeller was more impressed with the shows of resistance by the regulars than he should have been, however. It was true in those days that party leaders had the greatest influence on nominees, but, as John F. Kennedy proved with the Democrats the same year, there were enough primaries to persuade the party leaders, and Rocky was a hot candidate. In the end, however, he decided against running in 1960, a decision he regretted for the rest of his political career. "I didn't know who to believe," he told me years later, "and I listened to the wrong people."

His regret was compounded by Kennedy's own view, expressed privately on more than one occasion, that if Rockefeller had run, he would have beaten both Nixon for the nomination and Kennedy for the White House.

There was an enduring lesson in Rockefeller's experience. It is foolish for any politician to try to find precisely the right time to run for an office, a time when all the stars are in proper alignment. There are too many variables in the political context of a campaign and in the cast of characters who will be involved. Instead, the prize goes to the candidate who seizes the moment. In Rockefeller's case it slipped by, although it took him more than a decade to realize it.

In Albany both Harriman and Rockefeller dealt with a Republican-controlled legislature that was a marvel of demographic and political complexity. There were blocs and blocs within blocs that competed against one another for power and public money—upstate against the city, upstate cities against the dairy farmers, the city against the suburbs, Long Island against Westchester, the Southern Tier against the Hudson Valley, Manhattan against Queens, Jews against Catholics, Catholics against Protestants, whites against blacks, business against labor, conservationists against developers. Coalitions were formed and disbanded, issue by issue. Democrats against Republicans was the least of it.

The key figures were the Senate majority leader, Walter J. Mahoney of Buffalo, and the speaker of the Assembly, first Oswald D. Heck of Schenectady and later Joseph Carlino of Long Island. They controlled the committees and schedules in both houses, which made them prime sources for reporters. Ozzie Heck, a crafty old pol who had made a de facto upstate–Long Island alliance against New York City, was particularly helpful. I could ask him about a piece of controversial legislation affecting upstate, where the Gannett papers were centered, he would reply with a thumbs-up or a thumbs-down, and I could write with confidence that the bill was going to succeed or fail. If the situation changed later in the session, Heck would remember my interest and let me know that thumbs-down was now thumbs-up, thus permitting me to write another piece and avoid being embarrassed.

During the Harriman years Mahoney was also a special help to reporters for upstate newspapers. Although he recognized the ascendant importance of *The New York Times,* he was assiduous about protecting his base. I found that he could be particularly helpful if asked about some Harriman plan on which he was informed although it had not yet been publicly disclosed. "Can you tell me anything about that?" I would say. "I don't want to read about it in the goddamn *Times.*" As often as not he would offer a couple of cryptic sentences from the corner of his mouth that would be enough to do the trick. There is always symbiosis in the relationship between reporters and politicians. All that mattered was that you didn't blow his cover.

Playing it straight and keeping your word were particularly prized in Albany in those times. And the informal rules had nothing to do with party lines. One year a Democratic assemblyman from Brooklyn whom we shall call Sidney asked Ozzie Heck, the Republican speaker, if he could have a vote on the floor on his Sabbath-law bill. This was a measure to allow Jewish proprietors of businesses, who often closed on Saturdays for religious reasons, to open on Sundays, which was then prohibited in most jurisdictions by the so-called blue laws. Sidney's bill was bitterly opposed by non-Jewish shopkeepers, who feared they would lose trade to their competitors or be forced to open seven days a week themselves. So the bill was obviously a touchy one for legislators, particularly in the city, who represented large numbers of both Jewish and Catholic constituents. No one wanted to be put on the record if he could avoid it.

Heck finally told Sidney that he would put the Sabbath bill on the legislative calendar if Sidney would promise to kill it instantly on the floor if the opposition looked strong enough to require a roll call rather than an unrecorded voice vote—a judgment that could be made by the number of hands raised to indicate opposition.

When the clerk called the bill, hands shot up all over the chamber, clearly enough to make it a close call, and Sidney swiveled around in his seat, scanning the room and taking a count. But when Heck said in an inquiring tone, "Mr. Sidney?" the legislator didn't respond. He was still counting when it was already apparent there was too much opposition to get away with a voice vote. "Mr. Sidney?" Heck asked again. When there was still no response, the speaker banged his gavel and ordered, "Third reading"—meaning that the bill now would be considered for final passage. Sidney finally reacted, leaping to his feet and calling out, "Mr. Speaker, Mr. Speaker." But Heck had cast the die. "It's too late, Mr. Sidney," he said, "We're on third reading."

The bill failed narrowly, but Heck used some arcane parliamentary device to erase the roll call and protect his colleagues. Sidney, however, had failed to meet a commitment at a cost I didn't grasp until the following Monday morning, when I was taking the Empire

State Special to Albany. That train left Grand Central at nine o'clock, and the usual drill was for legislators and reporters to fill the dining car for breakfast while rolling along the banks of the Hudson, after which many of them would play bridge or gin rummy. Sidney had been a regular in the card games, but this week he skipped breakfast and remained in his seat reading newspapers. When I asked another Democrat from Brooklyn what was going on, he told me, "Sidney really fucked Ozzie last week. Nobody wants to play with him." And that ostracization continued for the several Mondays left in the legislative session. The lesson was clear. You play by the rules.

There was an equally instructive example in the Senate one year. The Republicans held a single-vote margin but maintained a rigid party discipline, so that when majority leader Walter Mahoney would announce, "Party vote," the Democratic minority leader, another Mahoney named Francis from Manhattan, would acquiesce without requiring all the Republicans to be in the chamber to cast their votes. It was a courtesy, Frank Mahoney recognized, that the Republicans would reciprocate if the Democrats were to win control. There was no point in a lot of nit-picking and party bickering over technicalities.

But this year the situation was complicated by the election from a Hudson Valley district of a Republican amateur—a retired engineer-industrialist who had his own ideas about how the legislature should function. Until his personal legislative agenda had been approved, he told Walter Mahoney, he would not agree to the assumption of unanimity in the "party votes." The majority leader was outraged but unwilling to yield to blackmail by some hayshaker from the Hudson Valley. So weeks passed without any action on what were called program bills—meaning those that made up the principal legislative agenda of the Republican majority. Then one of Mahoney's advisers made an intriguing discovery. Their new colleague, it seemed, was a member of the board of regents of Rensselaer Polytechnic Institute, a noted engineering school just across the Hudson in Troy, New York. Moreover, they learned, he took his responsibilities to RPI very seriously. Mahoney called the president of RPI and suggested that he might want to hold a special meeting of his board over dinner some Monday night. The legislature would be holding its usual evening session to open the week, but if the engineer-senator was a little late, that would be no problem.

Mahoney was a forceful and influential man, and the RPI president understood that he might need his help someday. So he scheduled the dinner, and the unsuspecting senator went to Troy to take part. Imagine his surprise when he returned to the capitol shortly after nine o'clock and discovered that in his absence all the Republican program bills had been called up and passed without a murmur of dissent from the Democrats. The recalcitrant senator also learned, of course, that his own legislative agenda had no future, and after another term he went back to his retirement. That kind of thing probably couldn't happen today. Some goo-goo group—Bob Moses's term for organizations devoted to "good government"—would squawk. Or, even more likely, some Democrat trying to make a name for himself would rush to the television cameras to express his outrage. But in that time the first imperative was playing the game by the rules, and that had nothing to do with partisanship.

The rules did not mean, however, that individual legislators couldn't have an impact on how things turned out. There were, for example, legislators from both parties with a reputation for doing their work seriously enough that they had a special influence. Eugene Goddard, a conservative Republican from western New York, was known to spend his train ride to Albany actually reading and understanding the bills that would be on the assembly calendar. So when he rose to speak, his colleagues in both parties paid attention, as did the reporters sitting in a row of chairs under the podium. The same was true of Max Turshen, a Democrat from Brooklyn who was simply smarter than most people, as well as more colorful. When the word spread that "Maxie's up," everyone listened. If the topic was education, then Assemblyman Billy Passanante would be given the same attention. He might be a product of Carmine DeSapio's infamous Tammany Hall machine, but he knew what he was talking about. A talent for rhetoric was also prized. When Assemblyman Malcolm Wilson, a Yonkers Republican who later became lieutenant governor under Rockefeller and then governor, rose to speak, even the lobbyists would crowd into the back of the chamber to listen to the polished precision of his rhetoric.

There were many, however, who didn't inspire similar respect.

There were a few upstaters who seemed to take a special interest in bills affecting the Niagara Mohawk power company or the dairy industry, some from the city with a special concern for securities legislation that seemed connected to the lobbyists in black suits who stood in the rear of each chamber. There were members of the committee that wrote excise tax bills whose offices were stacked with cases of twenty-year-old Scotch. There were some who had to call their county leaders every day to get the word on how to vote. There were notorious characters. One senator was an extremely wealthy building contractor from the New York suburbs who kept a suite at the hotel and brought his barber along to shave him and his friends every morning. This guy gave a party once a year that offered food, drink, and in a couple of rooms just down the hall the services of prepaid hookers brought up from Manhattan for the occasion.

But there were as many more benign oddballs, such as Senator Pliny Williamson of Westchester County, an old man who wore a plum-colored suit and always carried a pocketful of honey drops. During long sessions he would totter up and down the press row, dropping a candy into each reporter's outstretched palm like a priest handing out communion wafers. The ranking Democrat on the Senate Finance Committee, Sam Greenburg of Brooklyn, was a brilliant and sometimes acerbic orator who, when not speaking, loved to give the hot foot to any reporter who had nodded off in the press row. In each chamber there were two or three dedicated drunks who after lunch often had to be roused by their colleagues to cast their votes. There were more than two or three committed womanizers who cut a wide swath through the pool of clerical talent. And there was some clerical talent who cut a wide swath through the legislators.

But the reporters blew the whistle only in cases where they could find public money being diverted to, for example, a no-show job or what were known as lulus—meaning "allowances in lieu of expenses" often buried in the fine print of legislation. The laws requiring financial disclosure and accountability for campaign costs were so weak, no one could be nailed unless someone told on him. And when that happened the whistle-blower almost always became a pariah. One year a young assemblyman named Mark Lane, who later became prominent in a whole range of radical causes, accused the speaker, Republican Joe Carlino, of taking a fee of five thousand dollars to his

Long Island law firm in exchange for legislation that would throw a lot of business to the "contributor." The first reaction in the capitol was that the notion of Carlino selling out for a mere five grand was preposterous on its face; nobody would sell out for that kind of money. The second reaction was the bipartisan ostracization of Lane. When I wrote a piece about it that appeared in the Gannett Albany paper, the *Knickerbocker News,* under the headline THE LONELIEST MAN IN THE LEGISLATURE, several of his colleagues congratulated me, for, as one put it, "You got that bastard good."

The "arrangements" between legislators and special interests were, as they are today, usually a matter of a wink and a nod, tacit understandings rather than contracts. When Representative William E. Miller of Niagara Falls was chosen as the Republican nominee for vice president in 1964, he had a reputation as "the congressman from Niagara Mohawk," although there never had been any evidence uncovered to suggest any payoff beyond the utility's eternal goodwill for whatever favors it received. But I wanted to see if there was more to it than that, so I called an old friend in Albany who had enjoyed the same reputation vis-à-vis Niagara Mohawk in the legislature and asked him where I should look. To which he replied, "Jack, there's never anything on paper, you can count on it, they don't put nothing on paper."

The reporters themselves were not as sensitive to ethical questions as they should have been or would be today. Every year the clerk of the assembly, Ansley Borkowski of Buffalo, threw a lavish seafood dinner for the press corps—lobsters, oysters, bay scallops from Long Island, ice fish (smelts) from the North Country, Prior's beer from Philadelphia. I think we all understood that Borkowski wasn't paying the tab himself, but we all lined up at the trough and didn't inquire.

Then there was "the legislative box." A few days after I arrived for my first session in 1956, a clerk from the speaker's office delivered a large cardboard box to every reporter in the pressroom. Inside was a leather suitcase, and inside the suitcase we found not just stationery and boxes of paper clips and rubber bands but such luxury items as a leather appointment diary, an expensive travel clock, and a Cross pen-and-pencil set. Nonplussed, I asked my new boss and was told it was "the legislative box"—the same "supplies" given each member of the legislature every year to see him through his labors. Take it home and forget it. Don't make waves. And that is what I did until the following year, when Ed Hale, a newly arrived free spirit from *The Buffalo Evening News,* and I decided to quietly return our boxes and ask them to take our names off the list. Several others did the same thing, but there was also some muttering about reporters who were holier than thou.

Most of the time, however, the relationship among the reporters was collegial as well as highly competitive. If the reporter with the bad drinking problem failed to file his story one night, someone else would do it in his name. If the correspondent for the *Worker*—no longer the *Daily Worker* by that time—was broke because the Communists were so damned stingy with their expense money, someone else would pick up his dinner tab or pay for his shoeshine.

For a newcomer it was a time of testing against more experienced men with extensive networks of sources already in place. By almost all estimates the top hand in Albany was Leo Egan, the chief political reporter on the city staff of *The New York Times,* who came up to Albany for three months of the legislative session every year. Indeed, his stature was so widely acknowledged that other reporters referred to him regularly, and without rancor, as El Supremo—as in, upon picking up the *Times* in the morning, "Goddammit, El Supremo's got a piece on that transit bill. How in hell am I going to match it?"

Egan's obviously superior position was easy for the rest of us to swallow because he was such a lovely human being. He was a gray-faced, middle-aged man whose glasses gave him an owlish look, and he was notorious for his dress; it was not a surprise if he showed up wearing one brown sock and one black. He spoke softly with a slight stammer, and he always seemed to take everything in stride. He laughed a lot and always had a story about some arcane political deal he'd heard about when he worked for the *Brooklyn Eagle.* Many of the stories gave rise to what became known as Leo Egan rules. He would tell a story about a time he was beaten by the *Herald Trib* because he held a story one day too long to check one more angle, then add: "Reporter who sit on hot story get ass burned." His most famous rule, however, was one I tried to follow for the rest of my life as a reporter: When all else fails, ask yourself what's logical. Younger reporters like Warren Weaver, Ed Hale, and I often said that you never had dinner with Leo without learning something, but you never got the feeling he was a teacher. He was just another guy at the poker table, another guy closing the bar and swapping stories. But he was better than the rest of us, and we knew it and, amazingly, didn't resent it.

Leo took a special interest in me and, without being obvious about it, became my rabbi. If he had a beat on a story that was important upstate, he would suggest quietly that I might want to look into the situation because it was coming to a boil, thus sparing me the embarrassment of being beaten on a story in my own backyard. Or he would unobtrusively pass me what was then called a black-sheet—meaning a carbon copy of a story he had just filed—so I wouldn't get a callback, meaning a complaint from an editor for having missed it. One of the proudest moments of my life was the day in 1958, my third year covering the legislature, when I passed a blacksheet to Leo that he used for his file. An equally proud moment was the day I learned, after Leo's death in 1962, that he had written a memo to the *Times* suggesting they hire me to succeed him.

There were a lot of good reporters covering Albany in those days. The *Times* had Weaver, a remarkably graceful writer with a knack for the felicitous phrase with whom I traveled on both the state and, from Washington, national political beats for thirty years. Weaver had many skills, not the least being a talent for euphemisms that would inform the reader in a time when newspapers were notoriously cautious. A legislator who was a confirmed drunk, for example, might be described as "having a reputation for excessive conviviality." A womanizer was a man, in Weaver lexicon, "with an appreciation for a well-turned ankle." In an age when newspapers routinely discuss oral sex, these circumlocutions sound bizarre, but at the time they were breakthroughs.

The *Times* had many able reporters in Albany at one point or another, including late in my era R. W. (Johnny) Apple, Jr., whose bumptious manner couldn't hide his remarkable energy and skills. The *Trib* had Charles Quinn, later with NBC, and David Wise, who subsequently became an expert on the Central Intelligence Agency and the whole world of international espionage. The star of the *Daily News* was James Desmond, a slender, elegantly dressed man who drank his Scotch in milk because he had a bad stomach and who could summarize a busy day's activity in the legislature in 350 words without missing anything important. Gannett had Bill Ringle and our bureau chief, Emmet N. O'Brien, who covered the beat by knowing about the personal interests of everyone from the governor to the capitol elevator operators. Emmet was a kind man, who took it upon himself to train the young reporters in how to get along with the home office. When I once turned in an expense account that showed I had spent eighty cents on breakfast, he chastised me. "Breakfast is at least a dollar fifty," he told me. "Don't cheapen the beat."

There were a few curious cases as well. One was Raymond I. Borst, the longtime resident year-round correspondent for *The Buffalo Evening News*. In those days the *News* had pronounced Republican sympathies, to which Borst paid obeisance while covering the Democrat Harriman. One day Harriman held a press conference at which he announced that, yes, he would sign a bill passed routinely to grant franchise tax relief to city bus companies that were in serious financial trouble upstate. Harriman also said that he would veto a series of "humanizing amendments" to the income tax law that had been passed by the Republican legislature to give special breaks to the aged, the blind, and working mothers. The problem with the bill, the governor said, was that it wasn't generous enough in those benefits, so he would insist on a more liberal Democratic version. When the press conference ended Borst rushed to his telephone—his desk was right next to mine—and I heard him dictate his lead: "Governor Harriman announced today that he would grant tax relief to bus companies but deny it to the aged, the blind, and working mothers." Beautiful.

Borst was also part of one of the strangest pressroom card games any of us had ever seen. He didn't often join the regular poker games or the four-handed rummy we sometimes played to kill time during the day. But he had a long-running gin game with Tom Stowell, a white-haired, semiretired man who acted as a stringer for some trade publications and earned a few dollars as a kind of pressroom attendant by straightening out the piles of handouts and distributing the mail. What made the game so intriguing was that the two players distrusted each other so thoroughly. They played across a desk with a row of books in the middle so they could hide their hands from each other. And each of them kept a separate score, which they compared for accuracy after each hand. As Ed Hale put it one day, "It's nice to see two old friends enjoying their golden years together."

Then there was Arvis Chalmers, a dapper man with a slim mustache and a charm that dazzled a series of women twenty years his junior, each of whom he referred to as Mother as he drove them around town in his yellow convertible. Chalmers was the chief capitol reporter for the now defunct *Knickerbocker News* and the year-round stringer for *Newsday*. The second job paid him handsomely, but *Newsday*'s operating methods were sometimes hard to take. They had a habit of sending a reporter from their staff in Garden City, Long Island, up to Albany to do the story on "what's really going on" in the legislature. The implication was always that those of us who had been covering the session for months had gone into the tank for the politicians rather than find out "what's really going on." Listening to one of these new arrivals, Arvis would wince, but, what the hell, it paid well.

On one occasion, faced with an evening with another emissary from Long Island, Arvis called and asked me if I'd go along to dinner with them. Maybe I could cool this guy off and keep him from making a total ass of himself. We had dinner at Yezzi's and listened to a *Newsday* reporter we shall call Bob explain how we were missing this or that aspect of the story. He kept it up through dinner and several hours of barhopping ending in an after-hours place that admitted us only because the proprietor knew Arvis and me so well. Bob announced that he would spring for a bottle of champagne, "if they have such a thing in this dump," which was clearly the last straw coming from this clown from Long Island in our joint. So, although it was only about three, Arvis suggested maybe it was time to pack it in. But Bob had another idea. He was really ready "to buy a good piece of ass," he confided. He was willing to spend up to fifteen dollars. What a sport. Arvis was speechless and then even more dumbfounded when I told old Bob, "I know just the place, let's go." Arvis was baffled, but I reassured him, and we all piled into the convertible. Then I directed Arvis down the hill a few blocks to the Railroad Hotel, an old wood structure next to the train yards where railroad workers could stay overnight cheaply. "You register as George Washington or something, give the guy five bucks, and just go up to the room," I told Bob. When we saw him go through the door, Arvis and I both broke up and decided to go back to the after-hours for one more pop.

The next morning Bob arrived in the pressroom and said in accusing tone, "I did what you said and nothing happened. I was there all night and nothing happened."

"Did you knock on the wall?" I asked.

"What are you talking about?" said Bob.

"You're supposed to knock on the wall, you dumb shit," I replied.

That was the last I ever saw of Bob, but I followed his byline at *Newsday* for years. He wasn't covering politics.

CHAPTER 4

A CRITICAL DIVORCE

On the Friday after the New York mayoral election of 1961, Bob McManus, Nelson Rockefeller's press secretary, called me at my office in the Time-Life Building in New York. I had been transferred from Albany to open a one-man bureau for Gannett. I should come to the governor's Manhattan office at 6:00 P.M. for an announcement, McManus said. When I asked him what it was about—this was a Friday and I was thinking of knocking off early—he replied that he could say no more but that it was something I wouldn't want to miss. I took him at his word; he was an old and close friend who didn't play little flack games. The only inference I could draw was that it was bad news, because politicians always operate on the theory, usually mistaken, that if you break bad news on Friday afternoons, fewer people hear about it because they don't read the Saturday papers or watch the weekend news.

I showed up at 22 West Fifty-fifth Street, the town house backing up to the Museum of Modern Art that Rockefeller had converted into his New York City headquarters, at ten minutes to six. McManus invited me into his office and told me to take a seat. Then we sat there in funereal silence for eight or nine minutes until the second hand showed the time had reached precisely 6:00 P.M., whereupon he reached into his desk drawer and handed me a single sheet of paper. It was being delivered to the New York papers and wire services at precisely the same moment, he assured me. The brief hand-out announced that Rockefeller and his wife of thirty-odd years, Mary Todhunter Clark Rockefeller, were separating. Stunned, I began asking the obvious questions. Were they to be divorced? Did the governor plan to marry someone else? Did he plan to run for re-election again next year? Or for president, as we all assumed, in 1964? McManus pulled another sheet of paper from his desk. It spelled out the precise answers he was allowed to give to each question, none of them particularly revealing. But the whole process was choreographed down to the point that McManus told me he could add nothing to the written answers, even off the record or for my guidance. Not so much as a nod and a wink.

These days this elaborate staging seems a little overdone. But at that time the breakup of the marriage of someone as prominent in American public life as Nelson Rockefeller was such a big story that the effort to control the way it was handled made some sense. Al-though Adlai Stevenson had twice been nominated for president de-spite a divorce in his background, the conventional wisdom still held that a divorce was a heavy political burden.

Moreover, there had been no hint of trouble in the Rockefeller marriage. After the fact some reporters claimed to have known something was fishy when a fire in the executive mansion in Albany revealed that the governor and his wife occupied separate bed-rooms. But none of us really knew anything about their relation-ship. His wife, who was called Tod, came from a Philadelphia Main Line family, and they had been married shortly after he finished Dartmouth. She was a tall, slender woman who was not particularly attractive at first glance. But those of us who came to know her a lit-tle found her charming if somewhat reserved, and she was both well read and intelligent. Indeed, I had suspected that she was smarter than the governor. And those who knew her better than I said she was more liberal than he. The one thing about her on which every-one seemed to agree was that she did not really enjoy the public role she was expected to play as the wife of a glad-handing politician. Nonetheless, she did it.

The story exploded, and not just in the tabloids. And the question was obviously, Who is the Other Woman? None of us knew a thing, but we began to develop suspicions. I dredged up two incidents involving one of Rockefeller's executive assistants, a leggy, late-thirtyish woman named Margaretta Fitler Murphy, known to everyone as Happy. On one occasion, explaining Rockefeller's thinking on some initiative he had just announced, Happy referred to him as "Nelson" in speaking to me when "the governor" would have been more usual. On another occasion I was riding in a staff car with Happy following Rockefeller in a two-car motorcade careening along the Long Island Expressway toward Idlewild Airport at rush hour. His car kept veering wildly between lanes, narrowly avoiding one collision after another. I was struck by the fact that Happy seemed more concerned with what was happening to the first car than with the one in which we were riding. But that was all I knew, and it wasn't enough to even hint at in print. In fact, I never mentioned it to anyone but my wife.

As it turned out, Happy was the Other Woman. For months the press chronicled the divorce of the Rockefellers, Happy's divorce from Dr. Joseph Murphy, and the child custody arrangements until, in May of 1963, all the legal barriers removed and Rockefeller having won a second term as governor, Nelson and Happy were married. The man with $200 million now had a wife twenty years younger.

These days the popular attitude probably would be acceptance. Things happen in marriages that outsiders cannot know, and it happens in most families. Judge not lest ye be judged. But in this case the wise guys of politics were convinced Rockefeller had suffered a grievous blow to his presidential prospects. The story was too sensational to be put aside. It was seen as an example of how the rich and famous flout convention in ways the rest of us are not permitted. The whole thing was a particular affront, the political strategists said, to the middle-class white Americans who made up the core of the Republican Party.

In this case, too, Rockefeller paid an especially high price for his celebrity. He was not just another politician but a golden figure different from everyone else, so more was expected of him. Why did he have to humiliate the tall and awkward fifty-year-old wife? Why didn't he suck it up and stick with her? And what about Happy's four children—how much would they suffer? Opinion polls and anecdotal evidence made it clear that women in particular were outraged. A Gallup Poll taken shortly after their marriage found Senator Barry Goldwater of Arizona leading Rockefeller, 59 to 41 percent among Republicans as their choice for the presidential nomination in 1964, a reversal of their earlier positions. Even among independents it was Goldwater 56, Rockefeller 41. There was only one possible explanation, and it was a story that would not die.

Rockefeller himself didn't believe it. But as he began laying the groundwork for his 1964 presidential campaign, he was forced to face the fact that it would not be easy. In September 1963 I came up to New York from Washington (I had been transferred there two years earlier) to join him on a trip to Illinois, his first political foray since the wedding four months earlier. He would attend the annual Republican corn roast in Ogle County, held in a cornfield in Oregon, Illinois, some eighty miles west of Chicago. As we flew west that morning Rockefeller read *The New York Times* and a column by James Reston saying his chances for the nomination were "not worth a plugged nickel." He handed me the paper, pointing to the column, and asked whether I agreed. I thought Reston had gone a little too far, but it wasn't my business, so I passed it off with some wisecrack about how a quarter might be more accurate.

When we arrived at the cornfield, however, the evidence seemed to support Reston. This was a political event ordinarily considered a "must" for Illinois Republicans, but not this time. Everett McKinley Dirksen, the Senate minority leader and the state's most prominent party figure, didn't show up. Neither did Charles Percy, the ostensibly progressive businessman Rockefeller had befriended in 1960 who was running for the Republican gubernatorial nomination in 1964. The local Sixteenth District congressman, John B. Anderson, sent word that he had a previous commitment to speak at a party training school in Michigan. But when I called his home in Rockford, he answered the phone and muttered some awkward explanation about how he was just leaving. The crowd of several thousand was curious about Rocky the celebrity but restrained in reacting to his speech. The corn, taken off the stalk and plunged directly into the kettles of boiling water, was delicious. But the message to Rockefeller was clearly that he was not someone with whom Republican leaders wanted to be photographed.

Rockefeller was not fazed. He would not, perhaps could not, accept the notion that his personal life had scuttled his political career. He would demonstrate he was viable by defeating Barry Goldwater in the primaries, as John F. Kennedy had defeated Hubert H. Humphrey in the 1960 Democratic primaries in West Virginia and Wisconsin to prove that a Roman Catholic could win. There were not enough primaries in those days to provide a majority of the delegates to the national convention. They were chosen by party leaders and state conventions, where Goldwater had far more strength. But the theory was that Rockefeller would demonstrate that, given a chance, rank-and-file Republicans wanted someone in the political mainstream, not an extremist of the right.

It was a valid theory, but it didn't help Rockefeller. Campaigning in New Hampshire with Happy at his side in January and February 1964, he continued to attract the curious, who wanted to see the celebrity who had become so notorious and the Other Woman who had led him to do so. But commitments of support from local party leaders were hard to nail down. Happy was four or five months pregnant, and privately the New Hampshire elders speculated about what would happen if she had a miscarriage in the middle of the campaign. She shouldn't be riding over these icy roads in that campaign bus, they warned.

Goldwater had his problems as well. The senator from Arizona was an extremely likable man, plainspoken and blunt. But his penchant for tossing out wild ideas about privatizing the Tennessee Valley Authority or making Social Security voluntary made the primary voters uneasy. And late in the campaign those voters were given an alternative when two political amateurs from Boston, a businessman named Paul Grindle and a lawyer named David Goldberg, opened an office on Main Street in Concord, just across from the statehouse, with the declared purpose of running a write-in campaign for Henry Cabot Lodge, the 1960 vice presidential nominee, then serving as ambassador to South Vietnam.

The political reporters, myself included, were skeptical. Lodge, after all, had been less than a rousing success on Nixon's ticket in 1960. He had earned a reputation as a lazy candidate who broke into his schedule every afternoon for a nap, and, some horrified staff members confided, he was so effete he put on his pajamas to take the nap. And although there had been some impressive write-ins in previous New Hampshire primaries, they had been accomplished when there were no candidates competing actively, as both Goldwater and Rockefeller were doing. In 1956, for example, a write-in for Nixon for vice president attracted 22,000 votes to rebuff suggestions from some Republicans that President Eisenhower should drop him from his ticket in running for his second term.

But Grindle and Goldberg had a scheme. They obtained the mailing list of all Republican households in the state and sent each a two-part postcard. These voters were asked to detach the second part of the card, sign the pledge to vote for Lodge printed on it, and mail it back to the Concord office. I was still skeptical, until Goldberg urged me to come into their headquarters the next morning and open the mail with them. It was impressive, several bags of mail and hundreds of the signed cards, enough to persuade me the write-in could take a lot of moderate Republican votes from Rockefeller. I was still too locked into conventional thinking, nonetheless, to foresee what happened on primary day: Lodge won outright with 35 percent, leaving Goldwater a distant second with 22 percent and Rockefeller third with 21. He wasn't even comfortably ahead of another write-in for Richard Nixon, which attracted 17 percent.

Lodge remained in Saigon and never came home to capitalize on his showing by becoming an active candidate. The Goldwater and Rockefeller partisans insisted his triumph was a product of New England regional pride. After all, he had been a senator from Massachusetts when Nixon put him on the 1960 ticket. But the story was too thin to be convincing. The message in the results was plain to everyone: Neither Goldwater nor Rockefeller was acceptable to these Republicans. Neither was likely to put together a coalition within the party broad enough to make a Republican ticket competitive with President Lyndon B. Johnson only a year after the death of John F. Kennedy.

The Rockefeller-Goldwater competition continued through the spring, nonetheless. In May, Rockefeller won the Oregon primary when Goldwater refused to campaign in the state. John Deardourff, a perceptive young consultant working for Rockefeller, came up with an idea for capitalizing on whatever resentment Goldwater's decision may have caused—a series of television commercials depicting Rockefeller as the candidate "who cared enough to come," and Oregonians bought it. Then it was on to the showdown primary in California the first Tuesday in June, the contest that proved to be Rockefeller's last hurrah as a serious possibility for the White House.

The New Yorker entered the final weekend of the campaign holding a clear although tenuous lead in the opinion polls after spending heavily on television commercials that depicted Goldwater as a dangerous extremist. But over those final days Goldwater closed the gap and won the primary. The conventional wisdom held that Rockefeller lost because Happy gave birth to a son during that final weekend, thus reminding the primary voters of the two messy divorces that had led to their union. In fact, the critical decision was one Rockefeller made to coast to victory by surrendering options on a heavy television buy in the last few days. The Goldwater campaign bought the time suddenly available to them and used it to run a spot of the senator from Arizona speaking softly, twirling his horn-rimmed glasses, and projecting an image that clashed with the notion of him as an extremist.

Rockefeller had made the decision on the advice of some of his New York staff and contrary to the counsel of Stuart Spencer, a street-smart California consultant who believed that if you have an opponent down, as Goldwater was, you pound him into the sand. On that Sunday, two days before the primary, he told me, "I think we've blown it. Barry is everywhere [on TV]." Long after the fact Rockefeller told me, "I listened to the wrong people. That happens sometimes."

Rockefeller was essentially finished as a national candidate after that primary, although he made an awkward attempt again in 1968 and was still nourishing dreams-while-shaving when he was chosen to be President Gerald Ford's vice president in 1974. But he continued to be viewed with so much suspicion by the controlling conservatives in the party that Ford dropped him from the 1976 ticket in favor of a senator from Kansas, Bob Dole.

The saddest thing about Rockefeller's political career was not that he failed to reach the White House. That happens to a lot of them; he had his chance and he blew it. The sad thing was that over the sixteen or eighteen years he spent on the national stage the ebullient Rockefeller became so much like other politicians. It would have been too much to expect him to retain the freshness of those early days in Albany. But it was a shame to see him abandon the candor and directness that made him different. By the end he was shucking and jiving just like all the rest, no longer a candidate who would confess he might have to raise your taxes. He had accumulated so much scar tissue that the punches seemed to slide off him. In 1975 I wrote a condescendingly negative piece for *The New York Times Magazine* about him playing out his string as a lame-duck vice president to whom no one paid any serious attention. There had been a time when Rockefeller would have reacted intensely and aggressively to defend himself, but by this point he simply shrugged it off. "If that's the way you see it," he told me with heavy sarcasm when I ran into him shortly after the piece was published, "then I guess that's the way it is." It was clear that he didn't believe it but that he didn't give a damn either.

Rockefeller had not reached that point, of course, in 1964, when Californians rejected him in the primary. But he was realistic enough to fold his campaign. Given the support he had locked up in nonprimary states, Goldwater was now assured of the nomination. The eastern liberals continued desperately seeking a way to stop him, finally putting forward Governor William Scranton of Pennsylvania as a "mainstream" replacement for Rockefeller. Scranton proved ineffectual and served only as a resting place for the diehards against Goldwater. Even among middle-road conservatives, however, there were doubts about Goldwater's viability. Republican congressional leaders were particularly uneasy about the prospect of wholesale losses in the Senate and House. At one point Richard Nixon began making small gestures of his availability. His loss in the California gubernatorial election and that "last press conference" were only two years in the past, but apparently it would take a stake through the heart to discourage him.

The divisions in the party were spread for all to see at the tumultuous convention at the Cow Palace in San Francisco. Those of us sitting in the press section next to the podium were impressed by the vehemence of the Goldwaterites in their hostility toward us and toward Rockefeller and the remnants of the eastern liberal establishment. Circulating among the delegates on the floor, I encountered several who screamed obscenities at me, not because they knew who I was but only because I was wearing a press pass around my neck.

There were some moments. When the roll call on the presidential nomination reached New York, the state party chairman, Fred Young, a free spirit installed by Rockefeller, called out, "New York casts eighty-seven votes for Governor Rockefeller, five votes for Senator Goldwater." I couldn't imagine who those Goldwater delegates might be, but because I was working for a chain based in New York, I had to find out. I quickly got a floor pass and ran down the aisle to the delegation.

"Freddy," I asked, "who are the five?"

"Anybody who needs them," Freddy replied, "anybody who needs them."

The divisions in the party were not hard to find. Nor was the bad blood. When Senator Jacob K. Javits, the liberal New Yorker and ally of Rockefeller, walked out of the convention, the *Chicago Tribune* published an angry editorial under the headline SOREHEAD JAVITS. That, in turn, prompted Charles Percy, once again a profile in courage, to tell the *Trib* he was "reconsidering" a plan to bring Javits into Illinois to campaign for him. When I told Javits what Percy was saying, he replied icily, "It wasn't my idea in the first place. He's got a problem with the Jews, and he wanted me to help him."

The general election campaign changed nothing, although, to his credit, Goldwater never gave up. In the final month there were stretches of five or six days in a row in which he began the day with a breakfast in the eastern time zone and then flew west, taking advantage of the time change, for more appearances in central and mountain time, sometimes even Pacific time. He would finish the day, then fly back east, arriving at midnight or later for four or five hours' rest before doing the whole thing all over again. The goal was to touch as many media markets as possible every day on the theory that the local news coverage would be friendlier than what he was getting from the networks. It was futile and exhausting. The saving grace, I found, was that when we boarded the campaign plane at seven in the morning the stewardesses would be waiting with hot bouillon, an effective restorative for at least a couple of hours.

The one man in the Goldwater campaign who seemed to have the proper perspective was William E. Miller, a congressman from up-state New York and former Republican national chairman whom Goldwater had chosen as his running mate on the mistaken theory that his acid tongue would bother Johnson. From the outset Miller made no bones about the fact that he considered the whole thing a doomed enterprise but, nonetheless, a good thing for his future prospects. "How many lawyers from Niagara Falls get to run for vice president?" he would ask.

Miller spent most of the campaign playing bridge with reporters as his plane flew from one airport rally to another. I spent just a week on the Miller plane and, as it happened, filled in for one of the regular bridge players who was off that week and thus was able to watch Miller at close range. The rule was that when the plane pulled up to the gate, everyone would put down his cards and the bridge hand would be suspended. Miller would turn down his starched French cuffs, tighten his tie, and shrug on the jacket of his dark blue suit. He would go down the stairs, usually to the back of a flatbed truck, where he would deliver a canned speech attacking Johnson. (After a Johnson adviser was accused of soliciting a homo-sexual act in a public men's room, Miller would attack "Johnson and his curious crew." Subtlety was not his strong suit.) When he re-turned to the plane, he would shrug off the jacket, loosen the tie, turn back the cuffs, and reclaim his seat. Then he would say, "Now, let's see, that was one heart, two spades, pass, and I jumped to four spades. Your bid." He never bothered with any postmortems on the political event.

Perhaps the most telling judgment on Miller's qualifications for the vice presidential nomination was one handed down by a man named Tom Berrigan, who was the editor of *The Niagara Falls Gazette,* Miller's hometown newspaper. Berrigan was a close friend and one of those who had urged Miller to become involved in poli-tics. He and Miller regularly played golf and gin rummy together. But Berrigan published an editorial endorsing President Johnson for a second term and, more to the point, specifically endorsing the Democratic nominee for vice president, Hubert H. Humphrey, over Miller. It was a measure of how lightly Miller wore his responsibili-ties that he and Berrigan continued to play golf and gin together long after the campaign and the editorial.

After the 1964 election returns defined what was ever after called the Goldwater debacle, there was a great deal of hand-wringing by Republicans and in the press about the End of the Republican Party as We Know It. It was an exaggeration, as is usually the case with apocalyptic pronouncements in American politics. Two years later the Republicans rebounded to gain forty-six seats in the House. Four years later Nixon won the presidency.

But 1964 was the year the "eastern establishment" that had nominated Thomas E. Dewey and Dwight D. Eisenhower became a terminal case. Nelson Rockefeller was both the symbol and the personification of the liberal wing of the Republican Party. There was no one else with the potential for the presidency he had shown in his first days as a political phenomenon.

Through the rest of the 1960s and 1970s, there were still a number of influential progressive Republicans in the Senate—Javits of New York, Clifford Case of New Jersey, John Sherman Cooper of Kentucky, Edward Brooke of Massachusetts, and Tom Kuchel of California among them. And there were still some liberal Republican governors—Tom McCall of Oregon, David Cargo of New Mexico, Frank Sargent of Massachusetts, and Raymond Shafer of Pennsylvania, as well as Rockefeller. But most were picked off over the two decades, surrendering their seats to Democrats or more conventionally conservative Republicans. There was still a substantial moderate wing in the House of Representatives as well, but it atrophied over the next generation as more seats moved from the East and Midwest to the South and Far West. The party's political center moved so far that such conservatives as Gerald Ford and Bob Dole came to be considered moderates only a few years later.

The sins of the eastern establishment were never entirely clear. On national security, foreign policy, and budget issues, they generally were little different from their more conservative counterparts from the Midwest. The progressives were, nonetheless, much more inclined to rely on activist government to solve problems. And, above all, they were much different from their conservative colleagues in their aggressive support for civil rights, the issue that more than any other shaped politics for two generations of Americans.

CHAPTER 5

GEORGE WALLACE

The national press sort of missed the "other" campaign of 1964, the arrival on the national political scene of Governor George Corley Wallace of Alabama. We didn't exactly ignore his quixotic challenge to Lyndon Johnson in the Democratic primaries of Wisconsin, Indiana, and Maryland. There was some mild surprise at the Wallace vote—34 percent in Wisconsin, 30 percent in Indiana, and 43 percent, including a majority of the white vote, in Maryland. But it was written off as aberrational, cast perhaps by transplanted southerners who were responding to a rabble-rousing style with which they were familiar. We were slow to hear and understand the message in those primary results—that there was a huge reservoir of racial animosity in the North as well as the South that might be exploited in a more serious way by more respectable conservative candidates in the future.

Part of our problem was, of course, that we still thought of the war being waged over civil rights as an issue predominate in the South. It was there that the resistance to integration was based on state law and local ordinances as well as a century of custom. It was there that the young people marched behind Martin Luther King, Jr., and faced the wrath of Bull Connor in Birmingham and his imitators in places like Selma, Alabama, and Americus, Georgia. And it was in the South where reporters like myself from Washington and New York encountered such implacable hostility not just from the man in the street but from the local politicians and community leaders, including too often editors and publishers of newspapers. It was considered routine courtesy in the newspaper business in those days for a visiting reporter to be invited into a local paper's city room to use a typewriter to prepare his copy for Western Union to send back to the home office. But I remember being turned away from the Jackson *Daily News* on a trip to Mississippi and being refused an interview with an editor of the *Recorder* in Americus, Georgia, when the civil rights story boiled over there. So at first we tended to see George Wallace as part of that strange and isolated society, not really a national figure, despite his temerity in venturing so far from Montgomery.

Many of us, myself included, also were conditioned by our belief that the national ethic on race had been settled by this time. The March on Washington in August 1963 had impressed even the most jaded of our number, 250,000 people packed between the Lincoln Memorial and Washington Monument in a display of both civility and purpose few if any of us had ever before witnessed. Listening to Martin Luther King, Jr., from my perch above him on the memorial steps, I found myself almost convinced his dream could become a quick reality. We were convinced, too, that we had turned a corner when Lyndon Johnson and Congress approved the Civil Rights Act of 1964 covering public accommodations and moved toward approval of the Voting Rights Act of 1965. The national decision had been made, and neither George Wallace nor one of those other braying asses was going to reverse it. They were just playing southern politics.

Nor was Wallace himself impressive, at least on first acquaintance. He had been a bantamweight fighter as a young man and in middle age still looked the part, short and chesty with a meaty jaw but small hands and feet. He spoke with a pronounced nasal accent, punctuating his conversation with *heunh* (a spelling I have lifted from Marshall Frady's insightful biography *Wallace,* published in 1968)—as in "You be sure and vote for me, heunh" or "Y'all come visit, heunh." His speeches were largely unstructured rants about "pointy-headed intellectuals" and "bureaucrats who can't park a bicycle straight" but are quick to prescribe the proper behavior for "the average citizen—your steelworker, your taxi driver, and your beautician"—pronounced "b'yootishun."

Wallace's political history was well known. When he was a young member of the Alabama legislature, he had started as an ally and admirer of the populist Governor "Big Jim" Folsom. But when Folsom's brand of relative moderation on the race question cost Wallace a defeat at the hands of a hard-line segregationist in the Democratic primary for governor in 1958, Wallace made a vow: "John Patterson out-niggered me and, boys, I'm not going to be out-niggered again." Four years later he delivered on that promise and, in his inaugural address in Montgomery, delivered a diatribe against integration and declared: "Segregation now! Segregation tomorrow! Segregation forever!"

Wallace had come to national attention "standing in the school-house door" to prevent the integration of the University of Alabama in 1963, but by the time of the 1964 primaries reporters knew that had been a carefully choreographed confrontation that had far more to do with politics than with policy. If there was going to be a southern demagogue riding the racial horse to national political power, the conventional wisdom held, it would be some far slicker article than George Corley Wallace.

In fact, Wallace's performance in those Democratic primaries was all the more impressive because he wasn't a slick article. In retrospect, over the next year or two, it became clear to me and to the other Monday-morning quarterbacks of the political press corps that since it wasn't his charm, it had to be his message. There were indeed millions of Americans from all parts of the country who might see George Wallace as the way to "send them a message" of their discontent. So over those years Wallace watched us all fly down to Montgomery to try to come to grips with this phenomenon. He loved talking about those 1964 primary results. He took particular delight for years from his vote in Maryland and the fact that early in the evening of election night he appeared to be actually leading until Governor Millard Tawes announced that a "recapitulation" of the vote showed him running behind President Johnson after all. "You have to watch out for that recapitulation," Wallace would say, stretching the word out syllable by syllable. "Yes, sir, anybody says he's going to re-ca-pit-u-late on you, watch out."

Until I started appearing on television regularly in later years, Wallace always had a little trouble figuring out just who I was. But he knew Gannett was a chain with a lot of papers somewhere in New York. "I've got a lot of support up there; you'd be surprised," he would tell me when I showed up to cover him. And he knew I came from Washington, Dee Cee, and thus qualified as a member of "the national press." Walking through an airport, he would gesture over his shoulder with his thumb and tell the waiting-room passengers, "I've got the national press with me. We're going on a distortin' trip." It was all part of his shtick.

"You fellows don't mind me saying that, heunh," he would tell us privately a little later. "The folks like it and I don't mean anything by it." And most of us accepted that explanation. He was just another politician living off the land and using whatever was available. What the hell.

Wallace was ambivalent about the national press. He was pleased, even a little flattered by all the attention. And he enjoyed the fencing. He particularly liked to cast anyone from Washington on the defensive, chuckling over a putative plan to build another bridge over the Potomac "for all the white liberals fleeing to Virginia."

One day he asked me where I lived, "out in the suburbs in Maryland or Virginia somewhere?" When I replied that I lived within Dee Cee itself, he was stopped for only a moment. "And where do your chillun go to school?" he wanted to know.

"They go to National Cathedral. It's a girls' school," I confessed.

"Now, that would be a private school, wouldn't it?"

When I admitted that it was indeed a private school and started in on a convoluted explanation of why my girls were not in the public schools, Wallace tuned out. "Nothing wrong with that, heunh, I was just curious," he said. But it was clear he thought he now held the moral high ground on the school integration issue or perhaps the hypocrisy quotient, at least in relation to this reporter.

But Wallace was also, like so many politicians, extremely sensitive to what was said or written about him. I went to see him in Montgomery one day shortly after there had been several articles about him in national magazines, including one in *Newsweek* (which he always called "the *Newsweek*") that referred, although only incidentally, to his fondness for ketchup and another that mentioned an incident in which his wife Lurleen had casually brushed some dandruff off his shoulder. When I said, without mentioning any specifics, that I had been "reading a lot about you in the magazines lately," Wallace bolted out of his chair, rushed around his desk to where I was sitting at a conference table, and presented his shoulder for my inspection. "You see any dandruff there?" he wanted to know. "You don't, do you?" Then, reassured, he went back behind his desk to continue the interview.

An hour or so later we went down to the cafeteria in the capitol basement to have some lunch, both of us choosing something—hot dogs and beans perhaps—that seemed to cry out for ketchup. Sitting across from me, Wallace reached for the red bottle, then thought better of it and stayed his hand at the last moment. But when I seized the ketchup and poured it liberally over my food, he was clearly delighted. Drowning his own food in the stuff, he hooted, "You like ketchup, too—that means you can't write about it, heunh."

Whatever his sensitivity to the national press, Wallace never missed a chance to exploit the political opportunity. At his rallies he loved to point to the press section and tell his audience that "the *Time*" and "the *Newsweek*" and "*The New Yawk Times*" were all there, maybe learning a few things. They might be looking down their noses, he would suggest, but they would learn that the "average citizen" had a lot more common sense than some of those ivory-tower intellectuals at Harvard and Yale and places like that. Quite beyond that, however, Wallace used the press attention as proof to Alabamians that there was a purpose in his national campaigning that went beyond self-aggrandizement. He was succeeding, he would tell his home-state audiences, in persuading other Americans to stop "looking down their noses" at his home state and its people. "Everywhere I go," he would report, "people cheer when I call the name of Alabama."

Wallace showed his special ability to make the most of every opportunity one day in 1970 when Jules Witcover, later my partner but then a reporter with the *Los Angeles Times,* and I caught up with him in Midfield, Alabama, a small industrial community near Birmingham and Bessemer. We sat down with Wallace while he ate his lunch at a Holiday Inn and endured the usual special experience of sharing a meal with him. Wallace ate his steak only after lathering it in ketchup, all the while chewing vigorously on his White Owl and keeping up a running conversation with us, the waitress, and any other diners who happened within range. He would cut a bite of steak, pick up his cigar for a puff, put it down, and salt his food carelessly enough so that others at the table had to shield their coffee cups, then cut another bite, take another puff, add some more salt. It was a tour de force and lasted ninety minutes or longer while the governor offered us his views on every issue on the table at the moment.

That night Wallace was scheduled to speak to the Midfield Chamber of Commerce at a dinner at the Veterans of Foreign Wars hall. Witcover and I showed up and stationed ourselves at the bar, where we could look into the dining room and hear the speech. We were nursing our drinks when we heard the master of ceremonies calling, "Is Mr. Jules Witcover of the *Los Angeleez Times* in the room? Mr. Jules Witcover of the *Los Angeleez Times?*" When the embarrassed Witcover acknowledged that he was there, the emcee went on: "Come up here, the governor wants to shake your hand." Witcover knew he was being used, but there was nothing he could do without seeming rude except comply. When he returned to the bar, another drinker made Wallace's point by asking, "You come all the way from Los Angeleez, sure 'nough?" Or, as Wallace himself put it a few moments later: "I've got the national press here with me tonight. They follow me everywhere, and tonight they have followed me to Midfield."

(Wallace always seemed to have a special problem with my future partner. He got into his head the notion that Witcover, a Roman Catholic, was Jewish. So every time Wallace would see him, he would say, "I saw old Dave Silverman the other day," citing a Jew who owned a store in downtown Montgomery. Witcover had no idea who Silverman might be, but Wallace seemed to think all Jews know one another. Eventually, Witcover tired of trying to explain and simply sent his best wishes back to old Dave.)

Wallace was a master at tailoring his message to fit his purpose. In Alabama he spoke without any self-consciousness about "nigguhs" and what they could and could not do in the southern society of the time. Testing his message in the rest of the country leading up to the 1968 campaign, he rarely talked about race directly. Nor did he talk about "nigguhs." Instead, he derided the ineffectual liberals trying to prescribe solutions for the rest of the country—and thus allied himself with that steelworker and beautician, who had more sense anyway.

But, most of all, Wallace connected with his audiences with vivid images, his personal force and acute insights. His listeners understood the code. When he talked about "popping some skulls" if demonstrators lay down in front of his car, they knew he was talking about the black skulls of civil rights protesters. When he talked about lawlessness running wild, it was clearly about the fear of street crime being perpetrated by blacks against elderly Americans. He touched all the sore spots—deriding, for example, the behaviorists' apologies for some kid who went bad. "Just because his daddy didn't carry him to a Pittsburgh Steelers football game," he would sneer. But he didn't talk in any detail, or even anything but the broadest outlines, about tax policy or foreign affairs. Nor did he offer ten-point programs of his own for American agriculture or small business. His whole message was about what was wrong with the elites running things and making all the decisions for those "average citizens."

It was, of course, the crudest kind of racism, and Wallace was, as Hubert Humphrey described him in 1968, "an apostle of hate and racism" in the way he played his politics. But what is most intriguing about George Wallace is that he really didn't give a damn about race. He used race as a political tool, but offstage he never showed any particular animus toward blacks. He attacked them because that was the way he would get where he wanted to go. If he had succeeded in that first gubernatorial campaign in 1958, he might have been an entirely different kind of pioneer cutting a populist path into national politics for southerners. "I know the nigguh schools are bad and we got to fix it," he told me once, "but most folks don't agree with me there, not yet anyway, and you don't get elected going against most folks. I already found that out." Wallace's racism was essentially a weapon of choice. It was just something he needed to campaign effectively.

Campaigning was the only thing he liked to do. With most politicians, reporters find times when it's possible to talk about something other than getting votes, matters either as substantive as the condition of the environment or as trivial as a golf game. But Wallace had only one interest, enlisting the support of voters he needed to achieve more power and ultimately the White House. He was happiest on the podium, reveling in the way he could elicit and even fine-tune the approving roar of the mob with his rhetorical skills. He particularly enjoyed the minutes after a speech when the folks would crowd up to the stage and he would lean down to touch their hands, one after another.

Later, chewing on a cigar, he would relive the moment. "You see all those folks," he would say to the visiting reporter. "You tell those people up there in New York about those folks, heunh. Those are good folks and they got their heads on straight. We got good people here in Alabama."

Wallace had no hobbies. He didn't drink anything stronger than Royal Crown cola; his friends said he feared the loss of control that might result from too much bourbon. Food was just a necessity that interrupted his quest for the approval of the voters. He had neither any intellectual interests that he would share nor any store of small talk about anything not directly related to the votes he was seeking at the moment.

The only other interest he seemed to have—and it was largely overlooked by the press in those prissy days—was women. His friends talked frequently about his appetite for women, but he was reasonably discreet about it with reporters, although apparently not conspicuously sensitive with the women themselves. I was sitting in a hotel lobby in Indianapolis one afternoon with Billy Joe Camp, his press secretary (whose lime green leisure suit made him a sartorial legend) and a couple of his bodyguards in their maroon polyester slacks when an elevator door opened and a blond country singer who warmed up crowds at Wallace campaign rallies bolted out. She marched over to us and plunked herself down with an emphatic flounce of skirts and legs.

"That damned George Wallace," she announced. "He didn't even take his shoes off." I found that little bit of information interesting, but it never occurred to me to report it; these days it could be Page One stuff.

Wallace's interests were so narrow that the paralysis he suffered when he was shot down by Arthur Bremer in Laurel, Maryland, in 1972 seemed uniquely cruel. It had robbed him of the two pleasures of his existence: women and, probably more important to him, the ability to reach down into those stage-side crowds to grasp the hands of all those admiring "average citizens" for whom he claimed to be speaking. It didn't end his career in politics, but it took away much of the zest he had shown for so many years. It is a measure of Wallace's ultimate driving ambition that he continued to press his case as a candidate into the 1976 campaign and made himself a source of worry among national Democrats until another and different kind of southerner, Jimmy Carter, defeated him in the Florida primary by three percentage points.

It was a measure of Wallace's message that he was able to be a factor in those 1976 primaries even campaigning from a wheelchair. Indeed, his high point—the one he liked to recall later—was the Massachusetts primary, in which he ran third behind Senator Henry M. Jackson and Representative Morris Udall but carried a plurality of the Democrats in Boston, the Athens of America. "Boston," he would say, "can you imagine that? It's no different from anyplace else. They've got some good people even in Boston."

In the end Wallace had more influence on Republicans than on Democrats. He proved there was a strong undercurrent of anger in the electorate directed at conventional liberalism and at social engineering. It evidenced itself most obviously in racist hostility toward black Americans, but it wasn't race alone that moved the steelworker and the beautician. It was their conviction that the government was spending their tax money to subsidize others who were not willing to work as hard as they worked and who were responsible for so much of what was wrong in American society—whether it be street crime or street protest. And these were the voters the Republicans enlisted in transforming southern politics over the next generation.

Wallace's influence waned rapidly once he was no longer seen as capable of having a direct effect on national directions. Back home in Alabama, moreover, there was another generation of voters and newcomers who wanted to move on. The state's reputation as the last bastion of resistance to racial amity was, among other things, bad for business. In Birmingham there was pronounced defensiveness about the days of Bull Connor and the city's reputation. The comparisons with Atlanta, only two hours to the east, were particularly hard to take.

Wallace threatened to run for the Senate in 1978 but backed off when the outlook looked less than promising. But in 1982 he made another run for governor. It was a peculiar campaign because Wallace talked almost entirely about the past. His rambling speeches reminded his listeners of his days as a presidential candidate and the glories of the crowds that packed the Cow Palace in San Francisco and the Civic Center in Milwaukee and lined the streets of Baltimore and Pittsburgh. His message was that because he had played in the big leagues he was more qualified to attract jobs to a state with an unemployment rate of 11 percent.

I went to see him one day during the summer primary campaign, and he asked me to meet him outside the Birmingham convention center so we could talk in the backseat of his limousine. It was, it appeared, one of the few places he could make himself at least momentarily comfortable, shifting his body constantly, sweat running down his face as he alternately sucked on a bottle of water and puffed on the ubiquitous cheap cigar. Although I wanted to interview him about the current campaign, he was focused on those great days, reminding me of what he did in Boston and how they recapitulated on him in Maryland and did I remember that rally in Syracuse?

He was rewriting some political history. By this stage he had convinced himself that Hubert Humphrey had wanted to put him on the Democratic ticket as the nominee for vice president in 1968 and had actually extended feelers about such a step—a notion preposterous on its face. And his relationship with blacks—they were no longer "nigguhs"—that had never been as bad as portrayed.

He won the Democratic primary for governor by a narrow margin but only because of a gaffe by his chief opponent, Lieutenant Governor George McMillan, a relatively moderate conservative. Trying to maximize the black turnout, McMillan brought Jesse Jackson into the state in the final days of the campaign. But Jackson's declaration that Wallace represented "a bloody chapter in American history" was broadcast repeatedly on radio stations all over the state and caused a backlash against "outsiders" and Jackson himself that probably sank McMillan. Wallace went on to defeat a highly conservative Republican in the general election to capture his fourth term as governor, but it was his last hurrah.

Four years later, faced with opinion polls that showed him losing three to one to Lieutenant Governor Bill Baxley, Wallace wheeled himself into the House chamber in Montgomery and announced his retirement. By this point he was alone both politically and personally. His third wife, Lisa, had moved out of the executive mansion and didn't show up for his swan song. He was alone most of the time, totally dependent on two black attendants provided by the state, who took him through a laborious two- to three-hour routine every morning just to get ready for the day. Most galling for him, perhaps, he was a man without a constituency or even a coterie of hangers-on. He had lost almost all of his hearing, and his illnesses had multiplied.

As much as I resisted it, I found myself feeling some sympathy for him. He had been a hateful politician during much of his career. He had played on the worst instincts of those he purported to represent solely for his own selfish purposes. But it was hard to hate him. He was so needy, so dependent on the approval of others—those average citizens and, for that matter, the press. And he was the quintessential politician who never hid his ambitions. If you spend your life covering politics, it is hard to hate someone who played the game so well.

He continued to rewrite his personal history. Later in 1986 I mentioned in a column that one of the candidates to succeed him, Attorney General Charles Graddick, was using a racial appeal more naked than any seen in Alabama since the first days of Wallace. When the column appeared in *The Birmingham News*, Wallace wrote me a long letter revising political history to make the argument that he had a lot more support from blacks than anyone ever realized—and, not incidentally, recalling the times and places I had covered his national campaigning. I wrote back that it was nice to hear from him, but I didn't bother to argue political history.

In practical terms it doesn't make any difference whether Wallace was a true racist or simply someone who used racism for political advantage. Either way his politics was reprehensible. But the example he set in the early 1960s was not lost on others. He demonstrated to Richard Nixon that it was possible to use the crime issue in a way that reached the fears of many Americans outside the South so long as you were careful not to employ the clumsy language that would make you vulnerable to charges of racism. He demonstrated to Ronald Reagan, in time for his first campaign for governor of California in 1966, that he could strike a chord with many voters by running against demonstrators and protesters, whether they were opposing Lyndon Johnson's policy on the war in Vietnam or trying to end desegregation.

Nixon and Reagan had never stood in any schoolhouse door, so they could take the high ground, untarnished by their history. And those who wanted to do so could join their campaigns without being accused of identifying themselves with racist leadership. But it was George Wallace who wrote the book on playing the race card.

CHAPTER 6

A YEAR THAT
MATTERED

For any political reporter of my generation, 1968 was a special year. There was one good story after another, and Gannett gave me a free hand in covering them. That is what reporting is all about, getting the chance to cover the "good story" or even the "great story" that is so interesting it will command the full attention of readers or so significant it deserves their full attention. These are the stories that make up for all those Friday nights flying standby out of O'Hare or Atlanta. In 1968 they came one after the other.

Just six years after his "last press conference" in California, Richard M. Nixon became the Republican Party's de facto presidential nominee even before the votes were counted in New Hampshire when his challenger, Governor George W. Romney of Michigan, failed to demonstrate convincingly that he would be a credible steward of policy in the war in Vietnam and withdrew. Nixon needed to fend off only clumsy late runs by Nelson Rockefeller and Ronald Reagan.

The Democratic campaign was bizarre from the outset. In New Hampshire, Eugene J. McCarthy won 42 percent of the primary vote to 49 percent for President Lyndon B. Johnson, a showing that made him the clear winner of the expectations game—and brought

Robert F. Kennedy into the competition as another critic of Johnson's handling of the war. When Johnson, facing the likelihood he could not be nominated on a first ballot, announced his retirement, we watched as Kennedy overtook and passed McCarthy to lay claim to the nomination after his triumph in the California primary—a triumph confirmed only minutes before Kennedy was shot down in a kitchen of the Ambassador Hotel.

Meanwhile, the country was going up in flames. The street protests against the war were at their peak. But they were exceeded in violence and rage by race riots that erupted in one city after another following the assassination of Martin Luther King, Jr., in Memphis.

The president's popularity had plummeted as the protests against the war spread beyond the young to engage many of their parents, neighbors, and teachers. With McCarthy defeated and Kennedy assassinated, the Democrats met in Chicago to nominate a candidate, Vice President Hubert H. Humphrey, who had taken no part in the long primary campaign and carried the burden of Johnson's war. The national convention was chaos. The streets were filled with young protesters clashing repeatedly with Chicago police under orders from Mayor Richard J. Daley to keep them under control—orders that ended in what an investigating commission later called a police riot. Inside the convention hall the confrontation was equally passionate—distilled for history in photographs of Daley shouting obscenities from his seat toward the speaker at the podium, Senator Abraham Ribicoff, a liberal from Connecticut. In the end Chicago sent the ticket of Humphrey and Senator Edmund S. Muskie into the general election campaign leading a party in perhaps unprecedented disarray.

But 1968 was a year of sudden and extreme twists and turns. Although the election of Nixon seemed foreordained in July and August, Humphrey closed the gap over the final three weeks to lose by a whisker—and inspire another round of what-might-have-beens. The principal question, of course, was always What would have happened if Bob Kennedy had survived? My guess is that he would have defeated Nixon, whose hands seemed to shake every time a Kennedy was mentioned. And my guess is that the war would have ended sooner and the racial rioting been less severe. But this may be only wishful thinking. One of the lessons of covering politics is that it is difficult, perhaps impossible, to forecast performance in office. You never know what the circumstances will be. You never really know how someone will use power once it has been granted. The political scientists devise all sorts of schemes and scales to predict how the electorate and the politicians will behave. But politics isn't a science. Who could predict some crazy Arab kid named Sirhan Sirhan?

From this great distance, the true lesson of 1968 is how random and capricious our political system can be. Neither events nor individuals are ever quite as easy to describe as they may seem. And the press never seems to get it quite right.

We were never totally fair, for example, to George Romney. He had been governor of Michigan for two terms after a successful career with American Motors, where he produced the Rambler. He was an intelligent and decent man with good instincts on social questions. He could have been a successful president, perhaps even an outstanding one, if he could have negotiated the tricky rapids that confront all candidates for president. Instead, he began his campaign for the Republican nomination in 1967 with a fateful mistake. He started to criticize Johnson's conduct of the war in Vietnam without offering a policy of his own for either winning or withdrawing. For those of us covering his candidacy, that was a red flag, and we pursued him on the question with unrelenting fervor. We hounded him because that is what we are supposed to do in our self-styled role as the representatives of the reading and viewing public. If he was going to criticize Johnson's policy, then he had to produce an alternative. It was one of the rules we live by, even if we're all a little hazy about who wrote them in the first place.

Early in 1967 Romney embarked on what became known as the Mormon tour, a trip through several western states with large populations of fellow members of the Church of Jesus Christ of Latter Day Saints. So we went along through Alaska, Arizona, Idaho, and Utah. The high point was Anchorage, where we attended a Sunday morning Mormon stake (congregation) meeting at which his wife, Lenore, delivered a barn-burning sermon on morality only a few hours after the hungover reporters had been watching an exotic dancer named Cha-Cha O'Brien demonstrate that she could make the tassels attached to her formidable breasts twirl simultaneously in opposite directions.

Romney's intention was to demonstrate a base of support beyond what he might expect to enjoy from Nelson Rockefeller's fading and discredited eastern liberal establishment. The day-after-day story, nonetheless, was the candidate trying unsuccessfully to explain what he would do about the war different from what Johnson was doing. The same thing happened later in the year, when Romney embarked on a trip through a dozen cities that became known as the urban tour. He seemed to make one mistake after another, to the point at which I claimed to have a special key on my typewriter that printed at a single stroke, "Romney later explained . . ."

Romney was a remarkably earnest and dogged man, easy to caricature. When he played golf he made sure he used his time most efficiently by playing three balls simultaneously, rushing across the fairway and back again from one to the other so he could play eighteen holes in six. Trying duckpin bowling in New Hampshire for the first time and faced with a lone pin still standing after the first two balls, he bowled thirty-four more balls until he got it. With Lenore at his side, he was determined to soak up every experience as a candidate along the way. When he visited San Francisco, it wasn't to enjoy dinner at Ernie's but to be with the young antiwar protesters in Haight-Ashbury. He sat in a circle with them in the park, listening and taking some notes and promising to send them some position papers of his own—all to the amazement of the baffled hippies. Who was this dude and what was all this about, anyway? The puzzlement was just as pronounced on the other side. At one point Romney's bodyguard, a crew-cut plainclothes state police lieutenant named Neil Bykerk, quickly moved his body to shield Lenore's gaze from a young woman's T-shirt that, he suddenly realized, carried the legend FUCK HATE.

Romney's efforts to learn were admirable in many ways. But they also violated the rules that require presidential candidates to be fully credible on every issue from the day they begin running. His problems with Vietnam crystallized when in August 1967 he told a radio interviewer in Detroit that on a visit to Vietnam two years earlier he had been "brainwashed" by the military officers briefing him and defending the Johnson policy. It was, he said, "the greatest brainwashing that anybody can get when going over to Vietnam, not only by the generals but also by the diplomatic corps over there, and they do a very thorough job."

The use of the term was disastrous for Romney because it made it so easy for the press and his political rivals to seize on the caricature of the naïve governor, out of his depth, being conned. In fact, Romney was trying to make the point that he had overcome these attempts to enlist him behind the policy and now had made a thoughtful decision that it was a mistake. But never mind. It was too tempting to make jokes about brainwashing. "I would have thought a light rinse would have done it," said Gene McCarthy, looking down his nose.

It was not until January in New Hampshire that Romney finally produced his own plan for ending the war, or at least American involvement in the war. Surrounded by some well-qualified foreign policy advisers, he outlined it for us in a long press conference at the Winding Brook Lodge in Keene. In fact, his plan for "deAmericanization" of the war was not much different from the one that Richard Nixon eventually followed as president. It was, however, too late to alter the perception that this "brainwashed" candidate was out of his depth dealing with the issue. Although there were few published opinion polls at that point in the evolution of the New Hampshire primary campaigns, both the Nixon and Romney organizations had conducted private surveys that pointed toward a debacle for the governor from Michigan.

We finally began to realize how serious his problem had become one night when Tom Ottenad of the *St. Louis Post-Dispatch*, Jules Witcover, and I had dinner with John Deardourff, a Republican consultant advising Romney as he had advised Nelson Rockefeller in other campaigns, and found him obviously depressed. At breakfast in Concord the next morning, Ottenad and I reviewed the conversation and suddenly realized that Deardourff had been speaking in the past tense. We quickly telephoned Bill Johnson, the bright young lawyer running the Romney operation in the state, and the three of us made a date to see him in Hanover later that morning. We took along another reporter, Ward Just of *The Washington Post*, who was doing his first coverage of the campaign or, for that matter, politics. We found Johnson no more optimistic than Deardourff, although predictably cautious. At one point I asked him if there had been any thought given to just conceding the primary, but Johnson avoided an answer. "All kinds of things run through my mind when I'm shaving," he said. He told us later, apologetically, that at the very moment we arrived at his office he was working on the draft of a Romney withdrawal statement; it was written on a yellow pad face down on his desk. What we had failed to ask specifically was whether there was any discussion of quitting altogether and going home.

Even with that failure to ask the right question, we felt confident in filing stories that night about the Romney campaign near collapse. Just filed a similar piece, although perhaps more qualified because he didn't know either of our sources as well as we did. And the next day we were all patting each other on the back—the high five had not been invented—when the word circulated that Romney would hold a press conference in Washington and quit. Our stories looked golden; only we knew how we had fallen just short. So we accepted the applause of our editors. Our colleague from the *Post* was unable to share in the self-congratulation, however. When Just called the office at midday expecting praise for the perceptiveness of his political reporting, he discovered that the editors had held up his story because they were uneasy about it. It was the kind of thing that would drive a good reporter into writing novels.

In any case, Romney was gone and Nixon essentially assured of the nomination. We overlooked the irony in the fact that he had no plan for Vietnam either, or at least not one he was willing to disclose. We all acceded when he primly declared a moratorium on the issue so he would not be in the position of making the sitting president's situation more difficult with partisan sniping. The difference was that, in contrast to Romney, Nixon wasn't attacking Johnson on the issue.

In retrospect, it is clear we were never entirely fair to Romney. By insisting on seeing his candidacy only through the prism of the most newsworthy issue of the moment, the war, we had given too little attention to his proposals, for example, for improving conditions in the inner cities, then called slums or ghettos. Nor had we ever given our readers and viewers a clear enough picture of his personal qualities, although he was a politician many of us liked and even admired. Such failures have always been common in the coverage of politics and are even more common today, when so many voters rely so heavily on television news reports, even more superficial than what we write in newspapers. Even if you cannot point to particular examples of unfairness in press coverage, the total picture of the candidate or the situation is too often flawed.

Gene McCarthy was another example, although our failure with him was the reverse of what it had been with Romney. We tended to give McCarthy the benefit of the doubt at the outset because he had the nerve to challenge an incumbent president of his own party on an issue of principle, which always qualifies as news in a world of go along, get along. We were also impressed by the legions of young people who invaded New Hampshire promising to be "clean for Gene" as they canvassed precincts in his behalf. It was essentially a case of allowing the senator from Minnesota to be defined by the nature of his mission and by his associations. In fact, as the campaign wore on through the primaries, McCarthy's mission changed, perhaps inevitably. Now he wanted not only to force a change in the policy on the war in Vietnam but to win the presidency himself. And increasingly he showed a waspish cynicism in his attitude toward the campaign and even toward those young people who were his most valuable asset.

After the fact McCarthy used to complain about how the press and the pundits had ignored his campaign until he achieved that 42 percent showing in New Hampshire against 49 percent for the sitting president. It was true, of course, that the possibility of McCarthy unseating Johnson was taken lightly when his candidacy was first being discussed in 1967. By the time the New Hampshire campaign was at full boil in February 1968, however, no reporter could miss the signs that something special was happening. Even in the absence of reliable polling figures, it was apparent a lot of New Hampshire Democrats didn't like LBJ for a variety of reasons. It wasn't only a case of Americans objecting to the war.

Talking to voters at random in Portsmouth one day, I found several who were suspicious of the president simply because he was a Texan with a pronounced southwestern accent and several others who believed the McCarthy making the challenge was Joe rather than Gene. "He chased all those communists out of the State Department," an old man told me, "so I think we can give him a chance."

The perception of Clean Gene was reinforced when Robert Kennedy made his belated entry into the competition after New Hampshire. The picture of the Principled Purist and the Ruthless Opportunist was one everyone could understand. McCarthy had shown the guts, Kennedy had held back. There was some validity in that argument, but also some limits. McCarthy had nothing to risk by running; he was going nowhere in the Senate, and, until the war issue came along, he was in no visible demand to take a place on the national ticket. He was just another liberal senator from Minnesota given to reciting poetry, for God's sake. Kennedy, by contrast, had become a leading candidate for the White House after his brother's death, whether he chose to risk that stature or waited until Johnson served a second term.

The students who had left school to canvass for McCarthy were particularly forceful in their declarations of loyalty to him and scorn for Kennedy. They were the kinds of idealistic and intense volunteers any campaign would prize. One of my favorites was Alice Krakauer, a skinny psychology major from City College who at nineteen had already taken on the persona of the classic Jewish mother. She worked for McCarthy in primary pressrooms in several states, answering the telephones and handing out schedules and speech texts—and, not incidentally, ministering to reporters who needed it. If you hung up a pressroom phone after a shouting match with an editor back home, Alice would be there with a cold drink. "You're feeling hostile today, Jack," she would lecture. "You need to drink this and just rest for a few minutes, then you'll feel better." She was one of those who would never yield to Kennedy. Clean Gene, she would say, was the one who stepped forward when everyone else was silent.

The Wisconsin primary campaign was the high point of Gene McCarthy's candidacy. His success in New Hampshire had given him a celebrity he had never enjoyed, and now there were many signs that he could defeat LBJ outright, not just in the expectations game, in a state with many liberal Democrats who were critics of the war and dubious about Johnson. McCarthy was still in the mode of being "willing" to run because there had to be a "personification" of the antiwar movement. He was enjoying the moral high ground of having made that initial challenge while the ruthless Kennedy waited on the sidelines. And he had the field to himself because Kennedy had declared his candidacy too late to qualify for the Wisconsin ballot.

I also enjoyed an extraordinary stroke of luck covering the primary, one that persuaded Gannett editors they had this remarkably perceptive reporter on the campaign. A week or so before the primary, Tom Ottenad and I flew to Oregon to cover a Kennedy visit there. Talking on the plane, we each remarked that someone—neither of us could remember just who—had suggested to us that Johnson might pull out if he was not assured of winning the nomination on the first ballot. There had been no suggestion of anything like that in the published speculation, but Ottenad and I began to pool our reporting on what was going on in various states. Counting delegates that might be lost in primaries or delegates that might be held back by favorite sons if the president appeared weak—and his approval rating in the Gallup Poll was now down to 36 percent—we were able to foresee a situation in which Johnson might fall short on that first ballot. It wasn't likely, but it was not totally unrealistic either. We were convinced, moreover, that someone as proud as Johnson wouldn't be willing to scratch for a handful of delegates to save himself. It was an interesting idea, but just idle speculation to pass the time on the long flight west.

In Portland that night, however, I ran into Representative Edith Green, an antiwar Oregon Democrat who had decided to support Kennedy. Chatting in a hotel lobby, she began to muse about the chances that LBJ could be forced to withdraw. I was struck by what she was saying but not enough to write anything about it. Then I flew back to Milwaukee. It was the Friday before the primary, and that was the day I regularly wrote my one weekly column to be published in our newspapers on Monday mornings. As it happened, I had scheduled a lunch that day with David Carley, a Democratic National Committee member from Wisconsin. He, too, it turned out, had been gossiping with other insiders about whether Johnson might withdraw. So I went up to my room in the Pfister and wrote a column about Democrats for the first time facing the possibility that Johnson would not seek another term.

The column was already in print in the early editions of the Monday papers when Johnson announced his withdrawal on Sunday night, March 31. In fact, I didn't have a shred of hard evidence, only the speculation among the politicians. It was a pop fly, but it looked like a line drive in the box score. My editors, always defensive about competing with the big guys, were impressed, and I accepted their praise with casual restraint, just as if I had known what I was doing.

Johnson's withdrawal changed the dynamics of the campaign. In a sense, McCarthy had been robbed of the lofty rationale for his candidacy. He was now simply another Democrat after the prize, and his first priority was to defeat Kennedy, against whom he was matched in the Indiana primary. Unsurprisingly, McCarthy began to behave much like most candidates do in such circumstances, trying to redefine the terms of the contest as it went along. When it became apparent he was losing in Indiana, he told us that the candidacy of Governor Roger Branigin as a stand-in for Johnson (or Vice President Hubert H. Humphrey) had clouded the waters and made it impossible for a real test against Kennedy. He was now aiming at the impending Nebraska primary, which, he told us, would provide "a direct confrontation" with Kennedy. But a few days before the Nebraska vote, having lost Indiana, McCarthy joined several of us at our dinner table in the old Blackstone Hotel in Omaha and confided that he was leaving the state before primary day. This wasn't the right time, either. The real test would come in Oregon.

McCarthy's charm began to wear a little thin. He was still complaining about Kennedy the opportunist, which was legitimate enough but no longer relevant. He was increasingly acerbic about the press. Reporters were like blackbirds on a telephone wire, he would say, one of them flies off and the others all follow. And, more distressing, he was dismissive of all those clean-for-Gene kids who had done so much to put him where he was. McCarthy still got all the best of it in press coverage as the professorial intellectual of principle leading a cause. But among ourselves many of the print reporters were becoming disenchanted.

By contrast, the Robert Kennedy we were covering was a positive surprise. My own experience with him was fairly typical of that of political reporters. We had seen him perform as the ruthless brother running John F. Kennedy's 1960 campaign and as an arrogant candidate who moved into New York in 1964 and defeated a well-respected liberal Republican, Kenneth B. Keating, to claim a seat in the Senate to which he seemed to think he was entitled.

That 1964 campaign spoke volumes, however, about how the brother of the fallen president would be received as a national candidate four years later. Entering the race against Keating less than a year after JFK's death in Dallas, Robert Kennedy evoked an almost hysterical reaction from voters that no one before or after—not John Kennedy or Ronald Reagan—ever achieved. On his first campaign trip upstate, he arrived at Glens Falls, a small city in the Adirondacks, after midnight, three or four hours behind schedule. There were people lined up all along the route of his motorcade to downtown, many of them parents holding up children in their pajamas kept awake for the historic moment. And in the town center several thousand more waited to cheer him. At Buffalo the next day, late again, the Kennedy motorcade found people all along the six-mile route from the airport to downtown, standing three and four deep along the last half dozen blocks. Neither I nor any of the other reporters with long histories in New York politics had ever seen anything like the special celebrity of a surviving Kennedy brother.

There were limits, of course. When Kennedy arrived at the tiny Ogdensburg airport in New York's North Country on another occasion that fall and found more than five hundred people waiting, I started to dictate a story to my desk describing the "unprecedented" crowd, then thought better of it in mid-sentence and checked with the airport manager, whose telephone I was using. "This the biggest crowd ever?" I asked. "Oh, sure," replied the manager, who then added, a few beats later, "except, of course, when Joan Crawford came up here last year to dedicate the new Pepsi-Cola plant." So much for our priorities.

The Kennedy of 1964 was not always easy to take. He and the people around him seemed to feel they were on a moral crusade in which reporters covering them were expected to enlist. I was particularly suspect because the headquarters of Gannett was in Rochester, the hometown of Keating, and because our publishers and editors had a close relationship with him. At one point one of Kennedy's chief advisers, Edwin Guthman, asked me in so many words if I was "with us or against us" and seemed to find it hard to accept my reply that I didn't give a damn who won. That is something a reporter is obliged to say in those circumstances, but in this case it was also true, as it usually is. The Kennedy challenge was a hell of a good story that I enjoyed covering before returning to the presidential campaign, in which Johnson was burying Goldwater. But I had no personal stake one way or another in Keating, and there was never any pressure on me or reporters I assigned to the campaign to tilt the coverage.

Over the next four years as Kennedy served in the Senate and came to know me and our staff in the Washington bureau, the suspicion gradually dissolved. Our bureau chief was still an ardent right-winger, but he was the chief in title only; I made the decisions on assignments and coverage.

It was also becoming clear, however, that Kennedy was changing in the job. He had always been essentially a staff person—for a Senate committee and for his brother, as his campaign manager and even as attorney general. Now, for the first time, he was the elected official responsible himself for meeting the concerns of his constituents. He was the one who had to assess the situation and make the decision. When he visited the ghetto in New York or Buffalo or Rochester, he was the one who had to look for solutions, not the one who worried only about how they would play politically. I found him suddenly intensely curious about upstate cities I knew so well because I had worked in Albany and because Gannett owned so many upstate newspapers. He seemed mildly surprised to discover that although the poverty in Mississippi or West Virginia might be more dramatic, it could be just as discouraging in Rochester.

As it turned out, Kennedy's concern for the underclass became the underpinning of his campaign for the presidency after Johnson stepped aside. He was still, like McCarthy, an antiwar candidate for shorthand identification purposes, but the war was not his only issue to the degree it was for McCarthy. In the first instance his connection to the disadvantaged, and to blacks and Hispanics in particular, was a product of his brother's history. But by the time he ran for president, Kennedy had made an emotional connection of his own that McCarthy did not share. Most important, he was now the principal.

He was particularly caught up by the children. One night, after a long day of trudging around the ghetto of Omaha in the rain, we boarded the chartered 727 for a three-hour flight back to Washington. Coming down the aisle, Kennedy invited me to join him in the back for a drink, something he often did with individual reporters. He ordered a bourbon and I a Scotch, and he asked me what I thought of "all those kids" we saw that day. Their life, I said, was a lot different from those of my daughters and their prospects even more different. Kennedy wanted to know how different. What were my kids able to do now? Where could they go to school? How many of these little Negro kids could ever get out of that ghetto? How? And look at my own kids, he said at one point, the children of affluence with nothing to fear from life and every opportunity available. Your kids and my kids, he said, they have no worries, they can enjoy being kids. Then he started talking about individual youngsters he had met that day. That little girl with the pink ribbon tying her pigtails, he said, she was bright as hell and what a smile, but where does she end up?

The conversation continued all the way to Washington, three hours or more. The Jack Daniel's and the Scotch continued to flow, and we were both slightly the worse for wear when we landed at Washington National long after midnight. But what was remarkable was that the topic never changed. We talked about children in America for the entire flight, swapping stories about what we had seen in Omaha and elsewhere, speculating about what might be done and about what would happen to those children if nothing was done. This was not a case of a politician conning a reporter by showing how sensitive he was to the disadvantaged. The conversation was, by tacit agreement, off the record and, in any case, not something that would be newsworthy. I wasn't going to write a piece about how Bob Kennedy loved kids. Given the fact that he had ten of his own and another on the way, that was hardly necessary. The episode was, nonetheless, a glimpse of a politician trying to come to grips with a troubling failure in our society. It was a rare insight even in a time when there was far less distrust between reporters and politicians.

Kennedy was a singular candidate in many respects. He felt very strongly that draft deferments for college students were a mistake. They allowed the young men of privilege to avoid the war in Vietnam while the blacks and poor whites fought and died. More to the point, he raised the issue with one campus audience after another, even while seeking student support in the primaries. It seemed to be a case of deliberately confronting a constituency whose support he needed but was unwilling to court by moderating his view on what he saw as a defining issue. A noontime rally at Creighton University in Omaha was typical. He cited the disproportionate number of blacks fighting in Vietnam, then asked, "How can you accept this? What I don't understand is that you don't even debate these things among yourselves. You're the most exclusive minority in the world. Are you just going to sit on your duffs and do nothing, or just carry signs and protest?"

Kennedy was not always a sainted figure, however. During the Indiana campaign he became concerned about the danger of losing conservative Democratic primary voters if he appeared to be soft on law-and-order issues, an accusation always directed at liberals making the case for the poor. So he began to tilt some of his speeches, perhaps going over the edge at times, even if you granted he had a genuine concern about the problem. That happened one night in Evansville and became the story of the day when we returned to the Holiday Inn at the Weir-Cook Airport in Indianapolis, which was our home base for the primary. After filing our stories, several of us went to the bar, where we had fallen into a routine of stretching the closing hour a little while David Breasted played his guitar and a waitress with a heartbreaking voice sang country songs. This night Kennedy showed up, sat down, and asked what we had told our readers. "That you sounded like Nixon," somebody said. "That you caved in to the conservatives," somebody else said. Kennedy was taken aback but not peevish, as McCarthy often seemed to be in such situations. You guys may be right, he said. Maybe I went too far, but we can't ignore the crime problem, the victims are right there in the ghetto. Then he listened to a song or two and went off to bed.

The candidate also had a sense of humor. When a single sheet of paper blew out of his hand as he prepared to make a speech in rural Nebraska, he shrugged with resignation and said, "There goes my farm program." Sometimes he would seem overcome by the artificiality and boredom involved in giving the same speech at one stop after another. So he would improvise. He would tell a rural audience that they should vote for him because he did a lot more for the farm economy than Gene McCarthy; with all those kids at home he had to buy a dozen quarts of milk every day. Or he would tell school-children in Oregon that if he was elected there would be four more holidays every year and you won't get that with Senator McCarthy. So tell your mom and dad to vote for me.

One day the campaign was using an ancient, oil-streaked Martin 404 run by a mom-and-pop charter service to make stops in several small Indiana communities. But leaving Columbus, the pilot sud-denly aborted the takeoff and, after much squealing of brakes and a shuddering stop, taxied back up the runway. He climbed out, and we could see him walking around under the wings and inspecting the two engines. Finally he reboarded and came on the loudspeaker. "We had a warning light on that number-two engine," he said, "but I can't find anything, so we're going to try it again." As he revved the engines, the cabin grew silent with tension until Kennedy said, "I hate to sound immodest, fellows, but if we don't make it, your names are going to be in very small print tomorrow."

The atmospherics on the campaign were favorable enough that, as we often did in those times, we wrote a parody song while riding a Kennedy whistle-stop train through Indiana—a takeoff, of course, on "The Wabash Cannonball." "The Ruthless Cannonball" dealt with Branigin's fondness for an occasional drink and Humphrey's support among the more conservative and establishment elements of the party. The writers included Jules Witcover, David Broder, David Halberstam, who was doing a magazine piece, Warren Rogers of *Look* magazine, and me. Then David Breasted played his guitar and sang it to the candidate:

Listen to the speeches that baffle, beef, and bore
As he waffles through the woodlands and slides along the shore.
He's the politician who's touched by one and all.
He's the demon driver of the Ruthless Cannonball.

He came down to Logansport one sunny April day.
All 'long the depot you could hear those Hoosiers say,
He's the heir apparent, full of chutzpah, full of gall,
I'll bet he wants our helpin' hand on the Ruthless Cannonball.

His eastern states are dandy, so all the people say,
From Boston to Virginny and New York by the way,
The blacks in Gary love him, the Poles will fill his hall,
There are no ethnic problems on the Ruthless Cannonball.

There goes Roger Branigin, the Hoosiers' favorite son,
He doesn't want the office, he only wants to run.
His highballing days are over, he's riding for a fall,
They're noted for long memories on the Ruthless Cannonball.

Now good, clean Gene McCarthy came down the other track,
A thousand Radcliffe dropouts all massed for the attack,
But Bobby's bought the right-of-way from here back to St. Paul,
'Cause money is no object on the Ruthless Cannonball.

Old Hubert's got Big Business, Big Labor, and Big Mouth,
Aboard the Maddox Special, coming from the South,
Lyndon's got him preaching so ecu-men-i-cal
But soon he'll be heaving coal on the Ruthless Cannonball.

So here's to Ruthless Robert, may his name forever stand,
To be feared and genuflected at by pols across the land.
Old Ho Chi Minh is cheering and though it may appall,
He's whizzing to the White House on the Ruthless Cannonball.

Kennedy also lost well, a talent reporters always admire. Defeated by McCarthy in the Oregon primary, he didn't do what so many politicians do by trying to find someone to blame. Some of his advisers, including Larry O'Brien, thought that William Vanden-Heuvel, the New York lawyer who had been in charge of the Oregon operation, had done a weak job as an organizer. But even within the inner circle Kennedy avoided recriminations. The real problem, he recognized, was that Oregon was a state without the kind of disadvantaged population he needed as a base. "One big suburb," said O'Brien. The morning after the defeat, at a press conference at the Los Angeles airport, I asked him how it felt to be the first Kennedy ever to lose an election. He gave me one of those mock glares and replied by citing Abraham Lincoln's story about the man ridden out of town on a rail, "If it weren't for the honor of the thing, I'd rather have walked."

For the press Kennedy's campaign of 1968 posed a special problem—how to keep a proper distance, how to maintain a professional detachment. To begin with, the emotional content was extraordinarily high. What you saw day after day was thousands of frenzied people trying to touch him as his motorcade passed, surging against police lines and gates to get into the places he would speak. Political reporters understand that the size of crowds does not necessarily correlate with support at the polling place, but crowds do give a measure of the intensity of the feeling a candidate evokes. And in Bob Kennedy's case the intensity level could not be ignored.

Most of us also liked Kennedy and the people around him. He was a wise guy, and so were many of those closest to him—Fred Dutton, Frank Mankiewicz, Dick Drayne among them. And even the young, earnest issue advisers—Adam Walinsky, Peter Edelman, Milton Gwirtzman, Jeff Greenfield—were not too hard to take. Dutton was perhaps the shrewdest analyst in the Democratic Party at the time.

Some reporters, particularly those assigned full-time to Kennedy rather than dividing their time covering McCarthy, became so caught up in the daily adventure they began to think of themselves as part of it. Most often these were people covering their first presidential campaign, but not always. One of the true tough guys on the story, Richard Harwood of *The Washington Post,* worried enough about his own objectivity that he suggested to his editors that he should be replaced for a time.

All of these feelings were, unsurprisingly, multiplied several times over when Kennedy was shot down at the Ambassador the night the primary voters had given him the victory over McCarthy that seemed likely to assure his nomination. It was a chaotic scene. Kennedy had just finished his victory statement in one of the hotel's smaller ballrooms and was heading through the adjacent kitchens toward a meeting room to do a postmortem for the press. I was making for the same room but along a corridor parallel to the kitchen when I heard the *whap, whap* of gunfire and the angry shouts of reaction. I went through a waiters' door into the kitchen, where Kennedy was sprawled on the floor and Sirhan Sirhan was being held by Rafer Johnson and several others jammed against a steam table. I began scribbling notes. I couldn't read them later, but it didn't matter. It was not the kind of scene you would forget.

In the ballroom young women were crying hysterically. In the lobby several older women had dropped to their knees to pray. Just outside the door, where I went for a cab to follow the ambulance, two men were fighting furiously. At the Central Receiving Hospital a few minutes away, several black women were waiting on a small lawn in front, wailing and keening. When Jean Smith, Bobby's sister, appeared as the ambulance prepared to transfer him to the Hospital of the Good Samaritan a few blocks away, they called out, "God bless you, honey, God bless you." At the hospital the reporters and camera crews milled around on the curb, watching those who went in and waiting for word from someone inside on the candidate's condition. About dawn an enterprising hustler showed up peddling PRAY FOR BOBBY bumper stickers. Later in the morning a student nurses' classroom was turned into a makeshift pressroom, and we all crowded in to set up our typewriters and begin writing the obituaries it seemed likely would be required. The vigil lasted just under twenty-six hours, until Mankiewicz announced his death.

Then, within a few hours the plans were announced for the body to be flown to New York, where a service would be held before it was taken on a train to Washington to a grave site at Arlington National Cemetery. Now the question was not simply whether you were going to cover this phase of the story and accompany the body to New York and Washington. It was whether you were going to "see it through to the end." It became some sort of test of your commitment, a way to demonstrate respect. But I decided against it. I was dog tired, but I was a young man with great stamina. What I understood, however, was that I was the wrong reporter to cover that story. I was no good at stories like this, and I had in the bureau a master of such stories, Bill Ringle. So I called Ringle and told him to meet the plane in New York and do the train trip.

Some of my colleagues were offended, and their questions made it plain how emotionally involved they had become. How could I peel off before the end? Didn't I want to see it through? For some of those who asked the questions, the Robert Kennedy campaign became the defining moment of their careers. But it was a professional decision I would make again. I, too, had become caught up in the drama of the story, but it was still a story to be covered.

I was not unaffected, however. Haynes Johnson of the *Post* and I took a red-eye back to Washington. We settled down in first class, drank several martinis and two bottles of wine with dinner, then several cognacs without ever being able to sleep. Instead, we speculated about what might have been the rest of the year if there had been no Sirhan Sirhan lurking in the kitchen of the Ambassador.

—

CHAPTER 7

FOREVER NIXON

If you are going to write about American politics of the last forty years, there must be a chapter about Richard Milhous Nixon, simply because he was always there. I wrote my first story about Nixon in 1954, when, as vice president, he passed through Rochester, New York, to deliver a speech and I was assigned to cover it as a city staff reporter for the *Rochester Times-Union*. I wrote what I thought would be my last column about him for the *Baltimore Sun* after he died in 1994. As it turned out, there were other columns as Nixon continued to provide rich material from the grave through the medium of the White House tapes. He was always there, even in death.

Nixon is particularly relevant here, however, because so much of his career was colored by controversy over his relationship with the press. In the most obvious sense there is nothing special about that. There is always a certain amount of tension between reporters and politicians, at all levels. The politicians want to be presented to their constituents in the most favorable light. The reporters strive to present them in the most accurate light. The two are not often the same. The relationship is further complicated by its symbiotic nature. They need us and we need them. And both of us hate admitting it.

But it was Richard Nixon more than any other political figure who crystallized the terms of the debate over the last two generations by defining the press as liberal, elitist, and hostile to Republicans, conservatives, and those who became known as middle Americans. The proof, in the view of Nixon and many of those closest to him, lay in the criticism he received for his tactics in his Senate campaign against Helen Gahagan Douglas in 1950, in the sneering way he was treated for his role in the Alger Hiss case, in the derision directed at him after the mawkish Checkers speech that saved his place on Dwight D. Eisenhower's ticket in 1952, and, especially, in many reporters' admiration for the élan of John F. Kennedy in the 1960 presidential campaign. So no one misunderstood the hostility Nixon was expressing when, after losing the California gubernatorial election to Pat Brown in 1962, he declared it was his last press conference and heatedly told the reporters, "You won't have Dick Nixon to kick around anymore."

Nonetheless, the relationship between the press and Nixon in particular or the press and conservatives in general has never been as simple as he made it appear. His own relationships with reporters were shot through with contradictions. It was said that he manipulated the press masterfully. It was said that the press was unfair and biased in its treatment of him. It was said that reporters had it in for him—and that he had it in for them as well. All those things were true, although none of them was the whole truth. Nixon was so self-conscious he could not ignore press coverage or even accept it with any detachment. He was so obsessed with how he would be regarded by his peers and by history that he could leave nothing alone, no slight unremarked. He was forever explaining his own motives and analyzing those of his political enemies and, for that matter, those of the reporters covering him whom he viewed as enemies.

It was equally true that most reporters didn't like Nixon. I never liked him. I disliked him long before Watergate proved to me how venal he could be. But that dislike had nothing to do with his Republicanism or his conservatism, although I never shared either. I really didn't think of him as anything but the ultimate pragmatist, who would do whatever it took to get where he wanted, a judgment that might be applied to many politicians across the ideological spectrum. So my dislike had nothing to do with ideology and everything to do with the kind of guy he was. He was not someone with whom a reporter would choose to have a friendly jar at the end of the day. He was always posing. And I knew that Nixon would never choose to associate with reporters if he could avoid it. In his view we were enemies bent on his destruction or, at best, trivial people deserving the contempt he turned on so many people he considered beneath him.

Nixon enjoyed fencing with reporters nonetheless. He fancied himself good at playing the game, able to divine our motives and then bend that knowledge to his own purposes. And he was. I remember asking him a question at a small press conference in Madison, Wisconsin, in 1966, when he was positioning himself for another run at the White House in 1968. Nixon ducked the question. When the conference ended he called me aside in the hotel corridor to explain that he knew what I was trying to get him to say but that if he had said that, there would have been the following consequences and implications. He was right on all points, but most politicians don't feel obliged to show off their analytical skills. It was important to him to demonstrate he had seen through my clumsy design.

Another time in the 1960s I went to interview him in his law office in New York armed with a yellow pad on which I had jotted down a few words as cryptic ticklers to remind me of questions I wanted to be certain to ask before my time ran out. Nixon could not see the words on my pad—we were sitting at opposite ends of a long leather couch—but once I asked the question triggered by the first of my notes, he went into a lengthy exposition that covered every subsequent point in order. It was impressive.

For all of Nixon's skill at playing the media game, however, it was always clear that his hostility was seething there just under the surface. And that resentment and antagonism were apparent even when he was at the peak of his power and popularity as president. I covered the White House during the first eighteen months of his presidency and, like most of my colleagues and competitors, was impressed by the "new Nixon" we were seeing. He was advancing interesting and innovative ideas on domestic policy, and the White House was relatively open in making its case. His chief advisers, other than the implacably hostile H. R. Haldeman, were available to have breakfast or lunch to discuss the rationale behind White House initiatives with reporters. His press secretary, Ronald Ziegler, was not much help, but, what the hell, he didn't get in the way either. And Nixon made himself accessible with press conferences.

But that atmosphere vanished when the president tried to nominate a southern conservative candidate for the Supreme Court who could be confirmed by the Senate. His first choice, a federal judge in North Carolina, Clement F. Haynsworth, had to be withdrawn because of conflict-of-interest charges raised by the press—charges that in retrospect probably were not legitimate. Nixon then nominated another district court judge, G. Harrold Carswell of Florida, only to learn that as a young man running for the legislature Carswell had made a racist speech. Again, it was the press that produced the crippling news.

With the nomination in trouble, I went to a press conference in the East Room of the White House prepared, like most of my colleagues, to pursue Nixon on the Carswell issue. Whatever he said about it, we were sure, would be news, so it was the logical topic. But I must confess that I—and, I suspect, many of my colleagues as well—were enjoying his discomfort in having once again screwed up the Supreme Court vacancy. Reporters are not supposed to revel in the troubles of the politicians they cover, but they are human, and this was a Page One story however it turned out.

As it happened, Nixon called on me early in the press conference.

"Mr. President," I asked, "if you had known about the speech in which he advocated white supremacy, would you have nominated Judge Carswell to the Supreme Court?"

I will never forget the small smirk of triumph that spread over Nixon's face as he listened to the question. I understood immediately that he was primed to put down me and any of my fellow travelers.

"Yes, I would," he replied. "I am not concerned about what Judge Carswell said twenty-two years ago when he was a candidate for a state legislature. I am very much concerned about his record of eighteen years—as you know, he has six years as a U.S. attorney and twelve years as a federal district judge—a record which is impeccable and without a taint of racism, a record, yes, of strict constructionism as far as the interpretation of the Constitution and the role of the courts, which I think the Court needs, the kind of balance it needs. Those are the reasons I nominated Judge Carswell."

Then Nixon slipped in the knife.

"I should also point out that, looking at a man's record over the past, any individual may find instances where he has made statements in which his position has changed. I was reading, for example, referring to the press corps here, a very interesting biography of Ralph McGill [a liberal and widely admired editor of *The Atlanta Constitution*] the other day. In 1940 he wrote a column in which he came out unalterably against integration of education of southern schools. He changed his mind later. As you know, he was a very great advocate of integration. That doesn't mean that you question his integrity in late years because in his early years in the South he took a position other southerners were taking."

It was a quintessential Nixon triumph. The message was clear: I may have screwed up, but you bastards have some skeletons of your own.

The triumph was short-lived, though. The Carswell nomination had to be withdrawn a few days later when it became apparent the votes weren't there for confirmation by the Senate. That afternoon Nixon compounded the political felony by marching into the White House pressroom and delivering an angry outburst against the conspiracy to prevent him from choosing a southerner who believed in strict constructionism for the Court.

"Judge Carswell and before him Judge Haynsworth," he said, his voice trembling with anger, "have been submitted to vicious assaults on their intelligence, on their honesty, and on their character. They have been falsely charged with being racists. But when you strip away all the hypocrisy, the real reason for their rejection was their legal philosophy, a philosophy that I share, of strict construction of the Constitution, and also the accident of their birth, the fact that they were born in the South."

The comparisons with Captain Queeg were obvious. What was

most telling about the episode, however, was the evidence that Nixon would put aside his analytical skills in a moment if he thought he was being mistreated because of his conservatism. Rather than being annoyed at the failures in the vetting process that had produced vulnerable nominees for the Court, the president saw this incident as Dick Nixon being kicked around once again, even after he had reached the pinnacle of power.

Those rare glimpses of the "real" Nixon we were all seeking were made all the more striking because he always took such pains to prevent anyone from seeing him as a human being, subject to human failings or even human feelings. He was always the imperial figure, the leader functioning far above the mundane, workaday concerns of his critics. There was a memorable day during the 1968 New Hampshire presidential primary campaign in which he was running against George Romney. Romney's campaign had been crippled for months by his inability to handle effectively the issue of the Vietnam War, and opinion polls showed Nixon far ahead with New Hampshire Republicans. But it was still surprising when late one morning word began to circulate through the political community in both Washington and New Hampshire that Romney was about to hold a press conference and withdraw. The implications were enormous—essentially a clear field to the Republican nomination for Nixon.

Nixon was handshaking in a restaurant when Patrick J. Buchanan, then a young member of his staff, learned about Romney in a call to Washington. Buchanan quickly ushered his candidate into a men's room to tell him what was happening. But when Nixon emerged and reporters crowded around to question him, he pretended to be getting the news for the first time and passed off questions with some predictable talk about how he was going to keep campaigning as hard as he could. And, to prove the point, he pressed on with his handshaking for another hour or more before returning to his motel in Manchester.

When we asked Nixon if he intended to watch Romney appear on television from Washington, he replied that he was too busy and vanished into his suite at the end of a long corridor, ostensibly to "do some work" that had been piling up. But when a campaign adviser entered the suite a little later, he found Nixon sitting before the television set, staring intently at the screen while Romney made his announcement. It was, of course, just the way anyone might be expected to behave in the circumstances. This was a critical moment in his quest for the White House, so what could be more natural than to savor it? But Nixon didn't want to seem too eager, too ready to enjoy Romney's collapse and his own success, too human.

I sometimes felt some sympathy for Nixon in those days because he was such a graceless man. He always seemed uncomfortable with anyone except those on his staff. He was impressed and perhaps intimidated by wealth. He was clearly discomforted, for example, by Nelson Rockefeller's fortune and gregarious self-confidence. He always seemed ill at ease with reporters, even when there was no reason to feel threatened and, in fact, he was getting the best of the relationship. During the 1968 campaign some political reporters, myself included, felt some collective guilt for the way Nixon had been treated by the press in 1960, when he ran against a candidate most reporters liked and enjoyed, John Kennedy. The first result was that we bent over backward to be "fair." And the second, perhaps inevitably, was that Nixon exploited the opportunity and took us over the jumps. He announced during that New Hampshire campaign that, yes, he had a plan for ending the war in Vietnam but could not spell it out publicly without intruding on the foreign policy prerogatives of President Lyndon B. Johnson. So, he said, he was declaring a moratorium on talk about Vietnam for the duration of the campaign.

We let him get away with it. In retrospect, I find our failure mind-boggling. Nonetheless, at the time it seemed to be a natural evolution of our general feeling that Nixon had been treated harshly in the past, if not by us then by others in our role, and was entitled to a fresh start. Herblock, the great liberal cartoonist for *The Washington Post*, perhaps reflected this sentiment most dramatically when, early in 1969, after years of drawing Nixon as a heavily bearded, slime-covered figure climbing up out of manholes, he drew a cartoon giving the new president a "clean shave" to say, in effect, that bygones were bygones.

Although the same attitude prevailed in the White House press corps in 1969, Nixon remained conspicuously wary. A few months after taking office, the new president moved into his renovated oceanfront home in San Clemente, California, and the traveling White House press corps, billeted at a surfside motel in nearby Laguna Beach, was invited for drinks one night to see the place. Nixon waited by the swimming pool, wearing the powder blue blazer that was a signal he was relaxing. In practice, Nixon could not relax. In those days there were few perils for a politician at such an occasion. It was understood that the conversation was off the record and, barring his confession that he was a transvestite or a Democrat, Nixon had no reason to fear that anyone would rush to the telephone with a cheap-shot story about some offhand remark he had made. But Nixon could talk or would talk of nothing except sports. Nor would he allow himself a drink while we were all swilling down several. After the proscribed hour we boarded our bus back to Laguna with the feeling that our host would then turn to the Filipino steward who had been serving drinks and say, "Now that those bastards are gone, you can bring me a double Scotch."

For me, all those unfortunate facets of the Nixon personality had been distilled several years earlier when I accompanied him on a trip that began with a speech in Sacramento. It was 1966, and Nixon was campaigning for Republican candidates for the House of Representatives, a first step toward clawing his way to another presidential nomination in 1968. For a political writer it was natural to spend a few days on the road with him and then write about this enterprise. I was the only reporter on this trip, but Nixon had one traveling aide, Patrick Hillings, a bluff, good-natured lawyer and auto company executive. Hillings had succeeded Nixon in the House for a single term, and, for reasons lost on me, he both liked and admired the former vice president.

We were spending the night in the old and now long defunct Senator Hotel, and Nixon's schedule called only for an afternoon press conference and a speech at a party dinner early in the evening. Waiting in the lobby to leave for the dinner with Nixon, Hillings and I noticed a photograph on an easel of a smashing young woman who, the sign informed us, would be playing for our listening pleasure in the cocktail lounge that evening. With a few minutes to kill, we popped into the bar for a quick drink and a little research that confirmed this was a piano player with a voice and style to match her beauty. The rest of our schedule for the evening seemed obvious.

We went off to the dinner with Nixon and returned to the hotel early in the evening, nine or nine-thirty at the latest. We showed him the picture on the easel, reported on our earlier finding that this was a special talent, and urged Nixon to join us for a nightcap. I could feel that he was intrigued and tempted but too self-conscious to do it. Muttering something about "work" he had to do, he went up to his suite.

As it turned out, Hillings and I had a grand evening at the piano bar, during which, my hotel bill later revealed, we drank thirteen Irish coffees. The piano player proved to be not only talented and beautiful but smart and funny. When the bar closed she loaded us into her car and took us to an after-hours joint that catered to entertainers, bartenders, and waiters when the legitimate drinking ended. There were more songs, a few beers with which to taper off, some scrambled eggs and coffee, and eventually a return to the hotel, only an hour or two before we were to leave for Chicago. I went to my room, took fresh clothes out of my suitcase, and spent almost an hour in the shower, running the water alternately hot and cold in a regimen that I somehow imagined would revive me for the day. Then it was down to check out in the lobby, where Hillings had told Nixon we'd enjoyed a long evening of Sacramento hospitality and were not in the best of shape.

When we boarded the plane for Chicago, Nixon invited me to join him for breakfast, so I took out my notebook to record an interview. But after a few minutes I realized Nixon was the one doing the interviewing. He wanted to know all about our evening with the piano player. Specifically, he wanted to know if either of us had taken her to bed, although he would never say as much in so many words. How had we "made out"? Who had "ended up" with her? Was she as "hot" as she seemed to be? He was like some prurient teenager living vicariously, and I reacted accordingly by being deliberately obtuse and failing to understand what he was getting at, for God's sake. In fact, the piano player had been so far out of our league that neither Hillings nor I was foolish enough to make a pass at her. But I was damned if I was going to make it easy for Nixon. So the conversation moved on to politics and the Republicans' chances in 1966 and 1968 and his own plans—only to return to the piano player every few minutes all the way to Chicago.

Looking back on the incident from a great distance, I realize it was an unkind and arrogant way for me to behave. I should have just laughed it off and told Nixon she went home with her husband. As we learned in so much detail from the Watergate tapes a few years later, the poor bastard wanted to be one of the boys, but he just didn't know how. That didn't make him a bad president or, for that matter, a good one. But it does explain why people like me never liked him. It had nothing to do with ideology or a press conspiracy. It was entirely personal. There was, of course, more to the reporters' mistrust of Nixon than the fact that he was not one of the boys. But, contrary to the suspicions of many readers and many politicians, it had little to do with his partisan and ideological identification.

It is probably true, as Nixon always insisted, that most reporters are liberal rather than conservative. That clearly was the case when I came along, and it wasn't hard to understand. As reporters we saw at firsthand far more than most Americans the underside of the culture—poor people, black people, the uneducated and unemployed. In my generation we were most impressed by both the human costs and the societal sickness that resulted from racial discrimination. More to the point, we looked to the government to provide the solutions—the laws and court decisions that would integrate the schools and build the housing and provide the jobs that eventually would correct all these flaws in our society. That was how you defined a liberal—by degree of reliance on government to provide the opportunity for economic and social equity. We had not yet learned that many of the liberal prescriptions don't work as well as we had hoped, if at all.

But political reporters don't sit down with lists of issues, checking off each candidate's position. They are far more interested in personal qualities. Is a candidate intellectually honest? Thoughtful enough to foresee national problems? Street-smart enough to find and promulgate solutions? Self-confident enough to understand the difference between enemies and adversaries? Or is he so obsessed with his own ego and image that every decision is made on the basis of the crassest political calculations?

That was the problem with Nixon. By almost any standard the domestic proposals he advanced as the new president in 1969 were thoughtful and balanced—disarming to many of his liberal critics. But behind that new Nixon you could always see the old one, with all the same grievances to be redressed. It was never going to be enough for him to win the White House. Once he had it, he had to grind the other guys into the dirt.

CHAPTER 8

WATERGATE

We don't like to admit it, even now, but the early days of Watergate were a nightmare for many reporters in Washington. The story was being written by two unknown punks from the metro staff of the *Post,* and they seemed to have the sources locked up tightly enough so that nobody could match them, let alone advance the story. Every few days we'd be whacked with another development by Bob Woodward and Carl Bernstein, whoever the hell they were. It is the kind of situation a reporter loves if he's the one who has it locked up, and we all have been in that position at one time or another, although not on a story of this magnitude. But if you're on the short end, there is always a lot of denial. The story is old stuff or it's exaggerated or it's just plain horseshit. There was a lot of that going around while we were getting our brains beaten out during the summer of 1972.

After a time, however, our attitudes inevitably began to change. For one thing, the story was simply too big to be brushed aside. And, as it took on greater and greater dimensions, it became possible for other reporters to plug into it. We may have missed the original story of the sponsorship of the break-in, but there were sources among the various investigators who could be reached and mined for other developments. That change in the dynamics didn't occur, however, until after the 1972 presidential election campaign, in which Nixon buried the hapless George McGovern, a story that in itself was fascinating to report.

After the fact, it became a part of the conventional wisdom that the original stupidity of the White House was bothering to break into the Democratic National Committee headquarters in the Watergate Office Building in the first place. The theory was that McGovern never had a chance to defeat Nixon anyway, so it didn't matter what might be in the files of the DNC chairman, Larry O'Brien, that had been targeted by the burglars.

In fact, that revisionist history is dead wrong. Richard Nixon was never a beloved figure nor a politically unassailable incumbent president. He won with 43 percent of the vote in a three-way election in 1968, and the share of Americans who believed he merited reelection four years later was about the same. In the spring of 1972, the period just before the break-in, there were opinion polls that showed both McGovern and Senator Edmund S. Muskie of Maine running essentially even with Nixon, well within the statistical margin of error. The White House was fully aware of that; in American politics both sides operate off the same basic data.

McGovern was an unlikely candidate for president. He represented a small state, South Dakota, at a time when that seemed important, and he had never been a major force in the Senate, although he was respected by his colleagues because he paid attention to the fine print of many issues. On the stump he was an unprepossessing figure. He spoke with a bland nasality that didn't seem to light any fires in his audiences. And, perhaps most to the point, he lacked strong connections to the traditional centers of power in the Democratic Party, including organized labor, the big-city mayors, and the black leadership. He wasn't exactly an outsider, but neither was he someone who would show up on every list of Democratic heavyweights who might qualify for the national ticket. For one thing, he was probably a little too liberal even at a time when liberalism was still in fashion.

But McGovern had made a political base for himself among the opponents of the war in Vietnam by serving with restraint and dignity as a stand-in of sorts for the late Robert F. Kennedy at the Democratic convention in Chicago in 1968. And over the next four years he had established himself as the leading voice of the movement, within the political community at least. What made McGovern a genuine threat to Nixon, however, was the way he took the nomination from the prohibitive favorite, Muskie, during the primaries. Americans love winners, and they tend to invest them with all sorts of qualities previously undetected once they have won a few elections. So any candidate who runs through a string of primaries looks impressive.

McGovern had been campaigning assiduously for well over a year before the primary campaign in New Hampshire began in earnest in 1972, an approach that was as unusual then as it became routine later. And he had two pronounced advantages in that opening primary. The first was a superb organization put together by a brilliant but sometimes abrasive young party activist, Joe Grandmaison, who built an instant machine out of the young antiwar protesters who flocked into the state to volunteer for McGovern much as they had for Eugene McCarthy in 1968. But even Grandmaison would concede that organization is worth only a few percentage points and that there has to be some other dynamic driving a candidacy for it to succeed.

For McGovern, that critical element was the inordinately high expectations for Edmund S. Muskie. He was the senator from next-door Maine and the clear favorite for the presidential nomination in national polls after his impressive performance as the vice presidential nominee in 1968 and an election-eve national television appearance in 1970 in which he made an eloquent plea for civility in American politics. Muskie's position was so strong on paper that it led his state campaign director in New Hampshire, an activist named Maria Carrier, to become incautious enough—or perhaps honest enough—to set the bar too high for her candidate. When Tom Ottenad and I asked her one morning if she thought Muskie would win at least half the primary vote, she replied that she would be "very disappointed" if that were not the case. As a result, although Muskie won the primary with 46 percent of the vote, he was written off as falling short of what he should have done, while McGovern's 37 percent was seen as the first evidence of a rising star.

More to the point, in "losing," Muskie had shown a human weakness that raised questions about whether he was too emotional to be president and made things difficult for him in later primaries with electorates that didn't know him as well.

Those of us who knew Muskie were aware that he had a volatile temper. Riding with him in a car during his 1970 campaign for re-election to the Senate, along with a young reporter from the Portland newspaper, I had raised the question then circulating in the political community about whether he wanted the presidency badly enough to do the things necessary to win it. Muskie, sitting in the front, wheeled around and shook a long finger in my face.

"That's that 'fire in the belly' shit," he shouted, pounding the back of the seat, "and I'm sick of hearing about it."

I protested that I hadn't made it up but was reflecting a common reservation.

But Muskie would have none of it. "You're repeating it," he shouted, "and I'm telling you it's just bullshit."

I will never forget the shocked look on the face of the young Portland reporter, seeing a different side of his state's elder statesman for the first time.

On another occasion Muskie had come to dinner with a background group of reporters we archly called Political Writers for a Democratic Society. There were ten or twelve of us—Jules Witcover, Tom Ottenad, David Broder, Robert Novak, Paul Hope of the *Washington Star,* Loye Miller, then of Knight-Ridder, James Large of *The Wall Street Journal,* James Doyle of *The Boston Globe,* Warren Weaver of *The New York Times,* Bruce Biossat of Newspaper Enterprise Association (a syndicate), Ted Knap of Scripps-Howard, and one or two others in a sometimes changing cast. We would have dinner with a politician, usually at my town house in southwest Washington, with a few drinks before and after the meal. The meetings were on what we called deep background, which meant we could never refer in print to their having been held or quote directly or indirectly anything the politician said. If, for example, someone outlined his strategy for winning the nomination, as McGovern did one night early in 1971, we could write about it but only without any attribution to any sources, however vague. (In McGovern's case it seemed so improbable nobody exercised that option.)

The intention was to get to know the candidates better in an informal setting, and with Muskie it worked just as we had hoped.

When we continued to press him on what we considered his failure to take a clear position on the war in Vietnam, Muskie, who had been into the bourbon, exploded in a red-faced denial—shouting at us so loudly that my wife could hear him clearly although she was watching television two floors above us and behind closed doors. There was nothing to write that night, but we had learned something valuable about Ed Muskie.

The result was that none of us who had been there was surprised when Muskie lost his temper in New Hampshire and, standing on the back of a flatbed truck in a snowstorm, assailed William Loeb, the vitriolic publisher of *The Union Leader,* who used the Manchester newspaper to club anyone who did not meet his right-wing proscriptions. The list was long, and Loeb was never subtle. In this case the paper was taxing Jane Muskie, the candidate's wife, for ostensibly telling dirty jokes with reporters on a press bus. It was no big deal to anyone but Ed Muskie, to whom it was a very big deal.

I missed the event, but I didn't miss the point. I had gone back to Washington for a weekend at home with my wife and daughters when I saw the film of the outburst on the CBS news Saturday night—Muskie on the truck, his face contorted with anger, tears or melting snow running down his cheeks. An hour later I was on a plane to Boston on the way back to Manchester, where I had breakfast the next morning with Tony Podesta, Muskie's state campaign director. He was too much the professional to try to hide his chagrin and, instead, was grasping for ways to repair the damage that was already apparent. Nothing helped. Muskie loyalists kept insisting that Americans admire someone who sticks up for his wife. But the Cold War was still being waged, and the American people didn't want someone given to emotional outbursts in charge of the red telephone.

In any case, there were enough doubts about Muskie to make McGovern a growth stock throughout the 1972 primaries and up to the point of the Watergate burglary in June. But the issue rarely came up during the general election campaign, in which McGovern suffered from several classic blunders, the most serious being his choice of Senator Tom Eagleton of Missouri to be his running mate for vice president only to discover that Eagleton had suffered from an emotional depression serious enough to require electric shock treatments. By the time McGovern replaced him on the ticket with Sargent Shriver, any chance of a competitive campaign had ended. But McGovern still found the lack of focus on Watergate galling.

About ten days before the election I interviewed him at an airport fire station in Cedar Rapids, Iowa. It was one of those interviews intended to summarize the entire campaign for publication in the Sunday newspapers, then an important news outlet. In fact, it was more of a postmortem, since both McGovern and I knew he would lose, and, unlike many candidates, he wasn't trapped in self-delusion. He was generally at peace with himself and the world about the whole experience. Yes, he conceded, there were some things he would do differently, but, what the hell, politics is an imperfect craft.

But then I asked him if he thought the American people had been given an accurate picture of the kind of man he was.

"Accurate?" he protested, pounding the firehouse dining table, his face reddening. "I'm running against Richard Nixon and people think *I'm* the dishonest one! How can that be accurate?"

It was a valid point. When he lost every state but Massachusetts and the District of Columbia, George McGovern became a political laughingstock in a way that was all out of proportion to his qualities as a public official and political leader. He had made some serious mistakes in his campaign—in his handling of the defense spending issue, in his tax and welfare proposals, and, most of all, in choosing Eagleton for vice president. But he also had been victimized.

Eagleton's failure to inform his benefactor of his medical history is the single most flagrant betrayal I have ever seen in a life covering politics. The senator from Missouri essentially allowed his ambition for the place on the ticket—and unquestionably his dreams of his own time in the White House—to cloud his judgment. He deliberately withheld the information about electric shock treatment because he knew it would be disqualifying. That may not have been fair or enlightened in what it suggested about Americans' view of mental illness. But in 1972, and I suspect today, the notion of a vice presidential candidate who had been, as Lee Atwater put it about another Democrat later, "hooked up to jumper cables" was too much baggage.

McGovern made the mistake of temporizing when he learned of

Eagleton's medical history. He didn't know what to make of it, he told me later. His wife, Eleanor, was furious at Eagleton, but some of their advisers were saying he had to do the "right thing" and move Americans out of the dark ages in their attitude about emotional illness. By the time Eagleton had been forced to withdraw from the ticket—it took several days—the damage was done and McGovern was never competitive.

But that failure certainly did not justify the opprobrium heaped on McGovern's head after that election. With Democrats, losing seems to be the ultimate sin. The Republicans will forgive a Gerald Ford or George Bush who kicks away the White House, or even a Barry Goldwater, who pulls the party down around his ears. But Democratic losers—Jimmy Carter, Walter Mondale, and Michael Dukakis as well as George McGovern—are savaged by their own party simply for losing. Indeed, McGovern became a nonperson within the party until he competed in the Iowa caucuses in 1988 and handled himself especially well in a televised debate in Des Moines. (When I remarked on all the praise he was receiving, he replied, "Where were they when I needed them?")

Although there was never any evidence of Watergate becoming an influential factor in the 1972 campaign, the story boiled up repeatedly over the next few months. Woodward and Bernstein were still delivering evidence of corruption and cover-up in the White House, and now other news organizations were getting a piece of the action. And, most important, Senator Sam Ervin of North Carolina was leading the investigation that would culminate in televised public hearings that spread so much of the story on the record in the summer of 1973.

Watergate also played an important part in the direction of my own life as a reporter. By the time of the Senate hearings I was in my twentieth year with Gannett and my fourth as chief of the Washington bureau. It had always been an uneasy relationship, but I knew a certain tension between the home office and the outposts was inevitable. I had been six years in the Albany and New York City bureaus and another eleven in Washington, so I had learned to roll with the punches. I was paid well and given extraordinary benefits— what Bill Ringle called "the bricks and mortar of the twenty-five-year club"—as well as annual bonuses amounting to 30 percent of my salary, paid in a lump sum every January.

Money aside, most of the time I controlled my own assignments and those of the reporters who worked in my bureau. I had been allowed to assemble a staff of a dozen, several of whom were as good at their beats as anyone in the business. I reported to John C. Quinn, the vice president for news at Gannett headquarters (then in Rochester), a good newspaperman with whom I had built a warm relationship.

Control of my assignments was an asset of inestimable value because it meant I could decide which political story was the one that required coverage and, equally important, because it allowed me to travel and build a bank of sources around the country upon whom I could rely. It meant that even though I worked for what I once incautiously called "a bunch of shitkicker newspapers" rather than the *Times* or the *Post,* I could get my phone calls returned and compete with the David Broders and Johnny Apples on more or less even terms.

There always seemed to be considerable ambivalence in the way I was regarded by the corporate brass in Rochester, however. Over the years they let me indulge myself and cover politics as thoroughly as any reporter for any news organization. But they also used me to do some heavy lifting as an investigative reporter. When Utica, New York, developed a problem with Mafia influence in the city government in 1959, I was assigned there for three months to conduct— with the help of Bill Lohden of the *Observer-Dispatch* staff—an investigation that led eventually to the appointment of a special prosecutor, a long list of indictments and convictions, and, not incidentally, the newspaper's winning a Pulitzer Gold Medal for public service, the first ever won by a Gannett paper. When racial tensions began to surface in Rochester the following year, I was sent there for two months to work with Desmond Stone, a solid reporter from New Zealand, on a series for the *Times-Union* called "The Winds of Change" that accurately forecast trouble in the streets if the concerns of blacks, then called Negroes, were not recognized and met. When there was evidence of some corruption in the Camden, New Jersey, police department, I was dispatched there to help the

Courier-Post find out how easy it was to get down a bet (answer: very easy) and how many cops might be on the pad (answer: lots).

But the chairman of Gannett Co., Inc., Paul Miller, was not comfortable with me as a political reporter and even less so with me as chief of the Washington bureau, the job that I obviously wanted from the day I went to Washington in 1961. It wasn't a question of my politics. Although the Gannett executives knew I was more liberal than they, nobody accused me of slanting my copy to the left, and, more to the point, no one ever tried to skew it to the right. By the 1960s we had reached a point at which newspaper publishers were like aging Mafia dons. They wanted respectability and knew they couldn't earn it by playing the kinds of games Eugene Pulliam played in Indianapolis or Bertie McCormick played with the *Chicago Tribune*.

What they didn't like about me, I came to realize long after the fact, was that I didn't fit their notion of what the Washington bureau chief should be. Miller himself had been the bureau chief for the Associated Press in the years right after World War II and had become friends and golfing buddies with many of those in power. He was a tall, handsome man who always looked as if he had just left the barber's chair. His suits were invariably pressed, his shirts crisp, his ties knotted perfectly, his shoes discreetly clean without being vulgarly shiny. He liked the idea of holding dinner parties as a way of building "contacts" that would be valuable in covering Washington. He took the Gridiron Club, an organization of fifty Washington newspapermen that held an annual white-tie dinner roasting politicians, very seriously indeed. He wanted someone, in short, to "represent" the Gannett Newspapers in the way he might have done.

But what he got was a fat, bald guy who looked unkempt even in a freshly pressed suit and a Brooks Brothers shirt, who played poker and the horses rather than golf, who didn't give dinner parties except for friends, and who sometimes drank too much. I was, in Paul Miller's eyes, a cultural misfit. In a history of Gannett published almost twenty years later, Vincent Jones, the chain's chief news executive at the time, described what happened when he sent me to Washington. "That didn't please Miller because Jack Germond is sort of a fat little guy and he's not a Paul Miller type. In fact, Al

Neuharth (who was in line to succeed Miller in running Gannett) and I went down to look over the bureau one day and Al asked his Detroit friends what they thought of Jack Germond. This Detroit guy said, 'Well, he's a blue-collar bureau chief. I'm a white-collar bureau chief.' " It is a description that, in retrospect, I find flattering but not one I would have welcomed then if I had known about it.

The result of Miller's resistance was that I didn't get the bureau chief's title, or money, until 1969, at least four years and probably six years after I began running it with one gimcracky title or another—news editor or deputy chief or whatever. And that was the case although they were determined to replace the longtime bureau chief, a man who met Miller's requirements of dress and demeanor but also combined a talent for writing right-wing diatribes with an unfortunate habit of vanishing on three-day benders. And those were his good qualities. If he had ever had any newspaperman's instincts, they had vanished by November 22, 1963.

When the bells on the AP and UPI tickers went off, signaling a rare "flash" to announce that shots had been fired at the presidential motorcade in Dallas, four or five of us from the bureau were in the dining room of the National Press Club, one floor above our office. We had just started on some Bloody Marys and beers and were looking forward to a leisurely Friday lunch that would ease us into the weekend. Most of us had finished writing our Sunday pieces, and there wasn't a hell of a lot going on anyway with the president out of town. We would knock off early.

All that changed when those flashes came from Dallas and we rushed downstairs to see what we could do on the story. We didn't have a reporter traveling with the president, so I assigned one to see how quickly he could get to Dallas and the hospital. Another reporter was sent to monitor the office of Speaker of the House John McCormack, who was second in line for the presidency and had been instantly surrounded by the Secret Service. A third was dispatched to the Senate. Others began calling anyone they knew in the White House or law enforcement who might know something. For an hour or two that day there was great uncertainty in Washington. We didn't know about assassinations. The notion that this might be a plot to overthrow the government didn't seem as ridiculous as it does now.

All through the afternoon our bureau chief had remained in his private office off the newsroom. We couldn't see him, but we could hear that he had his television set turned on and we could hear the steady clacking of his typewriter. I couldn't imagine what he was writing, but I assumed he would let me know before it was time to file the news budget—a brief summary of the stories the bureau would be transmitting to our newspapers that night—about 5:00 P.M. Meanwhile the story had evolved. President Kennedy was dead. President Johnson had been sworn in, and both were returning to Washington. There were a hundred new angles to be explored in what clearly would be an around-the-clock work weekend. But not for the bureau chief. He emerged from his office shortly after five and dropped into the copy basket a long story about an impending Senate campaign in New Jersey. "That's probably out of date now," he said. Whereupon he put on his elegant black overcoat and went home.

But even when the bureau chief finally was squeezed out—to a job writing long, bloodless pieces for *U.S. News & World Report*—Miller wouldn't abide me as a successor. The first replacement was the editor of the *Hartford Times,* a man named Bob Lucas, who fit the Miller prescription. He was tall, handsome, and impeccable in dress and manner. He had been editorial page editor of *The Denver Post* before moving to Hartford, and he was a graceful writer. But he had done little or no reporting for years and knew nothing about Washington. He was a warm, outgoing man with whom I worked easily, and we both understood why he had the job and I didn't, and we didn't let it get in the way of our friendship. He was, nonetheless, crippled by his lack of experience on the street and particularly in Washington. Reporters in the bureau snickered when he referred to Scotty Reston, whose byline in *The New York Times* was James B. Reston, as Jimmy and to Pat Furgurson, whose byline in the *Baltimore Sun* was Ernest B. Furgurson, as Ernie. But it still took more than three years before Lucas was given another assignment and Miller caved in so I could have the job.

With that history, it was inevitable there would be trouble over Watergate and Richard Nixon. In his own time in Washington, Miller had been particularly close to the young senator from California and later, in his days as president of the Associated Press and chairman of Gannett, to him as vice president and as president. So it may not have been surprising that he was one of the last prominent figures in American journalism to accept the reality of Nixon's personal culpability in the scandal. His attitude was the classic defense—that is, that Nixon hadn't done anything wrong, but even if he had, it was no big deal. This was, after all, a man with whom he played golf at Burning Tree and a president who would accept his telephone calls. What was the point in being part of the establishment if you didn't defend it to the death—or at least to the point at which you became the object of ridicule. So Miller persisted. Even when John S. Knight, his opposite number with the Knight Newspapers (later Knight-Ridder), finally wrote off Nixon in one of his signed weekend columns, Miller remained loyal.

And here he was stuck with a bureau chief in Washington who was not only an unkempt fat guy but one who was writing front-page pieces two or three times a week reporting on and analyzing the growing case against Nixon. For Miller, a particular irritation was a column I wrote once a week for Monday publication. During that summer of 1973 it focused unsurprisingly on Watergate and Nixon and ran regularly on the editorial page of the *Democrat & Chronicle*, the morning newspaper in Rochester, where Miller lived. Although I didn't know it at the time, almost every Monday Miller opened his paper, read the column, and called John Quinn to rage at what I had written. As Quinn described it in that book in 1993, "We were having real problems between Paul Miller and Jack Germond. It was at the time of Agnew and Nixon, and Miller was very sympathetic to Nixon. Germond was getting pissed all over [by Miller] and [Neuharth] and I were trying to be buffers. I caught more of it than a lot of people realized because I didn't even want to admit to Jack that it was a problem. You could get paralyzed by it."

By September, however, Quinn was out of maneuvering room or stalling time. The column that was the last straw began this way:

WASHINGTON—If President Nixon has been chastened by the experience of presiding over an unprecedented White House scandal, it isn't obvious to the naked eye. On the contrary, he seems to think that the most expeditious route back to business as usual is scapegoating as usual.

He is telling us that Congress is to blame for not dealing with serious national problems, and that the press is to blame for weakening his prestige to the point that he cannot deal with those problems. But we have heard nothing about what blame should be assigned to the John Mitchells and John Ehrlichmans or their sponsor.

Congress and the press may make fine punching bags most of the time. Congress is organizationally incapable of making a coherent reply to a president on the offensive. And Nixon knows the press is irritating many Americans and boring others by tenaciously harping on the unanswered questions of Watergate. But this time the scapegoating won't wash.

Miller's anger had reached a point at which he could not be placated, so Quinn called me and told me the column had been canceled, effective immediately. The trouble, he said, was that readers would see my byline on Page One writing either straight news or analysis and then again on the editorial page writing opinion. It was too confusing and this was the way to straighten it out. I pointed out that Dave Broder managed the same thing at the *Post* and nobody seemed confused, so let's not kid the troops. Moreover, my column was the feature most used by Gannett newspapers of all the material the bureau sent them. I fired off a memo to Quinn that began, "You pay me to figure things out and you expect me to believe this?" After twenty years of writing politics at all levels, from city hall to the White House, without a single problem about slanting my copy to meet some political goal, I had broken my pick over Richard Nixon, for God's sake.

I stewed and muttered to myself for several weeks. Although I didn't know then how much heat Quinn had absorbed in my behalf, I didn't blame him for a decision that was obviously out of his hands. But I was less comfortable about Al Neuharth, who had left some bodies by the side of the road on the way to the top, and about the corporate game playing that had become so much a part of Gannett as its stock soared. I was forty-five, and I began to ask myself, Do I want Al to control my life when I'm fifty-five and out of options? So early in December I went to the editors of the *Washington Star* and told them they needed someone to compete with Broder. They agreed but doubted they could afford me. So I took a pay cut of about one-third, but it was the first smart career decision I ever made. I never looked back.

CHAPTER 9

POLITICIANS
RISING TO THE
OCCASION

The *Washington Star* that I joined on January 1, 1974, was a newspaper with a long list of troubles, not the least being the low morale of a news staff that had been so badly beaten for so long on the Watergate story. The paper had been owned and managed—or, more accurately, mismanaged—by several generations of two families of well-meaning people. They had not accurately gauged the menace to all afternoon newspapers in the increasing reliance of their subscribers on television as a prime source for news. And, specifically, they had underestimated the threat represented by the aggressive *Washington Post,* which had been apparent from the day Benjamin Bradlee took over as editor in the mid-1960s.

The *Star* was, nonetheless, a great place to work. There were many excellent editors and reporters on the staff. And, most important to someone like me, there was an ethic I could appreciate. This was what newspaper people call a reporter's paper, meaning one that did more than give lip service to the proposition that the reporters' product was the heart and soul of the paper, to be treated with respect by editors even when they saw significant flaws in a story that needed to be corrected. And there was nothing approaching a "company line" on a story. No one at the *Star* felt any need to protect Richard Nixon—or, for that matter, to pound him into the sand. The story was what was happening. I had no idea of the politics of Newbold Noyes, the editor at the time I arrived. He came from one of the owning families, and I knew him only as a man with the manner of a friendly patrician who wrote elegantly and performed wickedly funny skits of his own creation at the annual Gridiron Club dinner.

In several conversations that led to my being hired, the managing editor, Charlie Seib; the assistant managing editor, Dave Kraslow; and I had discussed in some detail what my role would be as senior political writer. My first responsibility obviously would be elections, the midterms later in the year and, of course, the presidential campaign of 1976. But I clearly would have to play a major role in covering Watergate as well. Being a newcomer on the staff was a break in the sense that I wasn't one of those who had been beaten for the last year by the *Post* and, as a result, were sulky and defensive. (In fact, I *had* been beaten, but moving to a new employer gave me a kind of clean slate.) There were also some fresh faces in key assignments covering Congress. Martha Angle, a fiercely aggressive reporter, was covering the Senate, and Walter Taylor, a reporter with a special ability to build sources, was covering the House of Representatives and, more to the point, the House Judiciary Committee, which would be handing down the judgment on whether Nixon would be impeached.

Our planning was based on two premises. The first was that the Congress would not act against the president until it was plain that the country was ready for action to be taken against him. The second was that the Democrats who controlled the process would not act until there was a majority of Republicans willing to go along with them. We assumed then that there was no place for partisanship in an impeachment proceeding. So, to deal with the first premise, my assignment would be to stay in touch with the national mood on Watergate. I would follow the opinion polls and keep up with those who qualify as opinion leaders around the country, and I would travel enough to listen to what ordinary Americans had to say. My role in covering the House process would be to keep in touch with those Republicans outside the Judiciary Committee who were especially influential with their colleagues because of their own intelligence or probity or both—people like, for example, Representative Barber Conable, Jr., the ranking Republican on the Ways and Means Committee and a man with a reputation as a straight arrow as well as a record of supporting the administration. The theory there was that if a consensus developed among these heavyweights, it would eventually translate into action by the committee and the House as a whole.

With a few conspicuous exceptions, those House Republicans behaved magnificently over the next eight months that culminated in Nixon's resignation. They showed that politicians could meet a responsibility under the most difficult circumstances. They took their jobs seriously and, somewhat to the surprise of many reporters, demonstrated that they could rise to the occasion even when the course they followed seemed most threatening to their careers.

The notion that impeachment would be seen as so traumatic that Americans could not accept it was quickly dispelled. In early January, on my first assignment for the *Star,* I spent two or three days in Illinois with each of three Republicans who spanned the ideological reach of the party's minority in the House—John B. Anderson of Rockford, a progressive with a reputation for independence; Edward J. Derwinski, a devout conservative from a district in the working-class suburbs south of Chicago; and Robert H. Michel of Peoria, a middle-of-the-road conservative who had been close to Nixon for years. I went along with each of them while they spoke to service club luncheons and Republican gatherings and walked the downtown streets, pausing here and there for a cup of coffee with a constituent. The message was clear: There was no grassroots demand that Nixon be impeached, but neither was there any rush to rally around him.

Anderson put it this way: "I don't find any heavy pressure to throw the bum out, but I don't find too many people doing a Mexican hat dance when I mention his name either." Said Derwinski: "Compared to the oil companies, Nixon is in excellent shape. Compared to anybody else, he's got a lot of problems."

The response of Michel, an ebulliently optimistic man who would later be the Republican minority leader, was particularly revealing because he was the closest to Nixon, a fellow member of the Chowder and Marching Society, an informal group of mainstream conservative House Republicans, and a politician who took party loyalty very seriously indeed. Enjoying a drink and a steak after a day of listening to his constituents in Pekin, he told me, "I don't want to say this in public right now, goldarn it, but there's nothing propping him up. People are worried about the gas shortage, but they aren't worried about the president getting himself kicked out of office. That doesn't have anything to do with their lives." And even publicly Michel left himself what he called "an escape hatch" from his position against impeachment. "If during the hearings they can prove there's been obstruction of justice," he said, "I'd have to adjust my thinking."

The system, however, required some more convincing evidence than the soundings of a few congressmen on recess or even opinion polls that seemed to support those soundings. Most politicians are slavishly devoted to polls, but there is never any substitute for the evidence provided by real voters casting real votes. And as the Watergate story was coming to a critical point, the political calendar for 1974 showed six special elections to fill seats in the House that had been vacated by either deaths or retirements. Now we would find out whether Republicans in general were being menaced by what they had tried to portray as a Nixon problem rather than a party problem.

In fact, reading cosmic messages into election returns is always a tricky business. Most voters don't make two-step decisions, saying they will vote for Mr. X to send a warning to Mr. Y. But that doesn't forestall either the press or the politicians from drawing such inferences from the results, and sometimes they are justified in doing so. That proved to be the case this time.

The Democrats won the first special by electing John Murtha in a western Pennsylvania district centered around Johnstown that Nixon had carried with 64 percent of the vote in 1972. Murtha ran on the slogan "One Honest Man Can Make a Difference," and his campaign used several similarly oblique messages in its literature. But the Watergate issue was never distilled, and Murtha, who was forty-one at the time, won largely on the strength of his personal résumé as a war hero and state legislator and on the herculean efforts of organized labor in a district heavily populated by union coal miners and steelworkers. The Republicans could claim, and did, that nothing had been proven about the electorate's attitude on Watergate.

Those claims sounded hollow after the two special elections in Michigan, however. The first was held in the district in western Michigan that Gerald Ford had represented for twenty-five years before becoming vice president. No Democrat had carried it since 1910, and the Republicans had a prominent and well-regarded state legislator from Grand Rapids, Robert VanderLaan, as their candidate. But a Democrat named Richard VanderVeen, a fifty-one-year-old lawyer who had lost similar campaigns in the past, ran on the premise that "the fundamental issue in this election is the question of Richard Nixon's moral fitness to govern." When VanderVeen won with 53 percent of the vote, the result could not be explained away or ignored by the White House or the Republican Party.

The prospect of the Republicans facing a debacle because of Nixon was confirmed in the special election in a district around Saginaw, in northern Michigan, that Republicans had held for forty years and Nixon had carried with landslide numbers in 1972. James Sparling, the Republican candidate, seemed to be holding at least a nominal lead over Democrat J. Bob Traxler on this friendly ground when the White House decided to make it a test case. Nixon would campaign for Sparling and, the theory went, the embattled president would get some of the credit when Sparling won. At the least the bleeding that had begun after the western Michigan result would be stopped.

It was a classic example of Washington myopia. The last thing Sparling wanted to do was raise the salience of the Watergate issue in his election. But Dean Burch of the White House staff and George Bush, then chairman of the Republican National Committee, both called to urge the candidate to invite his president. Sparling was a good soldier publicly and took "credit" for inviting the president. What an honor for the citizens of the Eighth District. Drinking a beer late that night, he kept muttering to himself, "What could I do? He's the president of the United States, so what could I do? You can't tell the president to just keep away, can you?" he asked me repeatedly.

Two days later the Nixon visit fulfilled all the predictions of political disaster—and one witnessed by an entourage of more than two hundred from the national and international press. The president was greeted at the Saginaw airport by Governor William G. Milliken, a popular moderate Republican who then found it necessary to flee to Toronto for a meeting on water pollution problems that simply could not wait. Then Nixon embarked on a four-hour, fifty-seven-mile motorcade that avoided the only two cities in the district, Saginaw (population 92,000) and Bay City (population 49,000). The White House strategists decided these were the only two places where there might be enough Democrats to produce a turnout of protesters sufficiently large to attract the television cameras. So Nixon visited no community of more than 3,000, his motorcade making its way from Bad Axe to Popple, Ivanhoe, Cass City, Deford, Wilmont, Herman, Decker, Snover, Elmer, and Sandusky. He was viewed by small clutches of people along the road while the television cameras focused on the empty spaces. If Republicans in Congress needed hard evidence that Richard Nixon was poison, it was right there, first in the reports on the trip fiasco and then in the narrow defeat Sparling suffered a week later when, significantly, Republican turnout ran well below the norm.

There were three other special House elections that spring, two won by Democrats and one by a Republican in a heavily Republican district. But the returns from the Michigan Eighth had made it clear the Republicans were facing a political licking in the November elections because their own people were disheartened and discouraged.

The results of those special elections did not, in themselves, seal Nixon's fate. There was still the need for the clear evidence that later defined his attempt to obstruct justice. But the results did tell the House Republicans that they had no selfish political reason to protect the president. And the results did tell them that Americans were quite prepared to confront the reality of a president being impeached or forced to resign. For those on the Judiciary Committee it was, nonetheless, a torturous process. The travail of Tom Railsback of Moline, Illinois, was similar to what many Republicans on the committee experienced in trying to decide what was "the right thing to do" and at what point.

At forty-one, Railsback was in his fourth term in the House and always had enjoyed his service on the Judiciary Committee. Now, however, he found himself agonizing over the meaning of the evidence being presented to the committee—and, specifically, at what point he would have to accept the fact that the scales had tipped in favor of impeachment.

The pressure was enormous. A colleague from Illinois, Les Arends, was the minority whip in the House and a close friend and ally of Nixon's. Frequently Railsback would return to his office from the hearing room late in the day to find Arends, a tough old-timer with an acid tongue, waiting for him with a warning that was always the same: You stick with the president on this or you're finished. There will be nothing for you in Illinois or the Republican Party if you go off the reservation on this one. What you heard today was just crap. On some occasions Railsback was confused enough that he would go down the hall to John Anderson's office to get his reading of the day's developments. Anderson wasn't a member of the committee, but he was bright and analytical.

Meanwhile, Nixon was trying to firm up his support among loyalists by inviting them to White House meetings and social gatherings, including candlelight dinners aboard the presidential yacht *Sequoia,* which would sail down the Potomac to Mount Vernon and then back again while the president and his guests enjoyed the early evening breeze on the water. These were the people Nixon was counting on to save his hide—people who had served with him in the House: Republicans like Bob Michel, Les Arends, Sam Devine of Ohio, and Glenn Davis of Wisconsin, conservative Democrats like Richard Ichord of Missouri, Joe Waggoner of Louisiana, and Olin Teague of Texas.

One of those regularly included was a twenty-year veteran in the House from Michigan, Elford A. Cederberg, one of those rare politicians who found it impossible to dissemble, even when talking to a reporter. Facing an early-afternoon paper deadline, I would call Al Cederberg about breakfast time the morning after one of these gatherings, and he would give me a rundown on what happened and who said what. He was such a trusting man he seemed to be taking Richard Nixon at face value. I think the president doesn't really understand how he got into this fix, Cederberg would say, and I guess it is hard to understand.

But over the course of several weeks I began to detect what I thought might be a more questioning tone, although Cederberg was by no means prepared to abandon his fellow Republican. Some of these things, he would say of new testimony, are a little bit disturbing, but I imagine the president has a good explanation. Some of my friends aren't as sure as they were a couple of weeks ago, he would say.

Nixon apparently sensed some softening of his backing and began to woo his supporters even more ardently, although not to the point of pouring his guests the high-priced vintage French wines he drank rather than the domestic vintages he customarily served them. After one sundown dinner on the *Sequoia,* cut short by winds and choppy water on the Potomac, the president directed that the floral centerpiece be sent to the room of Cederberg's daughter, who was hospitalized with a life-threatening illness. It was the kind of easy gesture any president can make, done with a word to a Filipino steward, but Al Cederberg was clearly delighted. Wasn't that awfully nice of the president, he asked me when I called him the next morning. I said something diplomatic, although what I really thought was that it was a typically empty Nixon gesture and what I really wished was that Cederberg had reached the point at which he might tell Nixon, in a nice way of course, to stuff the flowers and tell him the truth about Watergate. That is a problem in politics. There are always decent people who are exploited by the Nixons of the world because of their decency and, often, because of their loyalty to their party and its leaders. All that mattered to Nixon was saving his own skin. Presidents are users, and Nixon was world-class.

The drama finally played out predictably. The key point was the release in early May of the 1,254 pages of transcript of the White House tape recordings. Whatever excuses Nixon's supporters had made were now, to use the Nixon flack Ron Ziegler's term, "inoperative." The president of the United States had been shown scheming and plotting to cover up Watergate with hush money and perjury and the misuse of the Central Intelligence Agency and the Federal Bureau of Investigation and whatever else it might take. The cracks in Republican unity appeared quickly. Senator Hugh Scott of Pennsylvania, the minority leader and a longtime ally of Nixon's, said the tapes had shown "a shabby, disgusting, immoral performance." Representative John Rhodes of Arizona, the party leader in the House, made a point of telling reporters over breakfast that Nixon should be "considering" resignation. Two hours later John Anderson, the independent progressive from Illinois, publicly called on the president to resign. The following day the same call came from Representative Mark Andrews of North Dakota, a conservative far closer to Nixon than Anderson had been. Ed Derwinski said there were "not quite enough votes" for impeachment but it was getting close. When I reminded him he had said in January that there were no more than 120 votes for impeachment, he laughed and pointed out that "a lot has happened since then."

In July the Republican solidarity on the Judiciary Committee began to crack. Representative Lawrence J. Hogan of Maryland, who was running for governor, announced he would vote for impeachment. Seven or eight other Republicans, including Tom Railsback, described themselves as undecided. Representative Robert J. McClory, the second-ranking Republican on the committee, described himself as still undecided but conceded that "the chances are" the committee would vote for impeachment with at least four or five of the seventeen Republicans taking that position. As it turned out there were only four or five holdouts.

A week after the voting I tagged along with Railsback as he went home to Moline to face the music. I have rarely seen a politician more apprehensive. We flew to O'Hare and had an hour to kill in a United Red Carpet Club before boarding the commuter flight to Moline. Railsback spent most of the time pacing back and forth while his press secretary and I drank coffee. I don't know what we're going to find out there, he kept warning me. I don't think folks are very happy out there, you know. I just don't know what to expect.

Railsback's fears were justified, at least up to a point. Many of his constituents were hopping mad. At a senior citizens' center in La Harpe several old women went into another room rather than listen to him. A farmer sitting at the back of the hall called out to his congressman, "How come you voted the way the young people wanted? You've evidently been speaking to some of the pickets out in front of the White House." Another shouted at him: "Have you ever thought about resigning from the Republican Party and joining the Democrat Party? That would be a good one." At the town hall in Augusta an old political ally passed out flyers urging "concerned Republicans" to vote for Railsback's Democratic opponent in the November election as "an effective and orderly way to voice our displeasure." Republicans could correct the situation in a later election, he argued. At the chamber of commerce luncheon in Moline, one old political friend made a show of turning his back on Railsback.

But that anger seemed centered among older voters and, in any case, was only part of the picture. At the chamber luncheon, by contrast, William Hewitt, chairman of the board of John Deere & Co., Moline's prime industry, introduced Railsback as a man who had voted his conscience and added, "I am very pleased to stand up and be counted with you." As the weekend wore on the apprehensive congressman found many constituents willing to praise him as a man who voted his convictions. They seemed surprised—and obviously pleased—to find a politician who had acted out of principle.

Perhaps Railsback's most significant discovery, however, was the fact that television had made him a celebrity in the eyes of many of his constituents and that celebrity alone was a political credential of great value. What he had done seemed less important than the fact that he been involved in something televised nationally day after day. It was a lesson I saw taught time and again over the subsequent twenty-five years as television became even more dominant in our culture.

In the November election, a disaster for the Republican Party nationally, Tom Railsback survived the strong Democratic tide. Richard Nixon had been sent packing, and at least some of the good guys had earned some credit for it. It made me wonder if the system worked, after all.

CHAPTER 10

A SURPRISING

FAILURE

Even before the returns were in from the 1974 elections, I had 1976 all figured out. After Watergate Americans would be sick of anything connected to Washington, so the Democrats would nominate a governor. I even knew which one—John Gilligan of Ohio. As a former congressman he had the necessary Washington credential, but he had made his reputation as a governor with the nerve to promulgate a tax program needed to put Ohio's schools on a footing comparable with those in other industrial states. He was also a smart guy and good company, although perhaps a little acerbic for some tastes.

My scenario fell apart, however, when Gilligan lost his campaign for reelection to Republican Jim Rhodes, who had served two terms just before Gilligan and been ineligible for a third consecutive term in Columbus. (Why anyone would want to spend twelve years in Columbus, Ohio, is one of life's little mysteries.) Rhodes, who had refused to do the responsible thing on funding education, beat Gilligan by blaming him for the tax increase. And Gilligan's quick mouth didn't help matters. Touring the state fair with reporters in tow, he was asked if he planned to attend the sheep-shearing contest. "I don't shear sheep," Gilligan replied, "I shear taxpayers."

It was the kind of thing that did not make for a successful reelection campaign, although Gilligan lost by fewer than fifteen hundred votes. A couple of months after the election I ran into him in a hardware store back in Washington, where he was buying a rake. "Look at you," I said. "I thought you were going to be Leader of the Free World, and now you're raking your own leaves." To his credit, he laughed.

Losing to Jim Rhodes was no disgrace, however. He was one of those politicians everyone always describes as "canny" and "shrewd" because he manages to give everyone he meets the idea they are first on his list. He was also colorful and profane enough so that reporters enjoyed covering him although he largely ignored them. During his first two terms, in the 1960s, he had become an admirer of Nelson Rockefeller as a potential party nominee for president. But he clearly disliked the other leading progressive Republican at the time, George Romney of Michigan. Rhodes considered his Mormon colleague too prissy to play winning politics. When a couple of us cornered him one day to ask about Romney, Rhodes replied: "George Romney running for president is like a duck trying to fuck a football." Try using that quote in a family newspaper.

Even with Gilligan consigned to political oblivion, the Democrats were not short of governors who might become prospects for my scenario, the most interesting being Jimmy Carter of Georgia. He was one of several moderate Democrats elected to southern governorships in 1970 and immediately designated by the press as the political pioneers of the "New South." In his inaugural address in Atlanta, Carter seized the role of leading spokesman for this group by addressing the race issue this way: "I say to you quite frankly that the time for racial discrimination is over. Our people have already made this major and difficult decision. No poor, rural, weak, or black person should ever again have to bear the additional burden of being deprived of an opportunity for an education, a job, or simple justice." Although it is language that sounds totally unremarkable today, it was considered daring in early 1971.

I began paying some special attention to Carter in the spring of 1974. There was a meeting of Democratic governors one weekend at a hotel near O'Hare Airport, and I noticed that he managed to make himself the lead of the story in the *Chicago Tribune* two days running. The next month the annual meeting of the National Governors'

Association was held in Seattle, and Carter was one of six governors on a *Meet the Press* panel leading into the conference. I was one of the reporters on the panel, and the question of the day was whether President Nixon could refuse to turn over the Watergate tapes if the Supreme Court ordered him to do so. Most of them gave predictably cautious and legalistic answers about the responsibility of any president to obey the Court, but Carter went a step further. Nixon would never turn over the tapes, he said, because he was guilty.

Viewed from a great distance, that comment hardly seems newsworthy, but at the time it was inflammatory enough so that—once again, I noted—Carter led all the stories on the Monday morning the conference opened. The following day this obscure governor of Georgia did it again. This time there had been an extended and acrimonious debate over land-use planning between two Republican governors, the conservative Ronald Reagan of California and the liberal Tom McCall of Oregon. Carter had been a minor player in the debate until near the end, when he injected himself in a way that made him appear in news accounts to be a principal figure and perhaps *the* principal figure. He had stolen the story still again.

The following night the governors were to attend their usual "state dinner," a black-tie event that I regularly skipped. So I had dinner with some other reporters and repaired to the hotel bar, where I ran into Jody Powell, Carter's press secretary. He and the Carters and a couple of other staff people were going to hear Billy Eckstine, who was appearing at a downtown nightclub patronized largely by blacks. Did I want to go along? I did, and soon the Carters and I were sitting at a ringside table drinking Scotch and listening to Eckstine prove he could still sell a song as well as anyone. Moreover, it turned out that the Carters were knowledgeable about jazz and knew Eckstine well enough so that he joined us for a drink before we returned to the hotel.

The next day I picked up *The Seattle Times*, and there was a modest story about how this Georgia governor bypassed the stuffy governors' dinner and went to listen to Billy Eckstine at a black nightclub. I immediately called Powell and made a date to go down to Atlanta for more conversation with this governor who seemed to be doing everything right and to have some dizzy idea about running for president. A week or so later I spent a strange evening at the governor's mansion eating fried catfish with Carter, his mother, Lillian, son Chip, and daughter Amy—Rosalynn was out of town—while he told me all about how he was going to become president. All the big-name candidates from Washington, he said, had been passing through Atlanta and spending the night with the Carters at the mansion. Now that he knew them, he figured, What the hell, if they can run, so can I.

He had already taken the first step by getting himself designated by Democratic National Chairman Robert Strauss chairman of the 1974 national campaign committee, ordinarily a meaningless title. But in this case it meant the DNC was paying Hamilton Jordan's salary and picking up the tab for Carter's self-promoting trips around the country ostensibly designed to help elect Democrats. Strauss, who was hoping Scoop Jackson might be the 1976 nominee, was both chagrined and admiring of the way Carter had conned him. "I didn't know what he was up to," he confessed later. "He had my pants off before I knew it."

I thought the notion of this jasper from Georgia winning the presidency after a single term as a governor was far-fetched. Just the idea of a southerner at the head of national ticket was hard to accept, simply because there never had been one other than Johnson in modern politics. But Carter was too intelligent and too self-assured to be shrugged off. He had a campaign plan that made a kind of rudimentary good sense, and he already had shown—at those governors' conferences—that he had some ability to play the press game. Dismissing him as an impossible long shot would be a classic example of the Washington reporter imprisoned by his own provincialism and determined to fight the last war once again, as we were always tempted to do.

Carter had some conventional assets. Although he was a southerner, he had an easy rapport with blacks and the early support of some key black leaders in his home state, most notably Andrew Young—an important credential in resolving any doubts about his commitment on civil rights. He was viewed by some calculating Democratic professionals, particularly in organized labor, as the man who might defeat George Wallace in the Florida primary and get that monkey off the party's back. Some liberal union leaders, including the United Auto Workers president, Douglas Fraser, viewed him as a stalking-horse who could perform that function in Florida, then be replaced by a more conventional liberal with whom they would be more comfortable. But the most impressive thing about Jimmy Carter was his extraordinary self-confidence. After spending a week with him on his first campaign trip in January 1975, I wrote about him for the *Star* in these terms:

> SACRAMENTO, CALIF.—The opinion polls show that almost no one knows him and when he passes through town he is regarded by the local news media as just more fodder for the television interview programs and a brief story on Page 6.
>
> His only base is a peanut farm in Plains, Ga., and his only political credential is a single term as governor that ended two weeks ago. And, of course, he is a Southerner.
>
> But to Jimmy Carter, this catalogue of handicaps seems beside the point, irrelevant in the face of a self-assurance that would shame Muhammad Ali.
>
> There are some problems, the 50-year-old Georgian concedes, but none of them is insuperable. And some of those disadvantages, he insists, may turn out to be blessings in disguise as he pursues what he calls his "absolute total commitment" to winning the 1976 Democratic presidential nomination.

On that same trip early in 1975, I had an experience with Carter that seemed to suggest a personal dimension not often found in politicians. We were eating lunch together on a flight from Albuquerque to San Francisco when Carter asked me if I had any children and where they went to school. I replied that I had two daughters who were attending a private school, National Cathedral, that I liked because it provided a protective environment for my elder daughter, Mandy, who was ill. Carter asked what the problem was, and I replied that she had leukemia. What's the prognosis? he wanted to know. Bad, I said. The drug protocol that works 95 percent of the time in producing a remission hadn't worked in her case. I had no sooner answered than his eyes filled with tears and he turned away and looked out the window. Then he asked me her name and her sister's name and said one of those things you say in a situation like that. That must be tough, that must be difficult, whatever. And that was the end of it.

About three weeks later a small package wrapped in brown paper and tied with string arrived at our home addressed in pencil to Mandy in Carter's hand, with a note that read:

> Here are two Indian arrowheads I found on my farm. They are about 1200 years old. You may give your sister one of them. I thought about you while talking to your father a few days ago. He is a fine man and a friend of mine, and he hates to have to be away from his daughters. I have a seven-year-old daughter Amy and I wish I could be with her more often.
>   Love, Jimmy Carter

I didn't quite know what to make of it. It was a warm and touching gesture, and Mandy was pleased at coming to the attention of someone from my other world. But as a reporter I had become suspicious of the motives of all politicians. As the chief political writer for the *Washington Star* I had some clout, so I wondered, however ungenerously, if this was an attempt to co-opt me. In the end, however, I concluded that it was an act of genuine kindness by a man quite capable of such gestures. Over the years I saw many instances of politicians capable of both extraordinary personal kindness and equally extraordinary acts of ruthless self-promotion. In the case of Carter and the arrowheads, I was struck particularly by the fact that his staff never learned about it until I told them some months later.

So it was no great surprise when Mandy died one night two years later that the first telephone call of condolence, at six-thirty the next morning, came from Jimmy Carter in the White House.

Mandy's death at fourteen, after five brave years of dealing with her illness with unfailing hope, was, of course, a signal event in my life as well as in that of her mother, Barbara, and her sister, Jessica, who was eleven. The loss of a child causes a pain that has no dimension and cannot be described to those who have not shared the experience. In my case it seemed to reinforce the detachment I felt from things going on around me. Politicians might tell me something was terribly important, but I knew that, whatever it was, it didn't really matter to me. Reporters working for me would whine about their assignments or the mishandling of their stories by the copy editors, and I would listen and make sympathetic comments, all the while thinking to myself, None of this really matters.

Although it was mostly a time of old and dear friends, there was also, inevitably for someone in my business, an element of politics in the aftermath of Mandy's death that night. The president's call was only the first of many that day, most of them motivated by the simple human sympathy anyone might feel. Ted Kennedy, who had a son suffering from cancer at the same time, called and sent a handwritten letter of several pages telling me of things I might read that had helped him in times of grief. George Bush, with whom I had little relationship then and a wretched one later, also wrote in personal terms about his own experience in losing a child to leukemia. Jody Powell and Hamilton Jordan came to the house one night and sat up with me, a bottle of bourbon between them, a bottle of Scotch at my side, while we spent several hours talking about all sorts of things that were diverting and distracting.

Some of the sympathy, I could not help but suspect, seemed to have political motives, coming as it did from potential presidential candidates with whom I had never been close. One of them, a midwestern senator, both called and wrote to express his sympathy at great length. Then, at a dinner two months later, he asked me: "How's that daughter of yours getting along?" It was so characteristic of this guy that I wasn't even offended, just amused.

Carter's election in 1976 raised a problem for me that I never faced before or would face thereafter. Because I had been the first national political reporter to pay any attention to his presidential ambitions, there was the danger that I would feel a proprietary interest in his success in the White House, as sometimes happens with statehouse reporters if their governor becomes president. There was also the danger that Carter and his people would believe, as so often happens, that a reporter who pays attention to them early in the game will have that proprietary interest. It was clear that Carter and some of those closest to him viewed me as a "friendly" reporter, at the least, if not totally in the tank. My wife and I were invited to the Carters' first state dinner, for the president of Mexico. And even when he wouldn't return telephone calls to congressional leaders, Hamilton Jordan would always call me back. When Bert Lance, Carter's budget director and close friend, was forced to resign one night in the first summer of the administration because of irregularities in the conduct of his banking business back in Georgia, Jordan and Powell invited Jules Witcover and me into the White House and spent two hours outlining the way the crisis had developed and been handled, thus allowing us to beat *The Washington Post* with the detailed account—called a tick-tock in the business—of the resolution of the controversy. When the Carters began holding private dinners with a few journalists and their spouses in the family living quarters, Jules and I were included in the first, along with our editor, Jim Bellows, and John Chancellor and two other people from NBC News.

The truth was somewhat different from what Carter believed. As I came to know him through 1975 and 1976, I thought Carter probably would make a strong president. I admired his intelligence and his basic decency. I didn't think the little political games he played—exaggerations, cautious locutions, selective memory at times—were any different from those played by all of them. And I agreed with most of his goals. In fact, however, if I had been a Democratic primary voter in 1976, which I was not, I would have voted for Morris Udall. He was more liberal and thus closer to my own views, and, ideology aside, he was a man of such droll wit and genuine self-effacement that he was totally refreshing.

During the campaign, nonetheless, I was convinced Carter would be a stronger candidate and, more to the point, after the first few primaries essentially unassailable in the competition for the nomination. As a result I frequently wrote columns and analysis pieces that those outside the business saw as hard on Udall, soft on Carter because Carter was winning and Udall was losing. Indeed, at one point during the Pennsylvania primary campaign, one of Udall's daughters confronted me in a Philadelphia hotel lobby and said, "Everyone tells me you like my dad so much, so why do you write all those awful things?"

During the Michigan primary run, Udall's staff arranged an interview I had solicited as a 7:00 A.M. breakfast in the obvious hope of punishing one of the late drinkers for a column I had written chastising Udall for using cheap media stunts that were beneath him. But the candidate himself wouldn't play. When we met that morning he told me: "I'm supposed to chew you out for that piece you wrote yesterday," he began, "but what the hell, you're probably right. Let's have some eggs."

I wondered at times whether I was not bending over backward to be hard on Udall because I liked him so much. That happens sometimes with reporters. We want to prove we are not in someone's pocket, so we go overboard in demonstrating our independence or integrity or whatever we imagine is being challenged. All you can do is play the cards you are dealt every day and hope that over the long haul you will be evenhanded.

The problem with being viewed by the White House as friendly is that when I—or, later, Jules and I together in columns—wrote pieces critical of Carter's political handling of one situation after another, they were seen as something of a betrayal. The result was a slow but steady deterioration in the relationship I had enjoyed with the president and first lady. After he lost his campaign for reelection in 1980, Rosalynn clearly felt aggrieved. During their final Christmas season in the White House I took my daughter Jessie, then fourteen, to a press party I thought she might enjoy and remember. When we came through the receiving line, the president was cordial and gracious, but Rosalynn was cool—to the point that, as we walked away, Jessie said, "Gee, Dad, Mrs. Carter really doesn't like you, does she?"

Although I have been guilty of many misjudgments in a life covering politics, I have never been more mistaken than I was about Carter's potential as president. I was convinced he had both a commitment to social and economic justice and the political skills to use that commitment to right some of the wrongs in our society. Rising from a single term as governor of Georgia to the White House was, in itself, a testimony to his remarkable political skills. The only serious reservation I had about him was that he didn't have any close friends who were peers and perhaps capable of telling him when he was going wrong. Nor did he cast his net widely seeking advice outside his inner circle. Although they were derided by the insular old hands in Washington as southern bumpkins, Hamilton Jordan and Jody Powell were street-smart and perceptive political operatives whom Carter trusted. But they were a generation younger than their principal, and members of his staff, not old friends or peers. And he was so remarkably self-assured he needed somebody who would tell him every so often that he was full of shit.

In the end Carter was undone by a combination of factors beyond his control and by his own personal qualities. It is still impossible to see how he could have dealt more effectively with the effects of the oil crisis on the economy. And despite that failed mission that left helicopters burning in the desert outside Tehran, no one has suggested there was some easy course that might have ended the hostage crisis in Iran before it compromised any chance he enjoyed of winning a second term. But Carter was a prisoner of his own values as well. He had shown himself to be a world-class politician in reaching the White House. Once he got there, however, he resisted politics. He seemed to believe that his ideas would succeed or fail on their merits alone, that he could bring Congress along to do the "right thing" when it might be easier to do the wrong thing or nothing at all. But succeeding as president requires the assertion of strong political leadership. Governing successfully depends not on the free competition of ideas but instead on a president's ability to define problems, offer solutions, and then sell them both to the American people and, most often, to a Congress made up of 535 people with their own agendas and priorities.

As president, however, Carter seemed to think politics was a dirty business. Jules Witcover and I had firsthand experience with this when, after being competitors for fifteen years, we joined in writing a syndicated column for the *Star* in March 1977. We planned to write a column that was heavily reportorial or analytical, rather than ideological, so we were pleased when the president gave us an interview for our first. We wrote that his insistence on including human rights as an important element of his foreign policy allowed him to do the shrewd thing politically, by reassuring liberals nourishing questions about his commitment, while satisfying his personal need to take the moral course. Carter later complained that the column was wrong because he had no political motive whatsoever in making choices on foreign policy—a statement I took to mean no political motive he could bring himself to acknowledge.

Then there was Carter's relationship with Robert Strauss, who as chairman of the Democratic National Committee had given him a party generally united and prepared for the 1976 campaign that put him in the White House. Strauss wanted to be secretary of the Treasury, one of the ranking portfolios in any cabinet, but Carter always seemed to view Strauss as a little tainted because he was not just a consummate politician but unabashedly proud of it. Rather than weigh Strauss's skills as a negotiator and his insight into both politics and business as assets, the new president saw the irreverent and wickedly funny lawyer from Texas as too much of a political operator to have a ranking place in his administration. So Strauss swallowed it and took an appointment as the special trade representative, the so-called trade ambassador. "At least," he told me and Tom Ottenad one day, "you grubby little scribblers can start calling me Mr. Ambassador. From now on, it's not just 'Fuck you,' it's 'Fuck you, Mr. Ambassador.'"

Strauss, who had many cronies among the Old Bulls in Congress, like Russell Long, chairman of the Senate Finance Committee, continued to offer the new president political advice but found it wasn't easy. If he called the White House and asked to talk to the president about a festering political problem, it would be two or three days before he could get through. But if he called and said there was a trade matter that needed attention, Carter would call him back within hours. The priority was never politics or, at least, not by the name.

One of Carter's particular failings was his inability to use television effectively to control the national dialogue. Ironically, one of his favorite words was *vivid*, but he was anything but vivid on the television screens. I recall a day when he held a midday press conference at a time when there were several important issues on the forefront. Because the *Star* was an afternoon newspaper with a deadline problem, my assignment was to watch the conference on television and write the story "in takes"—meaning in segments of four or five paragraphs at a time so it could be quickly edited and put into type against a deadline our White House correspondent attending the conference couldn't meet. But as I watched I found that, even though under pressure to produce immediately, I was letting my attention wander unless I forced myself to bear down. Later that day I mentioned the experience in passing to a Democratic senator, John Culver of Iowa. He could certainly understand, Culver said. Whenever Carter went on television during the workday, all the Senate Democrats went into their cloakroom to watch. It was part of their job just as it was part of mine. But, he said, within ten minutes they would all be gossiping among themselves and paying little or no attention to what their president was saying. He was not vivid enough to hold their attention. "Hell," said Culver, "if we don't listen, who will?"

Carter's other pronounced weakness as a leader was his willingness to turn the other cheek rather than come down hard on the politicians or advisers who earned his anger. Presidents hold enormous power, and they have only to use it occasionally to make an impression on the political community. A little healthy fear can have a marked effect on other politicians or advisers or, for that matter, on reporters. You don't have to be as heavy-handed as a Lyndon Johnson or as vengeful as a Richard Nixon, but it doesn't hurt if the word around town is that there might be consequences if you don't go along.

The point was driven home to me in the late summer of 1979. Jody Powell called one day and asked if I would like to stop in at the White House for a drink with Carter late in the day. The three of us sat in rockers on the Truman Balcony, Carter with a gin and tonic, Powell and I with our poisons of choice. I was impressed. I had been in Washington for eighteen years and had never been invited for a drink one-on-one with a president. Not too shabby, I was thinking as I sipped my Scotch. The purpose of the meeting soon became clear. Carter was infuriated by the columns Jules and I were writing in the *Star* criticizing his handling of the politics of his job. He kept referring to the way we were "savaging" him day after day. The unspoken implication was that he had expected better of me considering how long and well I had known him. But no, I was just savaging him at every turn. I replied that he shouldn't take it personally because it wasn't meant that way. Ours was a column of political analysis, and his politics were not going well right then so it was inevitable the columns would be critical. The president clearly wasn't persuaded, although the conversation remained civilized and moved on to other topics, including his plans for the rest of the year after Congress returned and for the campaign year ahead. After I finished my drink I made getting up and leaving motions, but Carter stopped me. You never settle for one drink, he said, so he ordered the steward to serve another round, and we talked some more about his problems and savaging and whatever. With that second drink it suddenly struck me that there was something wrong. Here I am having a drink with the President of the United States and Leader of the Free World and he is monumentally pissed off at me and I don't give a damn. If this were Lyndon Johnson, I would be afraid my barn would be burning at this very moment. If it were Richard Nixon, I would be expecting the IRS on my case the next day. But there was nothing to fear here.

After an hour or so Powell and I left and walked across the park to the Hay-Adams to have another shooter or two. Then, about nine, I called my partner to report on the meeting.

"What did he want?" Jules asked.

"He's pissed off," I said. "He says we're savaging him in the column."

"Too bad," said Jules. "See you in the morning."

Carter had some extraordinary successes in the White House, but because of his personality and his disdain for conventional political exploitation, he never earned much credit for them. He spent almost a year bargaining with Menachem Begin and Anwar Sadat before the Camp David summit in 1978, at which they signed the peace agreement between Israel and Egypt. It was arguably the single most important step toward stability in the Middle East that had been taken up to that time, and Jimmy Carter had been the broker.

The day after the agreement was signed, I wrote a column that proved as grossly mistaken as any I ever wrote. The lead paragraphs read:

> With a single stroke—if a 13-day summit meeting can be described so cavalierly—President Carter has transformed the domestic political landscape.
>
> All the discouraging opinion surveys of the past, all the whispered calculations of the politicians, all the cruel judgments of the experts have been declared obsolete by the spectacular success at Camp David of what Menachem Begin said must be called "the Jimmy Carter conference." The political slate has been clouded, perhaps even wiped clean.

The piece went on to say that he had proven he was not some "hayshaker from Georgia out of his depth in the presidency." There were the columnist's usual caveats about how this didn't assure his reelection and about how he was quite capable of making a sow's ear out of a silk purse. But the burden of it was that he had turned around the political momentum.

Two or three days later a Gallup Poll conducted immediately after the summit showed Carter's approval rating had risen all right—by a single point. Once again we had learned that, barring a threat of nuclear war, Americans just don't pay attention to foreign affairs. Contrary to the column, Carter was right where he had been all along.

In the end the problem for Carter was that he allowed himself to be defined by his weaknesses rather than his strengths. His bizarre behavior in the summer of 1979 probably compromised any chance he had of winning a second term the following year.

All through that spring Patrick Caddell, the mercurial young poll taker from Cambridge, had been warning the Carters that there was trouble abroad in the electorate. The president's approval ratings were dropping rapidly, while inflation was rising and Americans were being obliged to sit through long lines to buy gasoline. The voters, Caddell reported in several memoranda, were growing increasingly pessimistic about the future, always a danger signal for an incumbent politician. So Carter announced that he would give a major speech on energy on July 5 and went off to Camp David for the holiday weekend. But in meetings with his staff it became clear that he had nothing really new to announce. The speech, his advisers feared, would be hooted off the stage as just so much fresh rhetoric describing stale ideas. So the president announced that the speech had been postponed indefinitely and summoned all of his closest advisers to Camp David for another round of meetings, designed to produce a broader and more reassuring agenda for the nation. In Washington we all speculated and gossiped about what was wrong with Jimmy Carter; presidents don't just postpone speeches without some reason.

Carter had canceled a weekend trip to Louisville, where he had been scheduled to appear at the annual conference of the National Governors' Association, ordinarily a high-visibility political event. To make up for the cancellation he invited a delegation of eight governors, seven of them Democrats, to come to Camp David for consultations on what steps he needed to take to deal with the energy crisis and to reassure Americans. But once the governors had been invited, the political imperative became either to invite other interest groups or to explain why the state executives had been given such privileged treatment. Carter chose the first option. Over the next eight days Marine helicopters carried about 150 people from the White House grounds to Camp David for one meeting after another. There were mayors, labor leaders, business executives, state legislators, city officials, and even a few preachers.

By now the whole exercise was being viewed as some kind of crisis. Each night we would interview some of those who had been to Camp David that day to find out what in hell was going on up there. Their reports were not reassuring. Both Jimmy and Rosalynn were involved in the meetings but mostly listening to their guests. There was no hint of what the president planned to do, and there was little if any evidence he was being told anything about the national condition that wasn't already apparent to any politician. And the Carters were now planning two day trips out of Camp David and beyond the Beltway to seek the wisdom of "ordinary people," one to Carnegie, Pennsylvania, and the other to Martinsburg, West Virginia. The address to the nation originally planned for July 5 was now scheduled for July 15. On July 13 eighteen journalists—network television anchors such as Walter Cronkite and John Chancellor, newspaper editors, and a few columnists, including me—were flown to Camp David for a luncheon briefing that, we were assured, would clear everything up.

For me it was an event that was unsettling to the point of being almost frightening. We were taken to a living room at Laurel Lodge, where we were offered fruit juice or drinks while waiting for the Carters to return from Martinsburg. When they arrived, Jimmy and Rosalynn circulated around the room, telling us in fairly breathless tones that the folks out there were concerned about inflation and the energy shortage.

It was never clear, of course, why it had been necessary for them to go to Carnegie and Martinsburg to learn something everyone else already knew. At lunch we were seated around a rectangular table with the Carters at the head, side by side, and some of his senior staff at the foot. What was particularly unnerving at this point was that the first lady spoke as much as or more than the president about what they had been told and what they needed to do about it. We all knew that the first lady was a significant influence on the president and, because she was so obviously bright and serious, most of us probably felt comfortable about it. But I was not the only one shaken by the reality of the president's wife behaving as an official equal in these circumstances. On the way back Joe Kraft, a columnist for the *Post,* kept shaking his head and muttering about how this was something very different indeed.

In the speech, finally delivered in prime time on Sunday, July 15, Carter complained about what he saw as a "crisis of confidence" across the country that had become a "fundamental threat to American democracy." This was what became known as the malaise speech, ending the "malaise summit," although neither Carter in his speech nor Caddell in his analyses of the national mood ever used the word. But the fact, malaise or not, was that the crisis of confidence was occurring inside the administration, not among Americans in general. In a front-page analysis piece I called it a "plastic crisis" that Carter had created himself, by accident. He had started bringing those people to Camp David and been unable to find a stopping place while the country watched uneasily to see what in hell he intended to do.

Despite my sour view the speech caused two or three days of euphoria in the administration as the president's approval rating rose 11 percent almost overnight. But Carter felt some more dramatic evidence of change had to be given to the public, so he demanded the resignations of sixteen cabinet and cabinet-level officials and eighteen members of his senior staff. The purge was aimed primarily at two cabinet officials, Secretary of Health and Human Services Joseph Califano and Secretary of Commerce Michael Blumenthal, whose resignations were quickly accepted. Secretary of Transportation Brock Adams also was sent packing after he refused to fire close advisers who had worked in the 1976 Udall campaign and were suspected of disloyalty to the White House. And Carter made the whole thing seem more dramatic by choosing that time to accept two other resignations that had been in the works for reasons unrelated to the summit—those of Attorney General Griffin Bell and Secretary of Energy James Schlesinger. The effect of the clumsy bloodletting was to wipe away whatever political benefit Carter had temporarily realized from the speech. It was clear that the lack of confidence was not in the country but inside the White House.

Carter was being depicted as a weak and ineffectual leader who had blown himself up trying to reassert some control over the national agenda. And standing in his road as he looked ahead to a re-election campaign in 1980 were two of the most confident politicians of the time—Ted Kennedy and Ronald Reagan.

CHAPTER 11

GOLDEN YEARS
WITH BELLOWS

The best years I ever had in the newspaper business were the three in the mid-1970s when James Bellows was editor of the *Star.* I did my best work, and I had more fun doing it. We didn't beat *The Washington Post,* and eventually they buried us. But we put out a newspaper that was a "must read" for the world of government and politics if not, unhappily, a "must buy" for advertisers. And we had a glorious time doing it.

The paper's parlous financial condition—it was always identified in those days as the "financially distressed *Washington Star*"—had been stabilized at least temporarily by a new owner, Joe L. Allbritton, a Texan who had made a fortune in everything from funeral homes to insurance companies and savings and loans. "Joe's got so much money," an admiring fellow Texan told me, "that he's got thirty million just in T-bills." I didn't know how accurate that might have been, but I did know that when Joe arrived from Houston and moved into the publisher's office, there was a sigh of relief in the newsroom. We were alive for a while at least.

Bellows had made his reputation as the last editor of the *New York Herald Tribune.* Although he had not prevented its demise, he had made the paper a great read, far more entertaining and interesting although less complete than *The New York Times* of the same period. Allbritton found him editing some of the soft-news sections of the *Los Angeles Times* and lured him to Washington with the prospect of competing with the mighty *Post* and Ben Bradlee. As a practical matter there never was any chance the *Star* would win. The *Post* wasn't just entrenched, it was very good. It had more reporters and editors and many of the bright lights of the business, including some who had come through the *Star*, such as David Broder and Haynes Johnson. For the *Star*, the realistic goal was to become an essential second buy in the hope that over a period of years there could be enough money saved on the production side—through attrition contracts with unneeded printers, for example—to at least break even.

Bellows was never given the kind of budget that would allow him to go outside for many "name" hires. But he did manage to persuade Pat Oliphant to be our cartoonist, and Edwin Yoder the editor of the editorial page. He also created a writer-in-residence program under which outsiders with some reputation and talent—Jimmy Breslin, Caryl Rivers, Jane O'Reilly, and Chuck Stone among them—joined us for a few weeks to write columns. We already had some significant assets: Mary McGrory's column, Andy Beyer reporting on horse racing, Lyle Denniston covering the courts, David Israel writing a provocative sports column. The national staff was less than half the size of the *Post*'s but included a corps of excellent reporters—Lee Cohn on economics, Fred Barnes on the White House, Jerry O'Leary on the State Department, Martha Angle and Walter Taylor on Congress, Cristine Russell on science and medicine, Roberta Hornig on the environment, and John Fialka, Phil Gailey, Ed Pound, Jim Polk, Lance Gay, Mike Satchell, and Bob Walters on general assignment. I covered politics with Jim Dickenson, a gifted writer who came to the *Star* from the *National Observer*, the Dow Jones weekly that was also on its last legs.

We also had a whole stable of excellent feature writers and a remarkable editor, Mary Anne Dolan, for what Bellows named the Portfolio section, our answer to the *Post*'s Style section. He created a gossip column called "The Ear" and written by a Brit, Diana McLellan, that soon became famous—or infamous—and the best-read feature in the paper. McLellan did not make a fetish of checking out fully every little nugget that came her way, which meant corrections—or what she called "grovels"—were sometimes required. On occasion, however, the grovels were as snide as the original items. So I often advised victims who called me to complain to forget it.

Bellows also introduced a daily Q-and-A that started on the left side of the front page and jumped for several columns inside the paper. Some of them were conventional. The first, for example, was an interview about politics with then President Gerald Ford conducted by Barnes and me as the chief political reporter. The second, more interesting, was with Wes Unseld, the center for the Washington Bullets basketball team, discussing the things a black athlete needs to do to be a proper role model. Bellows also ordered a daily Page One feature called "In Focus," which was stripped across the bottom of the page and then jumped inside, again for several columns. These pieces were frankly patterned after the front-page leaders in *The Wall Street Journal,* but the difference was we had only a dozen or so reporters capable of producing them. I can remember being called into the office long after midnight after someone else's Focus piece had fallen through so I could write a four-column profile on which I had already done the reporting. The essential was to fill the space by the time the first edition closed at seven or so. Somehow we always made it, although the quality of both the Focus pieces and Q-and-A's was extremely uneven.

By the time Bellows arrived at the paper, I had become assistant managing editor in charge of national news after David Kraslow left to become publisher of the *Miami News.* I was still the chief political reporter and still paid as such because the *Star* had no money to fill the Kraslow job. So I functioned like a bureau chief, overseeing reporters and editors while covering my own beat. The trick here was the competence of the people around me. Shortly after I took the AME job, I chose Barbara Cohen (later Cochran), a twenty-nine-year-old editor of remarkable ability, to be the national editor, which meant she ran the staff day to day in my frequent absences. When I was on the road I called in to her twice a day. The only flaw in the arrangement was that some of the reporters and editors felt neglected because the boss was not there in the newsroom observing their labors every day. The result was that when I came back from a trip there would be a parade of reporters into my office seeking a little therapy. The advantage in the arrangement was that, because I was reporting and writing too, I had the same complaints about the copy editors who wrote a bad headline or mangled my prose. When Henry Bradsher, our diplomatic correspondent, came in to complain about a headline on one of his stories, as he so often did, I would quickly point to a similar crime committed against me by some wretch on the copydesk. "And remember, Henry," I would say, "they do that to me and I'm the fucking boss."

In fact, even before Bellows arrived the national desk's contributions to the paper were carefully handled by editors—most notably Cohen, John Cassidy, Ken Ikenberry, Ron Sarro, Ross Evans, and John Oravetz—who usually took great pains to protect the reporters' prose. We even had vastly overqualified dictationists, including Maureen Dowd.

I've worked for a lot of editors of varying levels of competence. There were a few I thought were one step from the welfare rolls, but there also were some who were thoroughgoing professionals. John Quinn, my boss during most of my years at Gannett, was in that group. So were Jack Lemmon, John Carroll, and Bill Marimow of the *Baltimore Sun*, but by the time I went to the *Sun* I was writing a column and thus out of the daily flow of the paper's operations in Baltimore except on special occasions, such as national political conventions and election nights.

By contrast, for three years I was totally involved with Bellows on a daily basis in trying to produce a *Star* that would somehow sell enough copies to hold those precious advertisers. It was always a futile exercise, I suspect. Afternoon newspapers were being killed by television all over the country, and we had the special burden of competing with the *Post*. We knew we couldn't match the comprehensiveness of their coverage or the depth of their staff. But we also knew we could match them or beat them in some areas—politics being one of them, I liked to think—even with limited resources.

Our prime asset, however, was clearly our editor. Bellows had two special abilities. The first was a genius for assessing the talents and potential of everyone on the staff. After less than a month he knew the strengths and weaknesses of everyone on the national staff as well as I did. And he used that ability to fit both reporters and editors into the right slots, the jobs they could do most effectively rather than those into which they had drifted. Second, Bellows had a feel for the popular culture that is essential in editing newspapers these days. He understood that the standard fare—the coverage of politics, business, and sports—was essential but far from enough. So his idea of a strong Page One was one that displayed stories that would appeal to several constituencies of readers. He knew which stories people in Washington would be talking about at dinner parties for the next few days. If you wrote a column that was intrinsically interesting enough, he would start it on Page One, then jump it inside. For a while we carried Oliphant's cartoons on the front page in the early street-sale edition. The rules were there to be broken.

Bellows's willingness to ignore many of the conventions of journalism was particularly satisfying for me as a political writer for an afternoon paper often assigned to do a quick analysis piece about the political ramifications of some development. Most newspapers, even including the highly sophisticated *Post,* still went through the motions of calling up political scientists to get a few quotes to support the point they already knew to be true. With Bellows that charade wasn't necessary. He assumed, correctly, that I understood the political equation as well as an academic and thus could explain it with authority for our readers. There is, of course, an obvious danger in that kind of analysis, but no greater than conning the reader by giving weight to some professor at Georgetown or American University always available for the instant quote.

One of Bellows's many strengths was his knack for firing up the troops to be even more zealous in competing with the *Post,* which Diana McLellan always referred to in "The Ear" as "the O.P."— Other Paper—in her frequent reports on the activities of "the Fun Couple," her name for Ben Bradlee and Sally Quinn, the star feature writer the executive editor had married. The knowledge passed through the grapevine that Bradlee was irked about these mentions made them all the more prized in the *Star*'s newsroom.

One fall, at Bellows's instigation, our reporter Lyn Rosselini produced a groundbreaking series about homosexuality in professional sports. It was a subject no one had ever gotten around to covering, so the stories attracted a lot of attention, particularly after a backup fullback for the Washington Redskins chose the occasion to come out of the closet. Mike Royko, the Chicago columnist, wrote a piece about how the story had spoiled professional football for the guys who like to watch games on television. Now every time some player patted a teammate on the fanny, Royko observed, there was going to be all this speculation about sex.

As it happened, the *Post* rather than the *Star* had the syndication rights to Royko's column, so we were not free to reprint it. Bellows called Bradlee and asked for permission, promising to credit the *Post* for having allowed us to do so. Bradlee hemmed and hawed, then called back. You can reprint it, he told Bellows, if you give us a credit line and promise not to mention Sally and me in that damned column for a month. Bellows agreed and asked for a written confirmation of the deal. When it arrived, he promptly posted it on the bulletin board in the newsroom, to the delight of the staff. On the thirty-first day "The Ear" cooked up some item about the Fun Couple and, in parentheses, added, "Hi, Ben."

All of this suggests a kind of frivolity that perhaps seems out of place in the serious business of producing a newspaper that sells enough advertising to support itself. But it would be a mistake to infer that Bellows and the rest of us were frivolous people when it came to covering the news. And Bellows was clearly interested in stinging the *Post* even if they didn't feel it. He never pretended, for example, to have much interest in politics, although he understood how important it was for a Washington newspaper. But he let me and my staff have our heads in covering the 1976 campaign because he believed it was an area in which we could play even or better than even with the *Post*. Some days he was right, some days wrong.

It was during that campaign, however, that an incident occurred which began a long-term deterioration in the relationship between Bellows and the publisher, Allbritton.

On July 4, Joe and Barbara Allbritton were invited to dinner in the private quarters of the White House with President Ford, the first lady, and one other couple. After dinner the president and his guests were served coffee on the Truman Balcony while they watched, directly in front of them, the Bicentennial fireworks display on the Washington Monument grounds. It was, by any measure, the Invitation of the Year, and Allbritton was impressed, as he had every reason to be. Unfortunately, however, he was so impressed that he raced back to the *Star* later in the evening, wrote an editorial endorsing Ford over his Republican primary challenger, Ronald Reagan, and ordered it published the following day on Page One.

The news editor on duty called Bellows, who came into the office, read the editorial, and decided it would have to be held. What he was doing, of course, was sparing Allbritton embarrassment. Publishers don't leave dinner at the White House and immediately issue an endorsement. And in the big leagues they don't run editorials on Page One. That is strictly for the bushes. Explaining himself to Allbritton, Bellows didn't put it in those terms. He tried to be diplomatic with some blather, as I understood it when he explained it to me later, about how such an editorial endorsement could have maximum impact handled in a different way.

But Allbritton was not used to being crossed by someone who worked for him. And he may already have been growing a little weary of all the encomiums being heaped on Bellows's head as the *Star* gained critical attention from other journalists. He was the one who put up the money, after all, but he was neither having any fun nor getting any credit. It was no surprise if he was growing a little testy. It was true that he had been a model publisher, from the news side's point of view, by providing the money and keeping his nose out of the paper. He could be charming and thoughtful. After the 1976 election he invited me and the rest of the political staff to dinner to celebrate our campaign coverage, presenting me with an inscribed sterling tray from Tiffany and the others with Steuben paperweights, also inscribed. It was the kind of gesture that builds loyalty, and I was ready to walk through a wall for the *Star*.

But it was also true that all the stories about how the *Star* had improved focused on Bellows and the innovations he had made. Bellows himself was a self-effacing, almost retiring man who seemed inarticulate until you became attuned to the soft rhythms of his speech. I never saw him encourage press attention, and I saw him deflect it more than once. But if a newspaper becomes a story itself, the editor, not the publisher, is going to be hero of the story.

Allbritton seemed to grow increasingly irascible. Some days his wife called Sid Epstein, the managing editor, and asked him to pay Joe some compliment because he had risen from the wrong side of the bed that morning or he was ticked off because their son Bobby was eating Froot Loops rather than healthy stuff for breakfast. He also started issuing fiats without any consultation with his executives about the consequences. One day he ordered a hiring freeze and staff reduction that would have prevented two reporters I had hired, with his explicit approval, from actually starting work. Both of them had left their previous jobs, and one of them had moved from Chicago and bought a house in Washington. For me the situation was untenable. If the two reporters, Ed Pound from the *Chicago Sun-Times* and Phil Gailey from Knight-Ridder, were cut adrift, I was going to have to leave as well. The result was that, while reassuring them every night that it would work out, I was spending several hours a day with Allbritton trying to find other ways to cut the news department budget. In the end the publisher rescinded the decision and went into the newsroom to stand on a desk and announce it and then, of course, enjoy the plaudits of the crowd for rescuing us from himself. When I called Gailey with the news that he could report for work the following Monday, he was relieved. "You mean," he asked, "I don't have to get knee-walking drunk tonight?"

The relationship between Allbritton and Bellows deteriorated for several months until things reached a point at which Bellows left or was driven out, ending those three golden years. I remember getting off the third-floor elevator that morning and seeing Bellows at his desk, buttering a doughnut and wearing an amused expression. "I have been relieved of my command," he said. The paper survived another couple of years but was never the same.

Allbritton seemed ambivalent in his attitude toward me. On at least two occasions his intermediaries approached me about whether I was interested in becoming editor of the paper. I was tempted because I feared the alternative, but I knew I didn't want to be penned into an office. And I admitted to myself I wouldn't be as good as Bellows anyway. My interests were too narrow; a good newspaper needs more than politics and horse racing.

On other occasions Allbritton seemed hostile. At one point he stopped me in the newsroom and said accusingly, "I kind of thought you'd have gone out to Los Angeles with your friend Bellers." I replied by pointing out I had been here long before Bellows and covered politics so there would be nothing for me in Los Angeles, where Bellows was taking over the floundering *Herald-Examiner*.

But Allbritton kept making cracks about "Bellers"—to the point that I started taking personal files home over the weekend to guard against the possibility of being shut out of my office. Allbritton finally sold the paper to *Time* magazine and walked away with several valuable broadcasting properties and a reputation as a very difficult man.

The experience with Time, Inc., was a disaster almost from the first day. The company installed Murray Gart, who had been chief of correspondents for the magazine, as the editor and gave him substantial money to try to save the paper. Gart and the *Time* editors seemed to think it was necessary to undo everything Bellows had done and to do everything he had not done, whether or not it made any sense. For example, they set up an elaborate and enormously expensive system of regional editions, complete with satellite offices and staffs, on the theory that the way to compete with the *Post* was with comprehensive coverage of every school board and sewer commission in the suburbs. What they learned, as Bellows had known, was that in Washington the national story is also the main local story.

The principal flaw in the *Time* approach, however, was that Gart and his cohorts were too stuffy. They wanted to put out a staid newspaper of record that was not really any different from the *Post* except perhaps less interesting and less thorough. We were very big on publishing the texts of presidential statements that had already appeared in the *Post* and *The New York Times* and heaven knows where else. We were short on series about homosexuals in professional sports. Gart treated Jules Witcover and me well enough. We had started our column, with help from Bellows, in 1977, but Jules had not been a full member of the staff. Gart made us joint political editors of the paper with prime responsibility for covering the 1980 presidential campaign while also writing our column, an arrangement that continued until the paper folded in August 1981.

What was most stunning about the *Time* experience was the discovery that their top executives were so easily impressed by presidents and other politicians. When the deal was consummated, a half dozen of us from the *Star*, news executives and columnists, were invited to a dinner at the Metropolitan Club with some of the magazine's movers and shakers, Henry Anatole Grunwald and

James Shepley and the like. I was bowled over by the almost syco-phantic attitude they displayed toward the president and some of the senators and congressmen who came up in the conversation. I don't believe that old saw that the only way a reporter can look at a politician is down. But I surely do believe that we should look at them dead level. Whatever power they may have achieved, most of them are ordinary people and should be treated as such.

The following day the *Time* attitude became even more apparent. I stopped in Gart's office and told him that if there was anyone he wanted to meet, I would be glad to help. He was, after all, a new-comer to the city. He replied that although he had been involved in *Time*'s coverage of the 1976 campaign, he had never gotten to know Hamilton Jordan. So I called Jordan a few minutes later, and he told me to bring the new editor over to the White House for a sandwich. Jordan was on his best behavior, charming and friendly and what I considered mock candid. Gart was bowled over. When we got back to the paper he took me into his office, where framed pictures were stacked against the walls waiting for him to decide which to hang where. He rooted through them, found the one he wanted, and proudly showed it me. It was a picture of him and another *Time* cor-respondent with Carter next to his campaign plane, *Peanut One*, and signed by the candidate. "I guess I'll be hanging this one," Gart said. I went down the hall two doors to the office I shared with Jules. "Let me tell you," I said, "we've got a real problem here." And it was a problem. We soon discovered that analytical pieces tough on Carter were not welcome. And if one could not be avoided it might start on Page One, then be moved inside for later editions.

Gart would have lunch about once a month with Walter Mon-dale, and the vice president would always give him some sales job on a story the White House was trying to peddle. Gart would come back from lunch and stop in our office, where he would float these "story" ideas as if they were his own—until finally I started greeting them with hoots to the effect that "that sounds like one of those things Mondale is always trying to sell." Gart was one of those edi-tors who would never admit he didn't know everything, and Jules and I used to play on that fact by using arcane inside gobbledygook to see how far we could go before he would ask us what the hell we were talking about. Between ourselves, we called it "talking GRPs" because of an occasion when Gart heard us talking about gross rating points, a measure of the dimensions of a television advertising buy, and refused to concede he didn't have any idea what the term meant.

When I look back on it, I realize we weren't very kind to Murray Gart, but then I recall that it was the hubris he and the *Time* editors displayed that scuttled a good newspaper. On the *Star*'s final day the *Today* show came into the newsroom and interviewed me, among others, about the paper's demise. I blamed Gart on the theory that he would have been given the credit if the paper survived so he had to take the hit when it failed. After the broadcast I was back in my office when Gart came in and asked me, "Have you and I got a problem?"

"Nothing personal, Murray," I replied, "just professional."

"Oh," he said. Then he shrugged and walked out.

—

CHAPTER 12

PLAYING THE
PRESIDENT

I flew out to Los Angeles in the spring of 1979 to cover President Carter's appearance at the Cinco de Mayo parade in downtown L.A. and to talk to the people running the embryonic Ronald Reagan presidential campaign. With the election still eighteen months away, they had established their head-quarters temporarily in an office building near the airport with the idea of moving to Washington when the primary season began. When I stopped in to see John Sears, the Washington lawyer who was Reagan's chief political strategist, he asked me if I would like to have dinner with the candidate at the Reagans' home in Pacific Pal-isades one night. I had been writing some columns for the *Star* raising questions about Reagan's age, so I guessed that Sears wanted to demonstrate the candidate could stay awake past ten o'clock. When I tested that theory on Sears, an old friend from the Nixon campaign of 1968 and Reagan's previous run in 1976, he laughed and rolled his eyes but didn't deny it.

There were six at dinner—the Reagans, Sears and me, plus James Lake, an old friend serving as the campaign press secretary, and Michael Deaver, one of Reagan's most trusted California advisers. Reagan seemed to relish his role as host, mixing the martinis with great care, pouring excellent California wines to accompany dinner, and, along with Nancy, telling one vintage Hollywood story after another. As the evening wore on, I could understand why those close to Reagan seemed to like him so much.

There were, however, two or three points in the conversation when I found myself wondering if these people lived in the real world. While we were having our martinis, Nancy asked me if I had been watching a television miniseries about the wartime relationship between General Dwight D. Eisenhower and Kay Summersby, his attractive Army driver. I replied that I had seen the first installment because I was a fan of Lee Remick, who played Summersby, but had missed the subsequent installments.

"Do you know," Reagan said quite heatedly, "they're implying they had an affair. Can you imagine that?" I paused for a couple of beats to be sure I had heard him correctly, then muttered something about yeah, it was pretty suggestive all right.

At another point we were talking about an incident that had occurred when Carter had made his speech in Los Angeles a couple of days earlier. The FBI had detained a derelict in the crowd who was found with a starter's pistol in his pocket. There was no serious evidence of any genuine threat to the president, but Reagan began to wonder aloud if this might have been a put-up job because of what happened in 1976. That was the year Reagan had fallen just short of winning the Republican nomination from President Gerald R. Ford, an outcome that obviously still rankled. And now, reminded by the Carter incident, Reagan suddenly brought up the two assassination attempts against Ford. The timing of these episodes, particularly the second, he said, was just a little bit suspicious. Ford had been the beneficiary of "the sympathy vote" because of Squeaky Fromme, and he, Reagan, had always wondered about whether it might have been arranged for political purposes. Now he was obviously harboring the same dark suspicions about Carter. I looked at Sears and found him staring at the ceiling. Lake seemed to be preoccupied with his watch. So I allowed that I sort of doubted it, but who knows, a lot of strange things happen in politics, ha, ha, ha.

Then at dinner Reagan asked me if I thought Ted Kennedy would challenge Carter for the Democratic nomination. I replied that I had no idea but that I did know some members of his family were concerned about the danger of another assassin and hoped he would not run. Whereupon Reagan told me that a Secret Service agent had told him "that Teddy's a physical coward." I was flabbergasted. I couldn't understand why being afraid of an assassin's bullet made someone a physical coward. More to the point, I couldn't believe a presidential candidate was retailing the gossip of some Secret Service agent to a reporter. Again, Sears seemed to be finding something interesting on the ceiling.

Reagan's ruminations about both Ford and Kennedy were revealing enough as insights into the thinking processes of a leading presidential candidate so that I might have written about them for the *Star* and landed on Page One. But I had understood all along that the evening was off the record in the strictest sense of that phrase. Sears had never spelled out any ground rules, but it had been clear to us both that this was a social occasion and that there was a tacit agreement I was not free to write about it.

In fact, it wasn't so much a social occasion as a classic example of political-press symbiosis. They were trying to shape my thinking about Reagan and I was willing to let them in exchange for getting a closer look at the candidate. In any case, the most I could do was file the evening away in my head and look for other occasions on which Reagan would be similarly revealing in circumstances that allowed me to report on it. And, of course, with Ronald Reagan there were many over the next eight years. He was always a man with a very loose hold on the real world around him.

I first met Reagan in 1966, when he was running in a Republican primary for the nomination to challenge the Democratic governor of California, Edmund G. (Pat) Brown. It was Reagan's first campaign, and from the outset he demonstrated that the ability to connect with voters personally was a lot more important than knowing anything about state government. He was being advised by Stuart Spencer and Bill Roberts, the same consultants who had worked for Nelson Rockefeller in the presidential primary two years earlier. This time, however, they had a candidate who could exploit the best issue of the moment for a Republican—the demonstrators against the war in Vietnam who were causing so many disruptions on California campuses—without sounding at all like George Wallace.

Reagan was also such a quick study he was able to paper over his lack of familiarity with the usual fodder of a gubernatorial campaign. I was with him one day in Long Beach when he was asked at a service club luncheon about a problem with the state workmen's compensation system and answered with a long, rambling response about the unemployment insurance law. When he returned to his car to drive on to the next service club, he was joined by a young academic Spencer and Roberts had retained to ride along for just such a situation. There were two separate problems, the professor explained, one with workmen's compensation and another with unemployment insurance. Then he described each and outlined a set of proposals to correct them. Sure enough, at the next stop Reagan was asked about unemployment insurance and replied with a full exposition of the problem and how he would correct it. As a bonus for his dazzled listeners, he then brought up workmen's compensation and dealt with that one with equal facility. I never learned whether he retained that information long enough to use it in Sacramento, but I did see that in a half hour Reagan could absorb enough to speak with easy authority. Not a bad quality for a candidate, assuming the information he is being force-fed is accurate.

Reagan's opponent in that primary campaign was a former mayor of San Francisco, a commercial dairy operator named George Christopher. He was markedly less conservative on social issues and seemed to fit the mold of the kind of moderate Republican who had been succeeding in California in those years. But he was a burly man who appeared to have the charisma of a cauliflower when matched against Reagan.

Christopher had taken an apartment in Los Angeles on Wilshire Boulevard, near the Ambassador Hotel and the Brown Derby, to use during the campaign, and I showed up there about seven one night to join him for the drive out to a couple of rallies in the San Fernando Valley that were on his campaign schedule.

He met me wearing a bathrobe. We've canceled the Valley events, he told me, there wasn't going to be anybody there anyway, so they were a waste of time. But he had a half hour of television coming up the next day, and he needed to finish preparing his speech. I should come in and have a drink, then we'd go out and eat some dinner. So I watched a ball game and sipped some Scotch while Christopher sat at the dining room table muttering over his speech and a large file of papers. Finally, after perhaps an hour, he capped his pen, stood, and stretched. He would get dressed, he said; meanwhile, take a look at this. And he handed me the file. It proved to be what political professionals would later call negative research on Reagan. It was largely an assortment of newspaper clippings purporting to connect the actor to some unsavory people with a lot of money, but the connections were flimsy.

"They tell me I can beat him if I just use this stuff," Christopher said, "but I doubt it. I don't want to do it anyway, it's just the idea of losing to an actor." He tossed the file back on the table, shrugged on his jacket, and we walked down Wilshire to Dale's Secret Harbor, a restaurant that despite the nautical suggestion of its name served excellent steaks and pasta. We ate and drank heavily, and Christopher kept talking about how hard it was to lose to an actor. I felt sorry for him because the whole thing seemed to be a case of Reagan simply stepping over a Republican who had worked in the vineyards for years. But mine was a romantic view of a very practical business, as Reagan would demonstrate repeatedly. Paying your dues is fine, but winning is what it's all about. He defeated Christopher easily, then unseated Governor Pat Brown, an old pro who had staved off Nixon's challenge four years earlier. Indeed, Brown's experience was much like Christopher's—coming to a realization well before election day that he was being washed away by a tide he could not understand. "I never thought it would end up this way," Brown told me one day on a small campaign plane. "I never thought the day would come when I couldn't beat some tap dancer"—a reference that suggested he was equating Reagan with another Hollywood figure, the song-and-dance man George Murphy, who served briefly in the Senate. "Imagine that, a tap dancer after all this time."

In fact, there were a number of political reporters, myself included, who felt some vague sense of resentment at the spectacle of a movie actor, and not even a very good one, starting out in politics so high up the ladder. It didn't have anything to do with Reagan's conservatism. Instead, we were offended at the idea that the skills involved in political success could be created—or replicated—overnight by some lightweight from, of all places, show business. If you cover politics, you like to imagine you're dealing with serious people and serious issues. When John Sears signed on as Reagan's presidential campaign manager for 1976, I asked him if his candidate wanted to be the president or just play the part, to which Sears replied: "I don't know and I don't know if it matters." As it turned out, we never got the answer to that question, and it didn't matter.

Dealing with Reagan as a political reporter was a strange experience. It was clear that he never took any of us very seriously, but neither was he hostile or contemptuous, as Nixon had been. Instead, as a movie star he saw reporters as necessary supporting players although not worth a lot of attention. But neither did he take offense at persistent or skeptical questioning. He was one of those politicians prized by reporters who seem to understand that there is nothing personal in most political discussion. Someone who disagrees with you is not your enemy but only your adversary or, in the case of reporters, someone doing his job. And Reagan was often an excellent interview because he tried to answer questions, not just play back some boilerplate response.

He was notorious for his inability to remember anyone's name. His press secretary in Sacramento, Franklyn C. Nofziger, was forever saying, "You remember *Jack,* Governor," as he ushered me in for my interviews, which was enough to get him through an hour or so on a first-name basis with a reporter. The standard joke among the Reaganites was that Nofziger would take the governor home at the end of the day and when his wife greeted him would say, "You remember *Nancy,* don't you, Governor." I went out to Sacramento and interviewed him at least twice a year throughout his two terms as governor and then covered his 1980 presidential campaign, but it was not until I began to appear on television regularly that Reagan could remember my name. Being on television was clearly something he took seriously, although it didn't seem to matter much what you said about him there.

When Jules Witcover and I went to see Reagan in the Oval Office to interview him for our book on the 1984 campaign, the president greeted me by saying something about how I kept whacking him on television every week and he'd just about given up trying to find something I'd think was a good idea. I replied with some shucking and jiving of my own about how, yes, wasn't it awful all I could ever do was criticize, but you know how that goes, Mr. President, nothing personal. Reagan clearly wasn't angry, he was just making good-natured small talk to put his visitors at ease. But Donald Regan, the acerbic former secretary of the Treasury who had become White House chief of staff, was less welcoming. "Yeah," he said, "and if it was up to me, you wouldn't be here now."

I replied that "it's a good thing you're just a staff man, Don" and took the seat on the couch the ever-courteous Reagan waved me into. Then he proceeded to answer our questions for more than an hour, twice the time that had been allotted, while Regan fumed.

Reagan's political handlers were always worried about his tendency to toss out opinions without thinking through the ramifications. During the early stages of the 1980 campaign, for example, he had made a point of saying the United States had to maintain "an official relationship" with Taiwan, a statement that evoked an angry reaction in Peking. After a meeting with Christian fundamentalist ministers in Dallas, Reagan allowed that, yes, there were "great flaws" in the theory of evolution. From a reporter's standpoint, the most vexing thing about Reagan was his penchant for throwing out purported facts that weren't factual at all, then blithely ignoring the contrary evidence. Members of his staff would wince when he would pass on as gospel something he had been told in a conversation or had read in the conservative fringe press. At one point, for example, he became convinced that all the nuclear wastes produced in the United States could be condensed into a mass the size of a softball and dropped far out in the ocean. Problem solved.

During his campaigns he was always coming up with horror stories to illustrate his arguments. A few of them would be exaggerations of some kernel of fact, some simply wild notions that had impressed themselves on his mind. He drew many of them from filler items in *Human Events,* the weekly conservative newspaper— so many, in fact, that his staff sometimes plotted to keep him from seeing the paper. When he first became president one of the staples of coverage of his press conferences would be stories about the things he had said that didn't quite square with the facts. Jules and I wrote several columns carping about a president playing fast and loose with the truth, but nobody seemed to care. On the contrary, we would get letters or phone calls from readers telling us to stop nit-picking. On the big things the voters knew where Reagan stood; on the small ones they were willing to cut him some slack.

Many of his stories were enduring. Back in that first gubernatorial campaign in 1966, I heard Reagan tell about how a black cook came up out of the bowels of one of the ships at Pearl Harbor December 7, 1941, and manned a machine gun to shoot back at the Japanese Zeroes attacking the fleet. "From that day on," said Reagan, "the armed services were integrated." An hour or so later I asked him about how this story squared with President Harry Truman's executive order in 1948 that ended segregation in the military. I pointed out that I had been in the Army Air Corps in 1946 and stationed on bases where the troops were still segregated and there were race riots.

"That may have been true where you were, Jack," he replied, the implication being that I didn't know the big picture.

Fifteen years later I was in a group of columnists having a cup of coffee with President Reagan in the White House when the race question came up—and Reagan told that same story about how the black cook manned the machine gun and finished with the same punch line, "and from that day on, the armed services were integrated."

What was most striking was that Reagan never seemed at all defensive, let alone angry, at his facts being questioned. You fellows just haven't looked in the right places, he would say. When Jules and I went to interview him for our book on the 1980 election, we knew we were obliged to beard him on some of the wild statements he had made during the campaign. He was the one who had insisted that General Motors requires 23,000 employees just to fill out federal forms, that there are 103 separate taxes on a loaf of bread, and that trees cause more air pollution than automobiles. We had decided, however, that we wouldn't raise these questions until we had covered all the other ground, so that if the president became angry and cut off the interview, we would still have the material we needed. Not to worry. When, quickly consulting notes I had made in advance, I started running through the list of "facts" that might be questioned, Reagan took it all in stride. You fellows need to look in the right places, he kept saying, then you'll find I'm right.

Reagan got away with these things because he seemed so relaxed and self-assured. He said one day early in the campaign that his primary task was "to convince people I'm not some combination of Ebenezer Scrooge and the Mad Bomber." And that was precisely what he did during that campaign. The first indication of how well he was doing came halfway through the general election campaign, when he participated in a debate in Baltimore with the independent candidate John B. Anderson despite President Carter's refusal to join.

I had the benefit of a de facto focus group with which I had made a connection through a column in which I had described the affluent suburbanite who would be the "typical" Anderson supporter. The lead went this way: "She drives a Volvo. When she attends a League of Women Voters' coffee, she selects a prune Danish on purpose. She thinks wine-and-cheese parties are 'great fun.' She doesn't think Ronald Reagan and Jimmy Carter are any fun at all."

The column had been published in the Portland *Oregonian,* and a few days later I received a letter from a woman who lived in a Portland suburb. "Do you know me?" she asked. It turned out that she drove a Volvo, was president of the League of Women Voters, and had eaten a Danish (although not prune—what the hell, nobody's perfect)—at a League meeting just the other day. She had even been to a wine-and-cheese party earlier in the year. And, although a Republican, she couldn't accept either Reagan or Carter, so she was supporting Anderson. When I telephoned she told me that there were about twenty women in her LWV group and that most of them were Republicans who were supporting either Anderson or Carter because they feared Reagan was too extreme.

But when I called her again the day after the Reagan-Anderson debate, there had been a significant change. They had watched the debate together, and most of the Republican women had switched to Reagan. They thought, she reported, that Anderson had been excellent in the debate, but, more to the point, they weren't frightened by Reagan as they had expected to be. On the contrary, he was clearly acceptable and they didn't want to waste their votes. The next few days' national polls began to show the same phenomenon. Anderson was seen as having "won" the debate, but his support declined as Reagan's rose. Over a long liquid dinner in Philadelphia a few nights after the debate, one of the independent's principal advisers conceded that "it's all over." And, of course, it was. Over the final weeks Anderson's share of the vote declined from about 20 percent in most polls to 7 percent by election day.

Reagan's ability to offer reassurance through the television screen was, of course, the secret of his political success. Like him, most of the voters were not going to sweat the small stuff so long as they knew he was acceptable on the important things, like cutting taxes and fighting communism. Most of them never knew, of course, how far removed he was from reality on many occasions, and when we in the press tried to tell them, they resented it.

In the spring of 1984 I had a particularly eerie experience with Reagan. I was president that year of the Gridiron Club, an organization of sixty newspaper people whose sole purpose is a white-tie dinner every spring in which members lampoon political leaders in songs and skits. As president, an office achieved solely through seniority, I was seated next to Reagan for four long hours and, to my amazement, found him just as divorced from reality as he had been at that dinner at his home five years earlier.

The president was soon to make his first trip to China and had been getting briefings in preparation for the trip. He had found this an eye-opening experience, and he was brimming with details about the things he had learned. Did I realize, he asked me, that China had mountains and forests and lakes much like the United States? He went on describing his discovery until it became clear to me that he had always had a mental picture of China as a huge desert or perhaps an endless series of rice paddies and was only now being disabused of those notions. I suspected he had seen some movie version of a Pearl Buck novel.

Equally striking was Reagan's very tenuous grip on all those other men in white tie who came up to the head table to shake his hand during the evening's two extended table-hopping periods. I began to suspect that, without Lyn Nofziger at his side to do the prompting, he didn't recognize not only members of the Senate and House but some officials of his own administration. At one point, for instance, Secretary of Agriculture John Block, whose seat was down at a far end of the head table, came along behind us and leaned down to shake hands with the president and perhaps carry on a little conversation. When this happened I would sort of lean back out of the way so I wouldn't appear to be eavesdropping on affairs of state. But in Block's case it was clear Reagan had no idea to whom he was talking until, finally, I leaned into the conversation and said something inane like "How are things in *Agriculture, Mr. Secretary*?"

Then there was the case of the absent ambassador of the Soviet Union, Anatoly Dobrynin. He regularly attended and enjoyed Gridiron dinners, but he had informed the club the evening before the event that he was suffering from a gastrointestinal illness that would make it impossible this year. Then the day of the dinner Dobrynin called and asked me to tell the president personally that the illness was genuine and that his absence wasn't intended as any kind of diplomatic gesture. At an earlier dinner when U.S.-Soviet relations were testy, the ambassador had shown up not in the customary white tie but wearing his military uniform with a chest full of ribbons. This time, he made clear, he would be there if it weren't for the nausea and diarrhea, and he wanted to be sure that was clear to Reagan.

So I passed the message on to the president, and we talked about how much Dobrynin had seemed to enjoy these events and how he would be missed now that his posting in Washington was ending and he would be returning to the Soviet Union. Then, to my astonishment, Reagan began to talk about whether, when it came right down to it, Dobrynin would go home or decide to stay. At first I didn't get it, but then I realized the president was speculating about the possibility that the Soviet ambassador might defect. I kept nodding and controlling my face.

But the president wasn't through with his flight of fancy. He sometimes wondered, he said, about all those Soviet diplomats here and at the United Nations in New York, if a lot of them wouldn't like to live the great life offered by the United States rather than go back to the grim realities of the Soviet Union. He sometimes thought, he said, that you should just fly them over the suburbs or New York or Washington in helicopters so they could look down at all those swimming pools and see what life could be in a free society. Maybe a lot of them would decide to stay. Again, I kept a straight face. You had to like a president who felt so much pride in his country. But, ye gods, this was the Leader of the Free World.

I often wondered how Reagan functioned in the world of international diplomacy, where more than a few good Hollywood stories might be required. An Israeli diplomat once told me that Menachem Begin had been horrified to sit down in the White House with Reagan for a serious discussion of the Middle East only to realize the president of the United States was holding several five-by-seven cards in his lap and speaking almost entirely from the notes on those cards. Begin apparently was struck particularly by the contrast with Reagan's predecessor, Jimmy Carter, who characteristically had stored a library of information about Israel and its adversaries in his head and could call it up in an instant. But the diplomat assured me it didn't matter in the long run because the decisions were mostly the inevitable product of staff work on both sides.

Still, we had to wonder how the country made it through eight years with someone in the White House as vague and detached as Reagan always seemed to be. Part of it, of course, was superior staff work. In the first term Chief of Staff James Baker and several Republicans in Congress—most notably Senator Paul Laxalt of Nevada, Reagan's old friend, and Senator Howard Baker, the party leader in the upper house—formed what amounted to an unspoken cabal to formulate policy on many touchy issues. Reagan had a set of what Jim Lake, a shrewd judge of politicians, called value mechanisms—broad views of what he believed. He was determined to resist communism at every turn. He was determined to reduce the role of the federal government in the lives of most Americans. He was determined to lower taxes. But he never concerned himself with the particulars required to uphold those principles. He relied instead on those around him. Press critics accused the White House reporters of giving him a free ride, but it was more accurate to say they could never nail down his culpability for things that went wrong. And on the rare occasions when they did, their viewers and readers didn't want to hear about it.

Indeed, Reagan's vagueness was itself a kind of defense against critics. When the question arose during his second term about whether he had authorized the actions of Oliver North and John Poindexter that led to the Iran-Contra scandal, I guessed in a television appearance that Reagan had signed it and then forgotten the whole thing. The remark was meant to be facetious, but one of those closest to the president told me later that I had stumbled close to the truth. The president's denials of responsibility were true, at least so far as he knew himself.

In terms of domestic politics, Reagan's strength was his skill at producing just the right one-liner when the situation required. We always suspected that many of them had been prepared well in advance of, for example, a debate or a press conference. But what mattered was his ability to seize the sound bite that the television networks would use that night. Nowhere did he demonstrate that talent better than the one time his political future seemed to be at all in doubt, late in his 1984 campaign for reelection.

From the outset, the result that year seemed foreordained. Reagan had completed what was generally considered a successful first term once the country got past an economic downturn in 1982. And the Democrats had nominated Walter F. Mondale, who had been Jimmy Carter's vice president. Mondale was a capable and intelligent politician who was both popular and respected within his party. But he was also a protégé of Hubert H. Humphrey's and a certifiable liberal of the old school. So he carried the burden of his association with Carter and an ideology that was in great disrepute in the Reagan era. The result, to no one's surprise, was that Reagan held a lead of landslide dimensions as the general election campaign played itself out.

But in their first debate Reagan surprised everyone and set off alarm bells in his own campaign. He seemed uncertain at times. He stumbled over a few answers. He rambled away from the topic. It was not the kind of crisp, confident performance everyone had come to expect from the old Gipper, and we know-it-alls in the pressroom were at a loss to explain it. The obvious question, of course, was whether Reagan, now seventy-three, had lost it. Had he reached one of those points at which old people suddenly seem to age rapidly, almost overnight? We all imagine we have seen that in others; there was no reason Reagan should be exempt. So the compelling topic in the campaign suddenly became whether the president had grown senile. And the critical time for answering the question was the second debate, scheduled two weeks later in Kansas City. Meanwhile, the campaign seemed to be placed on hold.

As it happened, one of the panelists for the second debate was Henry Trewhitt, a colleague from the *Baltimore Sun* who covered national security affairs, the topic for the confrontation. On the day of the debate Trewhitt asked me, as he did others, for my ideas on how to frame the Question. He needed to get to the heart of the matter with a question that Reagan could not simply brush off or slide by. But it also had to be a question that the consummate professional Trewhitt agreed would fit within the framework of the topic for the debate. Finally, after two or three hours of crafting and testing, he came up with a formulation, and, when his turn came in the debate, he asked it this way: "Mr. President, I want to raise an issue that I think has been lurking out there for two or three weeks and cast it specifically in national security terms. You already are the oldest president in history, and some of your staff say you were tired after your most recent encounter with Mr. Mondale. I recall, yet, that President Kennedy . . . had to go for days on end with very little sleep during the Cuban missile crisis. Is there any doubt in your mind that you would be able to function in such circumstances?"

Watching it on a pressroom television monitor, I could see just the hint of a smile on Reagan's face, and I thought, Oh, shit, he's all ready for it and he's going to hit it out of the park.

And, of course, he did. "Not at all, Mr. Trewhitt. And I want you to know that also I will not make age an issue in this campaign. I am not going to exploit, for political purposes, my opponent's youth and inexperience."

Thus, with a single sentence Reagan had once again seized control of the news media just as he had four years earlier when he used his debate with Carter to ask the nation: "Are you better off than you were four years ago?" This was the sound bite for every television or radio broadcast, the essential quote for every newspaper report. It was the sentence that dissolved the age issue and, not incidentally, any lingering doubt about whether he would be reelected.

This is, of course, ridiculous on the face of it. We shouldn't be electing presidents on their facility for producing one-liners for television. Nor should a seventy-three-year-old candidate have been allowed to dodge a question about his stamina at a time when the

Cold War was still very much with us. But projecting the right image on television is the first requirement of American politics today and often the only one.

Back in 1976 John Sears had said it probably didn't matter whether Ronald Reagan was the president or simply played the part. He was right. With television defining the world, it's all the same.

CHAPTER 13

RACE AND POLITICS

Serving his second term as mayor of Atlanta in 1989, Andrew Young decided to look into the chances of winning the governorship of Georgia. The operative question clearly was whether a black candidate could win enough acceptance among white voters twenty-five years after the Congress and President Lyndon B. Johnson had passed and signed the Voting Rights Act.

When Young scheduled a day in south Georgia to test the climate, I flew down to Valdosta to ride along. The mayor would begin the morning with a breakfast with "community leaders" in that small city near the Florida border, make a few speeches, do some radio and newspaper interviews, and make his way north to Albany, where there would be a dinner. It was the kind of trip politicians routinely make when they are both trying to measure potential support and send a strong signal that they intend to run. This was different only because the candidate was one of those who had marched at the side of Martin Luther King, Jr., and the area was one in which resistance to the civil rights movement had been stubborn and violent.

Superficially it was a campaign day of a kind I have been through scores, perhaps hundreds of times over the years. The audience at the breakfast was largely made up of black people from Valdosta already heavily inclined toward Young. The women were turned out as if for Sunday services, in hats and veils and gloves; a surprising number of the men wore ties, many of them obviously with some discomfort. It was a show of respect.

The rest of the schedule was also largely predictable—a high school assembly, a meeting of college students, a speech before the Azalea City Kiwanis Club, several radio interviews, and finally, the putative high point, the dinner at a glistening new art museum in Albany. And, on the surface, Young went through his paces in an unremarkable way. This is what candidates do at this stage—meet a lot of people, write their names on little cards, give a basic speech, try to attract a little press attention, and then, at the end of the day, attempt to measure what they've seen and heard.

In fact, it wasn't quite that routine for Andy Young. At the high school assembly one group of boys—no more than eight or ten of perhaps three hundred in the audience—made a point of sitting with arms folded when others applauded politely. At the Kiwanis luncheon there was one table of seven or eight men who were less welcoming, applauding perfunctorily or not at all. White men in short-sleeved shirts with plastic pocket protectors, their arms crossed, sending signals of their skepticism.

The event at the museum in Albany was, however, conspicuously civilized. The guests were not necessarily Young supporters but instead a biracial cross section of prominent people in a city of seventy thousand who came out for dinner to show proper courtesy to the mayor of their state's largest city and a serious prospective candidate for governor. I was stunned, however, when I realized that the man presiding over the event was James Gray III, publisher of *The Albany Herald.* The last time Young had been in Albany had been more than twenty-five years earlier, when he was a leader of the Albany Movement, in which the Southern Christian Leadership Conference (SCLC) tried to register black voters. That effort and a subsequent one by the Student Nonviolent Coordinating Committee (SNCC) had enjoyed little success, thwarted largely by a police chief and by the publisher of *The Albany Herald,* James Gray, the father of Young's host tonight. Indeed, the elder Gray had been the leading voice of defiance and segregation at that time, so unrestrained that he became infamous in the civil rights movement. When I mentioned this history to the younger Gray, he turned it away with a shrug and a remark about how times change.

Young was finding it less easy to shrug off. The dinner broke up about nine, and, faced with a three-hour trip back to Atlanta, the mayor decided to do the driving himself, dispatching his security man and his longtime assistant, Carol Muldawer, to the backseat to nap so we could talk. How did he feel, I asked as we drove north, coming back to Albany after all this time under these circumstances?

There was a long pause, perhaps thirty or forty seconds, before he replied. "Apprehensive," he said. "Very apprehensive."

We began to review the day, one event after the other. And it soon became evident Young had not missed a thing. He could describe not only the high school boys who had been off to his right but another clutch of hostile louts down in the front row to his left, whom I had missed. He had noticed that table at the luncheon and indeed anything that might have seemed even minimally jarring at every event along the way. The Albany experience had been the most stunning, of course, but for Young the entire day had been a kind of a trial politicians rarely go through. He didn't complain about the way he was greeted; indeed, he made a point of saying that he never felt "alien" anywhere along his route. But he wanted to examine it. I had the feeling he was trying to fit the day into some rational picture of his world as a highly sophisticated mayor of a major city who had already served in Congress and as the United States ambassador to the United Nations and now quite naturally was considering a campaign for governor.

For me it was the kind of day that makes up for a lot of Friday nights on standby at some rainy airport. I didn't know Andy Young well enough to fully understand his experience. I don't know that any white reporter could have done that. But I knew this was one of those stories that keep me covering politics. Andy Young being introduced to speak by James Gray's son twenty-five years later, is that mind-boggling or what? Andy Young driving through the night to Atlanta, trying to figure it out.

As it turned out, Young had reason to be apprehensive about the politics of the situation, at least. In the end he lost the Democratic nomination, winning less than 40 percent of the vote against Zell Miller, a populist from north Georgia who had been lieutenant governor for sixteen years and had built an impressive army of supporters, including many blacks from communities other than Atlanta.

In a sense Young's experience in politics reflected the way the race factor had developed in the South since the Voting Rights Act. Black participation in the political process had risen to the point that black candidates could succeed in a city like Atlanta with even 20 to 25 percent of white voters supporting them. And, as both Andrew Young and Maynard Jackson demonstrated in Atlanta, black mayors could bring more and more white constituents along as they became more familiar—and less threatening—figures. But there was still a stubborn resistance to black officials among whites in both rural areas and the suburbs around Atlanta.

That evening in Albany might have seemed less exotic to me if I had covered more of the civil rights movement at the time it was the dominant national story. But one of the regrets of my life as a newspaperman is that the decision I made to specialize in covering politics as intensely as I did—if indeed it was a decision rather than an inevitable evolution—denied me the opportunity of covering many other stories that were both significant and rewarding. I didn't cover Birmingham or Selma or Freedom Summer in Mississippi.

There were, however, a few chances for me to get a piece of the civil rights story. One of them came in a county near Albany in 1963, when a politically ambitious local prosecutor named Stephen Pace charged four civil rights demonstrators with "inciting to insurrection" and "seditious conspiracy" under a state law that state courts had already declared unconstitutional. The critical point was that the law defined the crime as a capital offense; conviction would make the accused subject to the death penalty. Its use clearly was intended to intimidate the young people who were coming south in increasing numbers to press the campaign for voter registration.

I drove from Atlanta down to Americus because one of the young men being held in the Sumter County jail was from Hartford, Connecticut, which made the story of special concern to the *Hartford Times*, a Gannett newspaper. For some reason I couldn't learn then and never quite understood, there had been no reaction either publicly or behind the scenes from the Justice Department. And reports leaking out of the jail told us that the four young men, three black and one white, were being abused by the other prisoners.

Sumter County was surely among the ugliest pieces of real estate in this whole republic. There were some pecan groves, but mostly there were spindly pine trees and red clay. Americus, with a population of perhaps fifteen thousand, was a shabby town whose prime distinction seemed to be a main street six lanes wide with angled parking along both sides for customers of the lines of cafés and small shops. Jimmy Carter lived a few miles away in Plains, an even less prepossessing community. But, although he was a state senator at the time, his name never came up during my week in town.

Most of the people were real sweethearts. The editor of the local newspaper wouldn't talk to me, and neither would the president of the small college. The goal was to not "get involved" in what the paper referred to as Recent Events without being so crass as to specify that those events had included a demonstration downtown that led to several hundred arrests. On one occasion while I was there the local paper covered a demonstration, telephoned an account of it to the Associated Press bureau in Atlanta, then published the story with the AP dateline so it appeared to have come from an "outsider." A journalistic profile in courage. The only local white man who seemed unafraid to talk to a reporter was Warren Fortson, a lawyer who was trying to negotiate some racial amity.

The kids who did the marching and canvassing, urging their elders to register to vote, had been organized by a nineteen-year-old SNCC worker from Alabama, Bob Mants, who held his meetings at a funeral home operated by another brave black man. Almost everyone else seemed intimidated by Sheriff Fred Chappell, whom Andrew Young quoted Martin Luther King, Jr., as describing as "the meanest man in the world." Sheriff Fred, as he was called locally, was a short man with beefy arms and an attitude of implacable hostility toward both blacks and reporters, and the kids involved in the demonstrations were clearly frightened. On one occasion a dozen or so of the youngest—only nine or ten years old—formed a ring around me and began clapping and chanting, "Sheriff Fred gonna put you in the jail, reporter-man," then laughed themselves to the point of hysteria.

The responsibility for dealing with outside agitators seemed to fall on a special force that included Americus police officers, Sumter County deputies, and some state troopers. They patrolled together wearing light blue helmets and were called, at least by some of the blacks, the blue beetles. One of their cars was assigned to follow me from the moment I arrived and stopped at the jail to ask to see the prisoners. Sheriff Fred told me to forget it, and when I drove away I had the tailing car. I took a room at a motel on the edge of town, and they parked just outside the door, the police car next to my rental every night. When I went to breakfast each morning at a café on the highway, three or four of them sat at the next table, and, while I read *The Atlanta Constitution* along with my country ham and grits, they carried on loud discussions about how Sumter County really didn't need a lot of outsiders telling folks here how to deal with their niggers.

I kept showing up at the jail and being turned away in my effort to see the prisoners. Finally, after five or six days of rejection, I informed Sheriff Fred that I was entitled to be given some reason I couldn't see the prisoners.

"Because there's no need for them to be talking to any fat, nigger-loving Yankee reporters," he explained, clearing that up once and for all.

Meanwhile, the police car continued on my tail. When I drove along the main drag in Americus, which was posted for twenty miles an hour but was usually driven at thirty or thirty-five, I held it at nineteen. Sometimes I would drive into the black section of town where the streets were not paved so I could enjoy my escorts getting a nose full of my dust. The surveillance was so close and constant that one night I drove to Albany just to have a meal alone in what passed for civilization. But when I crossed the Sumter County line on the way back, a car picked me up right away and followed me to the motel. My only small triumph was a bottle of Scotch in my suitcase, which I nipped on in my room late at night while the cops outside drank coffee and stood guard in case anything seditious was going on.

I never did get to see the four young prisoners, but the story began to receive more press attention, particularly after SNCC's chairman, John Lewis, mentioned the Americus outrage in his speech at the Lincoln Memorial during the March on Washington. The capital charges were scotched by a federal court order, but only after the four young men had spent ninety-odd days in jail. The kids I left behind were, of course, in it for the long haul, and eventually the black vote came to Sumter County, although Sheriff Fred never made it easy. Even as the Voting Rights Act was being signed two years later, Sumter County was forcing blacks and whites into separate voter registration lines—and jailing two women who protested and then John Lewis when he arrived to protest their incarceration. By that time Warren Fortson was giving up on Americus and moving his law practice to Atlanta.

There was a postscript of sorts. During the transition after Jimmy Carter's election to the presidency in 1976, I returned to Americus on assignment and found a new and relatively elegant Best Western motel that served as an unofficial headquarters for both press and staff. One night several of us went to Fay's Barbecue, the restaurant of choice in Sumter County, for a steak, and while I was eating, a man who looked familiar came out of the kitchen carrying a large tray for one of the waitresses. He was, someone said, Fay's husband and a deputy sheriff. He was also, I remembered, one of those who had worn the light blue helmets thirteen years earlier. I asked him if he remembered me and if the blue beetles were still functioning. He behaved as if I had landed from Mars. Yankee reporters had become a great source of dollars for mediocre steaks, and, as for that old civil rights stuff, that was ancient history. Carter also seemed to have trouble remembering it all very clearly, although Fortson said years later that he was helpful "behind the scenes." When I asked him about the attempt to break the demonstrations with the "inciting to insurrection" charges, Carter allowed that he had known Steve Pace, the prosecutor, as a contemporary who had attended West Point while he was at Annapolis. But Carter was vague about the whole Americus episode. There seemed to be a lot of that going around fifteen years later.

Most of the reporting I managed on civil rights had some connection, however tenuous, to politics and government, which gave me what passed for a legitimate excuse to get out of Washington. In 1965, for example, I spent ten days driving across the South gathering material for a series of pieces on how the 1964 public accommodations law was being observed or circumvented.

I began in Atlanta, at Lester Maddox's infamous Pickrick, where the food was worse than the company. The fried oysters arrived in cube-shaped globs of batter, raising the suspicion the oysters were dropped into ice-cube trays full of flour and water, then quick-frozen and quick-fried. But the food wasn't much better elsewhere—bad enough so that I developed a theory that the white southerners were exacting their revenge on blacks by allowing them to eat cooking that would destroy their digestive systems overnight.

The story turned out to be largely predictable but, like many predictable stories, deserved to be documented. Some hotel and restaurant proprietors, particularly those few connected in any way to national chains, were ready to comply with the new law. They saw desegregation as inevitable, and they had grown weary of the constant arguments and lawsuits. Others were pleased to have the law because they could blame the federal government when their white customers complained. Others avoided complying by setting up "private clubs" or, in some cases, simply sending threatening messages to local blacks about just how unwelcome they would be. A few diehards just shut down.

The story had its moments, of course. One day I stopped at a roadside catfish shack in rural Mississippi. But when I ordered some fish and hush puppies, the black proprietor told me he couldn't serve a white man. I told him I was a reporter from Washington, D.C., and I asked him if he hadn't heard about the Civil Rights Act of 1964. He had heard about it, he said, shaking his head, but he wasn't sure about the sheriff, and the sheriff was the one he had to worry about, not anybody from Washington, D.C. I didn't want to press the point, so I thanked him and went back outside to my rental car. Before I could turn around to drive on, however, he came out the back door and signaled me to wait. A few seconds later he brought me a paper bag that held two fried catfish, a half dozen hush puppies, and a cold beer. I drove down the road a mile or two before I stopped in the shade of a huge live oak dripping with Spanish moss and enjoyed one of the great lunches of my life.

The trip also gave me a far less sanguine insight into race relations than many of us had in Washington after the 1964 bill passed. Those who were resisting integration most stubbornly were not just ignorant rednecks. They often included the business and professional people who usually were thought of as community leaders, as I learned firsthand from old friends.

I had scheduled my trip so that, like any sensible man with a proper regard for his own comfort, I would end up in New Orleans, reporting on how many blacks were being served at Galatoire's and Arnaud's. And I arranged to arrive at Baton Rouge the previous day and have dinner with several of my classmates from high school, whom I hadn't seen for twenty years. We met at a steak house that had been converted to a "club," and I was enjoying the evening immensely until they started inquiring into what I was writing about and the conversation turned sour. It wasn't all of them. My closest friend from the old days, Buddy Souter, was still the quiet, gentle man he had always been. But another old friend asked me if it wasn't a fact that the whole reason for *Brown v. Board of Education* was that "old Earl Warren's got a thing for little nigger boys." And the vivacious wife of another friend suggested in her soft southern tone that it was all the goddamn Communists determined to pollute the races. When I drove on to New Orleans the next morning, the bad taste in my mouth was from more than the Scotch.

It was another twenty years, however, before I learned how deeply ingrained in my generation these racial attitudes had become. In 1985 I went back to Baton Rouge for a fortieth high school class reunion and found the atmosphere on race still poisoned, although less blatantly. One of my classmates who showed up was John Parker, known as Pep Parker in our school days. We had belonged to the same high school fraternity and hung around together enough so I was delighted to see him after all these years. He was now a federal district court judge and thus by any conventional measure one of the class success stories. During the evening, however, I noticed that most of my old classmates were ignoring Pep. And the next day, when another classmate gave a brunch in honor of my return as the prodigal son who had become a celebrity by appearing on television, Pep wasn't there. What I learned when he and I enjoyed a long dinner together a year or so later was that he had been ostracized by many of his old friends. He was, it seems, not just a federal judge but a federal judge appointed by President Jimmy Carter, and not just a Carter appointee but a liberal judge who had handed down controversial decisions in some racially charged cases involving school busing to achieve integration. When it came time for the fiftieth anniversary, I thought about going, then gave it a pass.

For all the time and effort I have spent covering the question, I've never found a way to measure with any precision how racial attitudes affect our politics. But we have learned a few things. We know, for example, that opinion polls involving black candidates almost always overstate the support for those candidates among whites. In 1989, for example, several surveys showed Democrat L. Douglas Wilder, the black lieutenant governor, leading Republican J. Marshall Coleman by at least ten percentage points in the contest for governor of Virginia. The findings made sense. Wilder, after all, was a familiar figure to Virginia voters after sixteen years in the legislature and a full term in statewide office he had won four years earlier. I assumed he had passed the racial hurdle in that campaign for lieutenant governor.

As it turned out, Wilder won by less than a point. In fact, Coleman's campaign had been such a disaster, in terms of both his handling of issues and its mechanics, that Wilder probably would have won by twenty points if he had been white. A detailed study of polling data found many white voters who were Democratic by habit and inclination and who agreed with Wilder on most issues but still voted for Coleman. A Gallup Poll in 1984, the first year Jesse Jackson ran for president, found that 18 percent of whites said they would never vote for a black man for president. That applied only to presidential candidates and might have been skewed to some degree by the less-than-retiring personal style of Candidate Jackson. But it would be no surprise to learn that almost as many whites in Virginia felt the same way about a state governor.

We've also learned that there are tipping points beyond which whites are less inclined to vote for a black candidate or, more often, a white liberal Democratic candidate who has solid black support. Thus, it is easier for a black candidate to be elected mayor of a city with a small minority of black voters than of a city in which blacks make up a substantial minority but not enough of a bloc to win an election. And it was no accident that as a presidential candidate running in primaries, Jackson did better in states like Oregon and Vermont than he did in New Jersey and Massachusetts. In short, blacks can win (1) when they make up a majority, or (2) when there aren't enough blacks to appear threatening to voters in the white majority who blame blacks for crime or the costs of welfare or both.

The tipping-point phenomenon has been more responsible than any other single factor for the transformation of the Democratic solid South into a Republican solid South. In states like Alabama and Mississippi, blacks make up one-fourth to one-third of the electorate, which means Democrats need only 30 to 35 percent of the white vote to have a majority of the total and be elected. But for candidates like Walter Mondale in 1984 and Michael Dukakis in 1988, it was far more difficult to capture that small share than to win the 40 to 43 percent needed in states in which blacks make up only 15 percent of the total. The vehemence of the white reaction was sometimes frightening. I went into Mondale headquarters in Birmingham one day just as two carloads of teenage girls returned from distributing Mondale-Ferraro leaflets at stoplights and shopping centers. Several were in tears because of the epithets that had been screamed at them, almost invariably by men. Exit polls later found fewer than 20 percent of white men voted for Mondale.

Over the 1980s and 1990s whites in states like Alabama, Mississippi, South Carolina, and Louisiana have come to consider the Democrats "the black party" and are unwilling to identify themselves with the party. The result has been the dramatic movement of governorships and Senate and House seats into the Republican column.

When the Voting Rights Act of 1965 was signed by Lyndon Johnson, many political professionals foresaw a different picture in the South—a coalition of blacks with white populists, academics, labor leaders, and others who had demonstrated their liberal credentials during the movement. But these groups never made a majority, and after a generation no one seemed to remember why a civil rights movement had been needed. Our schools don't teach recent history. So it is not surprising that Americans who don't know anything about the Holocaust don't know anything either about Rosa Parks or Central High School or the bombing of the Sixteenth Street Baptist Church in Birmingham. Nor is it any wonder that so many voters can be twisted and turned by candidates who play on the images of the black welfare mother and the black street thug.

In national politics these racial resentments have been reflected most directly in the reaction to Jesse Jackson in the years since he so forcibly impressed himself on the consciousness of the electorate with his campaigns for the Democratic presidential nomination in 1984 and 1988. It is no exaggeration to say that the white view of Jackson played a role in the dimensions of the defeats suffered by both Mondale and Dukakis. Many of the so-called Reagan Democrats who voted for Reagan and Bush in those elections abandoned their party because they were convinced the presidential nominees had made too many special concessions to Jesse Jackson. It wasn't true, but the perception was certainly vivid and widespread. And it is also no exaggeration to say that Bill Clinton's success in reclaiming the support of those working-class voters in 1992 could be traced in part to his decision to deliberately affront Jackson early in the campaign.

Jackson showed up on the national political scene for the first time serving as a surrogate for George McGovern during his struggle with Hubert Humphrey for the Democratic presidential nomination in 1972. During the critical California primary campaign, Jackson and his entourage checked into the Wilshire Hyatt House, which was serving as the base for the McGovern campaign. He was supposed to be making speeches to encourage black turnout, but his schedule was less than grueling. What the reporters soon noticed was that every day, at breakfast and at lunchtime, Jackson and several of his hangers-on would establish themselves around the hotel's swimming pool, shortly followed by several carts of room service meals. Morris Dees, raising money for the McGovern campaign, used to look down on the spectacle from his bedroom and, if you caught his eye, shake his head ruefully as more checks were being signed. By contrast, Julian Bond, enlisted for the same mission, worked a full schedule every day.

But Jackson was not a major player in that campaign or in those of Jimmy Carter in 1976 and 1980, although he did travel the country encouraging black voter participation. As the leader of People United to Save Humanity, or Operation PUSH, based in Chicago, Jackson was concentrating on improving economic opportunity for blacks and enjoying some success in persuading businesses they needed black Americans as their customers and should show it. But he began moving inexorably toward politics after Reagan's election was followed by a sharp rise in black voter turnout in several off-year elections in 1981 and midterm elections in 1982.

Jackson's decision to run for president in 1984 was not universally applauded among leaders of the black political community. Some of them had frowned on his penchant for self-promotion since the night, April 4, 1968, that Martin Luther King, Jr., was shot down in Memphis. Jackson was then a young member of the SCLC staff, waiting in the parking lot with several others for a ride to dinner, when King was shot on a balcony outside his room at the Lorraine Motel. He was not one of those truly close to King—such as Ralph Abernathy or Andrew Young—but he was the one who flew back to Chicago that night and then showed up on the *Today* show on NBC the next morning still wearing a shirt stained with the martyr's blood.

Even for those who had put that episode behind them, there were other complaints about Jackson among some veteran black leaders. They saw him as too self-aggrandizing in the way he made the movement's case. They resented his ability to command the attention of the press and, particularly, those television cameras. They made jokes about how he was always onstage at every funeral or demonstration or political meeting. They were convinced that he was trying to establish himself as not just the black political leader but another Martin Luther King, Jr.

In 1984, however, there were other, younger blacks who hoped Jesse would become another King. These were people like Tyrone Brooks, a state legislator in Georgia, then thirty-eight years old, and the Reverend John Nettles, a forty-year-old preacher in Anniston and head of the Alabama SCLC. Like Jackson, then forty-three, they had been too young to have been on the ground floor, to get their tickets punched with King in the earliest days of the movement. Like Jackson, they had still been in college or perhaps even high school, so they'd missed out. When I met Brooks the first time, he told me within a half hour that he had been arrested a dozen times or more. I understood it; it was credentialing.

In the campaign few black leaders were willing to go public with their complaints about him. Shortly before the Georgia primary I remember telling Andy Young the story about Jesse Jackson "helping" McGovern in the hope it might lead the mayor to be a little more candid about his own feeling toward him. Instead, Young suggested my story might make a good column, why didn't I write it? That same day I went to see John Lewis, then a city councilman, because I had been told he was planning to endorse Mondale and held Jackson in what we call minimum high regard. Lewis is one of those too rare people in public life who are both incapable of dissembling and eminently courteous, and I could see him growing more uncomfortable as I pressed him to tell me what he thought of Jesse. He began to sweat and the flesh on his forehead started to wrinkle as he tried to be polite and still avoid saying anything unkind about Jackson—to the point that I finally said to myself, Fuck it, leave the man alone, and left.

By contrast, Julian Bond was unabashedly supporting Fritz Mondale and making no effort to hide his reservations about Jesse Jackson. He was the one who brought Coretta Scott King to a press conference in Atlanta a couple of days before the primary so she could endorse Mondale and send the clearest message. This independence was characteristic of Bond and had been in all the years from the time he was nineteen or twenty and serving as the communications director of SNCC and putting John Lewis and his organization high on the agenda of the national press. It was no surprise to anyone who knew him that Bond was the one black leader of prominence in Georgia who hadn't supported Carter when he ran for president in 1976.

For a national political reporter, covering Jesse Jackson presented a different set of questions. His campaign was, first of all, a hell of a good story. This was not another Shirley Chisholm, a black congresswoman from Brooklyn who had declared herself a candidate for admittedly symbolic purposes in 1972. Jesse was a "serious" black candidate. But how serious? No one in the political world imagined for a moment that the Democratic Party was prepared to nominate a black person for president in 1984. However, it soon became apparent that Jackson had evoked such pride and excitement in the black community and among some white liberals that his candidacy could affect the outcome. As a reporter I was quickly impressed by the reach of Jackson's appeal. It wasn't just the kids or the poor rallying around one of their own. Sophisticated and highly educated blacks were showing the same kind of pride, particularly after Jackson proved in the early primary debates that he could hold his own—more than hold his own—with the white candidates with whom he was competing. Most of them seemed to understand that he probably would not be nominated, but they didn't consider their votes entirely symbolic either.

In the end the news coverage was essentially a cop-out, in which I joined. For several reasons we didn't cover Jackson as critically as we did the other candidates. First, we knew he was not going to become president, so why bother quibbling when he used the wrong figures to describe the defense budget? Hell, no one was going to act on those figures. Second, there was a consciousness of race. I couldn't put my finger on any particular story that I handled differently for fear of being called a racist, but that concern was there all the time. I remember several of us being relieved when a story damaging to Jackson turned out to have been reported by a black reporter. Finally, we didn't treat him like the other candidates because those other candidates didn't do so either. When Jackson got caught calling Jews Hymies and New York Hymietown, his competitors for the nomination were extremely slow to criticize. And when they did, it was in the most mealymouthed language. These were all Democrats and most of them liberal Democrats, but they swallowed Hymietown and Jackson's association with Minister Louis Farrakhan, the militantly anti-Semitic leader of the Nation of Islam.

Jackson played on the weakness, jerking around both the press and his party all through the campaign. Even after Mondale had been nominated formally at San Francisco, Jackson refused to endorse his candidacy and kept bargaining through the press for concessions that were never spelled out. Finally, on Labor Day weekend the Mondale campaign convened a meeting of black leaders from all over the country in St. Paul for the express purpose of getting them behind the ticket and sending that message to their black constituents. But Jackson insisted on a separate meeting with Mondale at his home in suburban North Oaks, just as had been granted the several vice presidential possibilities the nominee had interviewed before the convention. Then, following a routine the campaign had adopted, the two went to a nearby schoolyard, where the national press waited.

It was, of course, the time for Jackson to endorse Mondale, but, as we all watched incredulously, he didn't do it. He said other things. "We have embraced the mission and support the Mondale-Ferraro ticket with great fervor. My support will be wide-based, deep, and intense." And: "We will campaign together and present the solid front we need for victory." But, offered one opportunity after another, he refused to use the word *endorse* when he knew the conventions required it. Through it all, Mondale stood off to the side, his smile fading, his eyes finally turned down to focus on his shoes as he dug a toe into the gravel. It was infuriating, but he took it. Later that night, under pressure from Maynard Jackson, Jesse's leading supporter that year, he finally joined the group in an endorsement. Everyone laughed when Coleman Young, the free-spirited mayor of Detroit, who made no bones about his dislike of Jackson, made a show of affixing a Mondale-Ferraro button to Jesse's jacket. The damage had been done, however, as Jackson was well aware. The whole fiasco solidified the image of Mondale as the weak liberal candidate who had allowed Jackson to push him around.

I had a different view of it. Mondale and I were born only twenty-five days apart and thus had many of the same life experiences. And I was convinced that, unlike me, Mondale hadn't gotten past the liberal guilt in a way that allowed him to say some black guys are okay and some are horse's asses and Jesse Jackson is behaving like one of the latter right now. When I tested that theory on Mondale in a long postelection interview, he brushed it off. If he had gone public with his displeasure right at the moment, he said, it would have made things worse. I thought he was dead wrong, and so did a lot of astute political operatives who had dealt with Jesse Jackson. More than anything else, Jackson was a man who wanted to be "in the room" when the door closed and the important decisions were being made. If Mondale had used that leverage long before the nominating convention, I'm convinced Jackson would have gone along and delivered an endorsement in June.

But if it is true that Jackson had become an albatross to the Mondale ticket, it is equally true that he brought considerable assets to the campaign. Because of his scowling, aggressive manner and his forceful speaking style, he was viewed by many whites as threatening. But the message he delivered to his young followers was anything but threatening. One of the few bright moments of the 1984 general election campaign was watching an audience of black college students in Pine Bluff, Arkansas, light up when Jackson delivered his standard message: Stay off drugs. Stay in school. Get involved. Get out and vote. You are some-body. You are some-body. The students cheered and screamed, and here and there a young girl cried with joy.

It was a special day. A few hours earlier I had started the morning in Little Rock attending a rally for Geraldine Ferraro at the Excelsior Hotel, where Bill Clinton was to meet Paula Jones a few years later. Ferraro had attracted hundreds of women, most of them young mothers leading or pushing their children with them. "I'm showing my girls they can be president," one of them called out to me from behind her stroller. Ferraro's message, like Jackson's, had evoked genuine emotion—women weeping and cheering much as those students did later in the day. It made me wonder why none of this purity of feeling ever gets through the television screens or, for that matter, the newspaper pages. Are we too busy reporting on the details of nine-part programs for reforming farm subsidies? Or is it that we have learned that constituents' displays of enthusiasm often don't translate into votes? Reagan, not Mondale, carried Arkansas in 1984, despite those black kids in Pine Bluff and those young mothers in Little Rock.

When Jesse Jackson ran a second time in 1988, there was less of a division among black leaders. He had shown his ability to enlist black voters in numbers impressive enough so it didn't make sense for them to alienate him. And, anyway, Mike Dukakis didn't have the kind of connection to the black leadership that Fritz Mondale had enjoyed. He was no less reliable in his commitment on the issues, but he had not been in the trenches. Nonetheless, the result was the same. Dukakis conceded nothing of real worth to Jackson but still projected the image of a soft liberal caving in to this loudmouthed black guy. Well into the fall I encountered voters who had made note of the fact that Mike and Kitty Dukakis had invited Jesse Jackson to dinner to celebrate the July 4 holiday. Jackson, disappointed because Dukakis seemed unwilling to discuss the possibility of putting him on the ticket, was his usual difficult self. He bitched after the dinner that the Dukakises had served him New England clam chowder and a big bowl of vanilla ice cream although he was lactose intolerant. And, listening to the Boston Pops play its Independence Day concert on the banks of the Charles River, he sent one of his aides for a box of fried chicken.

One politician who had followed this history closely and understood it fully was Bill Clinton, the upstart governor of Arkansas running for the Democratic nomination in 1992. In June, well before the nominating convention might offer Jackson a national forum for promoting his ambition to be on the ticket, Clinton appeared at a meeting of the Rainbow Coalition in Washington and deliberately and publicly affronted Jackson. With his host sitting by his side, the nominee presumptive criticized the group for giving a hearing to Sister Souljah, a rap singer who had made some rash and racist comments on the Los Angeles riots that grew out of the Rodney King affair. Then in a private session with Jackson, Clinton told him bluntly that he was not being considered for the vice presidential nomination. In a White House interview with Jules Witcover and me later, Clinton denied it had been an insult designed to fulfill a tactical purpose, but we already had learned that the new president was not always totally candid when lack of candor suited his needs.

In fact, the Jackson ploy served a strategic purpose. The important point was that word of Clinton's action spread quickly and widely among those working-class Reagan Democrats. Jackson, moreover, played into Clinton's hands by complaining bitterly for several weeks about how he had been disrespected by the presumptive Democratic nominee, thus making it even clearer to interested whites that this was not another liberal softie like Mondale or Dukakis. Jackson dropped the issue only after several black leaders, most prominently Maynard Jackson again, told him to forget it. The Reagan Democrats didn't, however. I heard about it in October from white voters in both the South and the industrial suburbs of the

Northeast. You can make a case that there was no single Clinton stroke that contributed as much to his success in bringing those voters back to the Democratic line and winning the White House.

Indeed, Clinton played the race card effectively all through the campaign. When his schedule called for a black event, it usually occurred either after the evening television network news broadcasts or very early in the day, when it would be overtaken by a more visually attractive event that would be catnip for the networks. Twelve years of Reagan and Bush had made black leaders very pragmatic. I learned that one day when I asked Lucien Blackwell, a militant black congressman from Philadelphia, how he felt about the Clinton campaign giving the black community a fast brush-off on a swing through the East. He turned me away with a soft answer. If Clinton is seen paying too much attention to people like me, he said, he won't be elected, and getting a Democrat in the White House is what matters.

Black voters as well as their leaders understand the importance of voting self-interest. This was never more clearly demonstrated than on election day of 1991 in the Louisiana gubernatorial election. The Democrat was Edwin Edwards, the notorious Cajun rogue who had served three previous nonconsecutive terms, and the Republican, David Duke, the former official of the Ku Klux Klan, whose glib manner couldn't hide his anti-Semitism and racism. By this stage of his long and colorful career, Edwards was damaged goods, but the entire state establishment—churches, business and industry, unions, professional groups, educators, newspapers—was in a state of panic at the prospect of Duke winning the governorship. Elect this Nazi, the message went out, and New Orleans will be a ghost town.

But the voters most alarmed were clearly the blacks who make up almost 31 percent of the voting-age population of the state. And they used their franchise fully. On election day I left my hotel in downtown New Orleans late in the morning, planning to kill the afternoon until the polls closed playing the horses at the Fair Grounds Race Track. On the way I drove through a half dozen black precincts and found the streets were alive with women, many pushing strollers or tugging toddlers along with them as they hurried to the polling places. Before noon, several poll watchers reported, most voters already had cast their ballots. When it was over the black turnout ran higher than in presidential years and overwhelmingly—probably 95 percent or higher—for Edwards, who won the election with 61 percent to 39 for Duke.

Like others covering the story, I first saw those numbers as an encouraging testimonial to the good sense and decent instincts of Louisiana voters. But on closer inspection, the story wasn't anything of the kind. Although he lost, David Duke carried more than 55 percent of the white vote and an even higher share of the white Protestant vote. No wonder Andy Young couldn't get elected in Georgia.

CHAPTER 14

LIFE WITH
MCLAUGHLIN

I made my first appearance on a national television show during the Democratic presidential primary campaign in Florida early in 1972. It was NBC's *Meet the Press*, and the guest was Senator Henry M. Jackson of Washington, one of several candidates being trounced in the primary by Governor George Corley Wallace of Alabama. I was pleased. My colleagues from the *Times* and *Post* and *Wall Street Journal* already were frequent panelists, but for a reporter from the Gannett Newspapers, it was a big deal. It was made all the more memorable by Jim Naughton, who was covering the primary for the *Times* and was, not incidentally, a world-class practical joker.

We were staying at the Four Ambassadors in Miami, but the program was to be televised from Tampa, so I was up early Sunday morning to catch a flight after a long night in the saloon. I was still in the shower washing out the cobwebs when the doorbell rang, so I wrapped myself in a towel to answer it. When I opened the door, there were Naughton and four or five of the boys, each carrying a box of talcum powder and a huge puff. They burst in, shouting, "Makeup, makeup, makeup," and covered me from head to foot. It took another half hour to wash it all off and rush to catch the plane.

There wasn't anything memorable about the program itself, but I conducted myself well enough so that over the next several years I became part of that stable of reporters from which the Sunday morning questioners were regularly drawn. Even those sporadic appearances, moreover, gave me a hint at the enormous power of television. Strangers began speaking to me in airports, and there would be an occasional call from a lecture agent recruiting me for a paid speech before some business group. Just being on television, even infrequently, was a credential as an important player you apparently could not earn simply by doing what I considered far more serious work, reporting and writing for a newspaper. It doesn't matter what you say, it's just getting your face on the screen.

I had my first chance at a regular television slot in 1980, when Steve Friedman of NBC hired David Broder of *The Washington Post* and me, by now with the *Washington Star,* to be on the *Today* program during the campaign. Tom Brokaw was the host, and we appeared with Tom Pettit, a droll and perceptive correspondent for NBC, once or twice a week during the primaries, usually once in advance of each event to talk about what was supposed to happen and then the morning after to explain why it didn't come out quite that way. For Broder and me, it was an ideal way to get a foot in the door without the television work interfering with our primary responsibilities to our newspapers. It was a totally unscripted four or five minutes in which we quarreled in a good-humored way among ourselves.

Brokaw was particularly good because he was so quick on his feet. On one occasion I appeared with a small Band-Aid next to my earlobe. As the segment ended, Brokaw told the viewers that next time he would find out what that bandage was all about.

"A beautiful young stewardess lost her head and bit me," I replied.

To which, without missing a beat, Brokaw added: "And immediately fell dead."

There were some obvious perils for Broder and me in doing political analysis on network television. We didn't feel comfortable going beyond what we felt comfortable writing for our newspapers. Still, we didn't want our analysis to be so bland that it would tell the viewers nothing they couldn't find in a wire story in their morning newspapers. Pettit, feeling no similar constraints, demonstrated how hazardous it could be early in the campaign.

We appeared the morning after the Iowa precinct caucuses, in which George Bush had scored an upset victory over Ronald Reagan. Although all of the political press corps had been reporting that Bush was showing surprising strength and that Reagan was appearing complacent, the reality of a Reagan defeat was clearly a major story made larger by the fact that it was unexpected. Asked by Brokaw what it meant, Pettit declared Reagan was "dead." There was a momentary pause until I offered a mealymouthed qualifier, "Dead is a long time, Tom," and we went on with a discussion of how it would affect subsequent tests. As it turned out, Pettit's conclusion proved premature. Twenty-eight days later Reagan won the New Hampshire primary and was once again on the road to a first-ballot nomination. Pettit's gaffe became a running gag on the show through the spring. And the morning after Reagan nailed down the nomination at Detroit in July, they opened our *Today* segment with a tape of Tom pronouncing him "dead."

Broder and I continued on *Today* for the next ten years, appearing with one of the New York anchors, Bryant Gumbel most often and occasionally Jane Pauley or, later, Katie Couric. After Pettit moved on to another NBC assignment, our partner during most of that period was Ken Bode, then the network's premier political reporter. Like Brokaw and Pettit, Bode was quick-witted and acute. More important, he had a firsthand knowledge of both the substance and the flavor of American politics not often found in television correspondents.

As a political reporter for a newspaper, I tended to categorize television correspondents who covered campaigns into two broad groups. One was made up of those who essentially covered the spectacle of the campaign and relied on their on-the-air skills to sound authoritative. The second, much smaller, was made up of those who covered the campaigns much as we did and always knew more than they could use on the air. Their reporting was their own rather than being derivative. The best examples of the second group were Bode of NBC, Bruce Morton of CBS, and Herb Kaplow of ABC, but there were others at different points along the way. They would include both Brokaw and Pettit, Richard Valeriani of NBC, Roger Mudd and Bob Pierpoint of CBS, Sander Vanocur of ABC, and Gene Randall of CNN.

You could tell the difference when you had dinner or spent an evening in the bar with them. Everyone, print or electronic, had the same database underlying his analysis of what was happening and speculation about what might happen. We knew the same statistics and the same people. By contrast, those in the first group, although they might be excellent reporters, lacked either the time or the motivation to learn enough about the political world to make them interesting companions. This was true even of some reporters with long careers in newspapers who moved on to television and simply stopped going to the trouble of reporting as thoroughly as they had before. More than once I can recall sitting down for a drink with an old colleague from newspapers who had moved on to television and learning that he wasn't keeping up with changing sources and demographics and campaign techniques. It was a matter not of him shirking some duty but of different priorities. The networks don't feel the need for full-time on-camera political reporters, in part because they have off-air experts, such as Hal Bruno of ABC, a longtime *Newsweek* correspondent, who keep up in the same way print reporters do.

Broder and I felt our segments with the *Today* show lost something when Bode left the network. We now found ourselves working with Andrea Mitchell, a White House reporter without Bode's familiarity with the material. Although she was the television professional and we the amateurs, she seemed ill at ease—friendly enough but not comfortable with the kind of badinage that had made the segments distinctive. On the contrary, we noted, she arrived for each segment armed with a sheet of paper bearing notes on points she intended to make, apparently whatever the direction of the discussion. The cameramen, we noticed, seemed to make a point of their own by showing those note sheets. Whatever the reason, the segments were far more orderly and dull than they had been. And soon the length was being trimmed to three minutes, which would turn out to be even less when the time came. We began to ask ourselves if it was worth getting up that early in the morning for something so unsatisfactory.

We also were uneasy about being presented as the equivalent of two other "Washingon insiders" who appeared on a different day of the week, Bob Squier and Roger Ailes. The difference, important to us but less so to NBC, was that Democrat Squier and Republican Ailes were partisan political consultants, a distinction that was sort of glossed over in the way they were presented on the air. All in all, it seemed to be time to move on, so in 1988 we left *Today* and went to work for CNN through the 1992 campaign.

By that time, however, I was already established on television as a regular on *The McLaughlin Group*.

When John McLaughlin called me early in 1981 and invited me to take part in a pilot for a new panel show, I knew almost nothing about him. He was, I knew, a Jesuit priest from Rhode Island who had ended up writing speeches for President Richard M. Nixon and defending him until the last disclosure on Watergate. Since then he had been hanging around town for several years doing talk radio and writing a Washington column for William F. Buckley's magazine, the *National Review,* which I read only occasionally. The other panelists for the pilot were Bob Novak, Judith Miller, who covered foreign policy for *The New York Times,* and Chuck Stone, a black columnist in Philadelphia. We apparently were going to have a politically correct cast, but McLaughlin's first goal was to produce a program that would supposedly replicate dinner party arguments in the nation's capital and be livelier than *Agronsky and Company,* the long-running talk show on the local CBS outlet chaired by Martin Agronsky, which had lost much of its bite with the death of Peter Lisagor of the *Chicago Daily News* five years earlier. The cast there was clearly more establishment oriented—Hugh Sidey of *Time* and the columnists James J. Kilpatrick, Carl Rowan, and George Will— and far better mannered.

Neither Novak nor I expected it to work. Driving back downtown from the studio in Virginia after taping the pilot, we agreed it was probably not going to fly, but, what the hell, at least we had been paid. By the time we went on the air, however, it began to look at least possible, although with a different cast of characters. On the pilot Miller clearly felt limited in what she could say by the fact that she was a hard-news reporter rather than a columnist licensed to spout off on any subject. And Stone had been handicapped by the simple fact that he worked out of town and didn't have day-to-day familiarity with the Washington topics that were fodder for the show. He later complained to someone in print that I had been condescending toward him, which he gratuitously attributed to racism on my part. My real complaint was that he didn't know his ass from third base about the issues we were discussing, but I didn't press the point. There are some arguments that aren't worth having.

In any case, by the time we went on the air, in May 1981, the panel included, in addition to Novak and me, the syndicated columnist Pat Buchanan and Morton Kondracke, then with *The New Republic* magazine. Kondracke was supposed to be the other liberal, arrayed with me against the full mooners Novak and Buchanan. But as the Reagan administration went along and the country moved to the right, so did Kondracke—to the point that he wrote a piece for *The Wall Street Journal* in 1984 about why he might vote for Ronald Reagan and was tickled pink when Reagan called him. Some liberal.

In those early days, the show was fun to do and McLaughlin easy to live with off the air even if inclined to periods of ranting on camera. He would telephone each of us on Thursday, the day before taping, to give us his list of topics and to solicit our opinions on both those he had chosen and those he had left out. Sometimes he even would make a change if several of us argued, for example, that you can't ignore such and such a development this week.

Unfortunately for the culture and the egos of the participants, the show was an immediate success. There never had been an ostensibly serious public affairs program in which people repeatedly interrupted each other, shouted for attention, delivered ad hominem attacks on one another, and derided the moderator. McLaughlin had guessed there was a market for such a program, and he was correct. The ratings rose rapidly on the five NBC-owned and operated channels, and, with the sponsorship of WTTW in Chicago, more and more public broadcasting stations began to show *McLaughlin,* sometimes at the expense of the far more thoughtful *Washington Week in Review.*

The audience was eclectic. In one week I ran into viewers who included a black kid parking cars at a garage in New Orleans, a truck-stop waitress in Iowa, and a stockbroker at the next table at a

Chicago restaurant. College students stopped me in airports and asked earnestly how I could stand being on the same panel with that fascist Novak. And when I would explain that, despite our different views, Novak was one of my oldest friends, they would walk away in disbelief.

The instant celebrity, limited though it was, was a heady experience. You could write your fingers off for twenty-five years, Novak and I agreed, and never get the kind of hearing you could get from shooting off your mouth on television for a half hour every week. The viewers obviously took the show more seriously than it deserved. I would get long, earnest letters and even longer telephone calls from people who felt their points of view were being ignored. There were also abusive calls and letters. In my case, the latter often focused on the size of my stomach. Such salutations as "Fatso" or (a particular favorite) "You Fat Fuck" were common. If the letters were signed—most of them were not—I would occasionally send one back, scrawling across the top my "thanks for pointing out the fat part—I had missed it." Or I would follow the example of Stephen Young, briefly a senator from Ohio, who dealt with his most outraged critics by writing, "I think you should know some lunatic is writing crazy letters and signing your name." Most people, however, are nice and their praise is flattering, even if I feel a bit of a fraud when I hear it. And many of the angry ones are people frustrated because no one listens to them about how to deal with the Taiwan question or Social Security or whatever. Then they turn on their television sets and see all these know-it-alls in Washington blathering away.

The politicians clearly took these talk shows seriously. We taped Friday afternoons, as did our rival program, *Inside Washington,* which succeeded *Agronsky* and was moderated by Gordon Peterson. So Friday mornings the panelists could expect telephone calls from parties to some controversy in Congress making sure that we understood their position and obviously hoping we would adopt it on the air. An aide to the Senate minority leader at the time, Senator Robert Byrd of West Virginia, called me almost every week to tell me the senator was available for an interview on the telephone that very moment. In fact, I had no particular reason to speak to Byrd, but it would have been unseemly not to take advantage of the "opportunity," so I would telephone, thank the senator for giving me a minute or two of his time, then listen to him describe the Democratic position on whatever issue was in the news. I also received frequent Friday calls from House members who had been assigned to attempt similar preconditioning of panelists. But most of them were candid enough to say something like this: "I'm supposed to give you a sales pitch on this thing, but I guess you already know where we stand, so, what the hell, have a good weekend." We both knew it was a game.

One of the special problems of the *McLaughlin* show was that so many people paid close attention to the predictions we delivered at the end of each program. Some of the panelists were so concerned about their "scores" they would telephone sources ahead of the taping trying to find something to predict with reasonable certainty it would come true. I would wing it, secure in the knowledge that if I couldn't think of anything on the air, I could manage by nodding sagely and saying, "Two more members of the Reagan cabinet will be gone by June 1"—a safe bet at any time in any administration. If McLaughlin demanded to know which two, I would simply look smug and tell him to buy my newspaper.

If you allowed a little fact to intrude on these predictions, there could be trouble. One day in 1986 I ran into Senator Charles Mathias of Maryland just outside the Senate Office Building. We stood on the street corner chatting for five minutes or so, and I was struck by how dispirited he seemed to be about the chances of his moderate Republican views prevailing on any of the topics we discussed. So that Friday, stuck for a prediction, I guessed out loud that Mathias would retire rather than seek another term.

Early Monday morning his administrative assistant called me. "Do you know something we don't know?" she asked.

"Not at all," I replied. "If I knew something, I would have put it in the *Sun*. I was just guessing."

When, three days later, Mathias suddenly announced he would not seek another term, I was given totally undeserved credit for having such good sources I knew about it before his staff. I accepted the plaudits with a proper show of modesty, muttering unconvincingly that it was "just a guess." Mathias sent me a note saying he decided to retire to spare me the embarrassment of being wrong.

If the viewers and politicians took the show too seriously, so did McLaughlin. He began to believe we were performing some educational function for the great unwashed. He wrote longer and longer introductions to issues, as if our viewers had been on the moon all week. And he became increasingly testy about the whole thing. He was always irked when I would be quoted saying that it was "just television" and that my "serious job" was writing a newspaper column five days a week for the *Sun*.

After the first year or two McLaughlin never bothered to consult us on the topics. Instead, some member of his staff would telephone us the night before the taping to tell us what the issues would be. And if we howled, we would be told that "Dr. McLaughlin," as they were required to identify him, thought the issues he had chosen were not getting enough attention. Sometimes he would indulge in what he called counterprogramming, meaning that he would consciously ignore the collective news judgments of everyone else during the week leading up to the taping and choose topics that had not appeared on a single front page or network news show.

McLaughlin also began to isolate himself behind the staff of young people for whom General Electric, the program's sponsor, paid the bills. This led to a strange situation when I complained about the way the money from our "McLaughlin Group Live" lecture fees was being divided. The standard had become $2,500 per panelist for these appearances, a more than adequate amount by any reasonable standard considering how little effort was involved. The only heavy lifting required was spending more time with McLaughlin, who became even more ambassadorial in his manner when some lecture client was paying the bill. There were even a couple of occasions when we arrived at the host city airport to find a limo waiting for McLaughlin and a van for the hoi polloi, meaning the panelists. The hidden advantage there was that you managed to spend less time in McLaughlin's company, always a blessing. On the road he was particularly hard to take because he would let the shows run an hour or more beyond the hour for which they were usually scheduled. So we earned our twenty-five hundred each.

Then I discovered that the gross fee for the group was often $20,000 or higher and that, even after a commission to the lecture agent, McLaughlin himself was netting $7,000 or $8,000, sometimes even $10,000 from each appearance. So I wrote him a note and said that although I agreed he was entitled to more than any of the panelists, there was a question of how much more was equitable. From that point on, I said, before I agreed to any live appearances, I would have to know the gross amount and how it was being divided. If $2,500 seemed reasonable in some cases, I would accept it, but I wanted to know the whole thing.

McLaughlin simply stiffed me. He never replied and never returned my telephone call. From that point on, I never did another McLaughlin lecture date.

In the summer of 1986 it began to appear that there might be a strike against NBC by the National Association of Broadcast Employees and Technicians, the union representing the cameramen and sound and lighting engineers. General Electric was playing hardball or, more precisely, practicing Boulwarism. This is a strategy, named after a GE executive of another era, Lemuel Boulware, for his tactics in a strike in Schenectady, that involves simply announcing that a new labor contract would be put into place on a particular date, signed or not. I told McLaughlin that if there was a walkout, I wouldn't be able to cross the NABET picket line. The strikers included not only those who taped his show every week but those whom I had come to know doing the *Today* show for all those years.

When the strike started I called McLaughlin to explain why I couldn't cross the line, but, once again, he would not talk to me. Instead, after two or three weeks, he directed one of his kids to call me with a message that "Dr. McLaughlin wants you to know that the strike might prove to be a long one." I replied that I hoped not, but if that were the case, so be it. A few more weeks and another call from an agent for Dr. McLaughlin telling me that the pickets were marching on Nebraska Avenue in front of the NBC entrance but I could come in through the Presbyterian church parking lot next door and not have to cross the line after all. So much for his understanding of how things work. Finally, a few weeks later a call from a somewhat higher up staff person telling me that since I had a personal services contract, it might be possible for McLaughlin to force me legally to come to the taping. I sent the word back: That would be beautiful. Make my day. It would look great in *The Washington Post*. Finally, after sixteen weeks the strike ended and I returned to the set. McLaughlin and I had not exchanged a word about it during the entire time.

The strike episode was revealing about how strong the appeal of television time can be, as well as perhaps how irrelevant unions have become to reporters in Washington. During that sixteen weeks only three people invited to replace me refused to do so—Mark Shields, the longtime Democratic political consultant who had become a columnist; Hodding Carter, the State Department spokesman in the Carter administration; and Gloria Borger, a talented reporter whose career I had helped along slightly when she was a beginner at the *Washington Star*. All the other liberals invited to occupy my seat found a rationalization for doing so. And as for my fellow liberal on the panel, Mort Kondracke, he was comfortable crossing the line because the unions had become "way out of control" and no longer deserved support.

As the program grew more successful, McLaughlin became even more difficult to abide. His ego, always greater than seemed justified by his charm or achievements, swelled to enormous proportions. He began to behave as if he could do the program with four clothing store dummies, and he grew more and more autocratic. The tapings took forever. Frequently he would force us to cool our heels in the green room for an hour and a half or longer after the appointed times while he sat on the set, surrounded by frightened young staff members, and revised and rehearsed his "reads"—meaning the introductory and transitional material that would appear on his TelePrompTer. In fact, none of this required the kind of time he was taking. He liked to show who was in charge, and he didn't have any serious work to do on a Friday afternoon anyway. If he found out that one of the panelists needed to catch a plane and was pressed for time, the reads would take even longer. The only times we seemed to tape quickly were the occasions on which he had a plane to catch.

Moreover, McLaughlin would grow angry when any of us—usually me—complained about how long the process took. He would never confront me, of course, but he would dispatch his principal producer, a young woman whom we all liked named Allyson Kennedy, to convey the message in the most indirect way.

One of the manifestations of McLaughlin's hauteur was his resentment of Novak's role in the show. The Prince of Darkness, as he has been known for years, had strong conservative views and a combative style. He made everyone else seem to be appearing on the air in black and white while he was in Technicolor. He was the star, and McLaughlin was clearly irked. He began assigning one of his young staff people to count all the words each of us said during the half hour show every week. To no one's surprise, these counts found that Novak most often said the most and that I most often said the least, findings that bothered neither of us. Nor did Novak take the hint as the counts continued to appear every week and McLaughlin continued to make oblique comments about them without, of course, confronting anyone. Novak was a voluble partisan, and it just wasn't his nature to worry about how many words he was uttering or, for that matter, what John McLaughlin thought about it.

The tension between them erupted on the set one Friday early in 1988. During a segment on the primary campaign, Novak accused McLaughlin of being opportunistic in trying to butter up someone in the Dukakis campaign he might need later on. It was an accusation we frequently made against McLaughlin and one that we knew was accurate. Usually he laughed them off. But this time, for reasons that never were made clear, was different. When we broke for a commercial, McLaughlin started screaming imprecations at Novak at the top of his lungs. His face was red, and the cords in his neck turned white. Novak tried to reply, but he was more startled than angry and McLaughlin wouldn't listen. He grew more and more offensive, suggesting finally that if Novak didn't like the way he ran the show, he could take a hike.

I finally told him to cool down, turned to Novak, and said, "If you want to walk out on this son of a bitch, I'll go with you." Novak shook his head, and by the time the commercial break ended a minute or so later, McLaughlin had regained control of himself. We finished the taping somewhat awkwardly.

But the next week McLaughlin used a substitute for Novak on the show following the Iowa caucuses. The rule generally had been that the four regulars would appear each week unless one of us was traveling on a story or otherwise committed or unless McLaughlin wanted to substitute a panelist with particular expertise on one of the topics for the week. Now, however, he began using the substitutes as a way of meting out punishment to those of us who displeased him. Leaving Novak off the panel after a major political event on which he had done a lot of reporting was clearly self-defeating, but McLaughlin was more interested in his control of the program than in its content. When it happened again shortly thereafter, Novak tried to arrange a meeting to deal with the issue directly, but McLaughlin sent word that he was too busy to see him. So Novak took matters into his own hands and set about producing a rival show. By fall it was accomplished, and Novak left to produce and appear on *The Capital Gang* on CNN.

Novak was replaced by another friend of mine from our days together at the *Star*, Fred Barnes. Fred was an accomplished reporter and one of many who, for reasons I never understood, simultaneously embraced religious fundamentalism and political conservatism as they approached middle age. He was also an articulate and forceful advocate on the panel. But Novak left a hole. *The McLaughlin Group* was never as much fun thereafter, either for me or, I suspect, for the audience.

My own break with McLaughlin came several years later and without a dramatic confrontation on the set. McLaughlin had become increasingly autocratic and egocentric—and increasingly irritated at my bitching about the time being wasted in taping the shows. The beginning of the end came at the 1996 Republican convention in San Diego, when, after taping our second show from the convention site, we all went to a luncheon with people described as GE executives who were in fact largely customers who bought a lot of GE appliances for their retail stores. During the lunch McLaughlin announced that the program was now going to be distributed internationally through some mechanism I never quite understood. Then, when he called on each of the panelists for a few words, I observed that now we could take credit for "dumbing down the whole world." It was said in good humor, and the appliance dealers laughed at what I think they saw as quintessential *McLaughlin Group* badinage. McLaughlin, however, was not amused, although he said nothing to me at the time.

A couple of weeks later I discovered that I was being replaced with a substitute for both of the programs being taped at the Democratic convention in Chicago. I was mildly annoyed because it would cost me twelve hundred dollars in lost fees. Nor did it make sense. I had better sources at that convention than any of the other panelists and also was old enough to have covered the 1968 convention, to which it inevitably was being compared. I did not learn until somewhat later, nonetheless, that I had been dropped as a punishment for my wisecrack about "dumbing down" the world—and even that information came to me by a circuitous route.

With Ally Kennedy long since departed and another producer in charge, the whole system changed. Rather than the assumption being that the regular panelists would appear each week, we were told every Tuesday by a telephone call from some frightened staff member that "Dr. McLaughlin would like you to be on the show this week" or, alternatively, that "Dr. McLaughlin won't be needing you this week."

Now I had reached the point at which I couldn't simply roll with the punches. I found that I was getting angry every Tuesday at having to wait for the moderator's blessing, angrier every Thursday when told the issues, and still angrier every Friday when we sat through the ordeal of waiting to do the taping. At this stage in my life I was rarely angry about anything, and I began to ask myself why I would allow something as trivial as a television program to set me off. So one week late in 1996 I sent McLaughlin a fax: "Effective immediately, I am ending all association with *The McLaughlin Group*. Good luck and bye-bye."

An hour later I sent a copy to John Carmody, the television writer for the *Post*, to whom I explained I was quitting because I had grown tired of dealing with McLaughlin off the set. I made a point of saying I was not complaining about the content of the show; after fifteen years it would be the ultimate hypocrisy to suddenly develop standards. My concern was that if I didn't take the initiative in describing the reasons for my departure, someone else would explain. The story would get around that I was a drag on the ratings or that

I had an inoperable cancer or that I was involved in an unhealthy relationship with a sheep. Washington can be a tough town.

The reaction to my decision spoke volumes about how powerful television has become. No one could imagine anyone walking away from a regular slot on a television program. I looked at it another way—that the proof of how compelling such a slot can be was the fact I had stuck it out with McLaughlin for fifteen years.

Most of it was money. I always told people I used the show to send my daughter Jessica to college and medical school, which was accurate but only up to a point. Jessie was such an outstanding student and worked so hard at after-school jobs that she would have made it on her own if necessary. The real reason was selfish. Appearing on television allowed me to enjoy the luxury of being a newspaper reporter without having to live on a newspaper reporter's salary. I could get an editor's pay without doing the work.

I didn't want to be the pale guy sitting in the office, shuffling budgets and expense accounts and envying the reporters on the street covering the good stories. Not all stories are exciting or interesting, of course. And for every good one, you spend two or three rainy Friday nights at the airport in Atlanta trying to fly standby and ending up as the fat man in a middle seat. But the important thing was the freedom to make your own assignments and to get out of the office to report and write.

The show itself paid only $600 a week, but my lecture fees rose to a respectable level for a shabby scribbler—topping out at $6,000 or $7,000 once in a while, although usually somewhat less. One year I earned close to $100,000; most years it was about half that much. I also had a modest salary and health insurance from the *Sun* and some income from syndication of our column by Tribune Media Services, from a column Jules Witcover and I wrote every week for the *National Journal,* and from books and magazine articles as well as NBC and CNN. The critical thing was that I was not so dependent on any single employer that I could be easily jerked around. Having gone down with the *Star,* I didn't want to be on the beach in what were supposed to be my golden years.

There was, of course, a price to be paid for doing the lectures— endless dreary arguments about "buckraking" journalists selling their souls for honoraria. My partner and I followed a policy of not speaking for money to any group that we might cover, meaning essentially any political organization. But otherwise I take the money. I didn't worry about conflicts of interest when I addressed the Grocery Manufacturers of America or the National Aggregates Association. And the fact was that no group who hired me for a speech ever tried to lean on me for a column.

I did have reservations about doing the *McLaughlin* show, however. I knew that my partner and such close friends as Dave Broder disapproved of my participation. And there is some validity in the old saw about lying down with dogs and getting fleas. Broder pressed me with particular urgency to leave when McLaughlin became the target of a sexual harrassment lawsuit brought by a former employee. But I felt that quitting then would send a message that McLaughlin was guilty. And, although I had seen him verbally abuse young staff members often enough that I had interceded on a couple of occasions, I had never seen a sexual element or even the hint of one in that abuse. As far as I knew, he was just a loudmouthed bully.

When I finally quit, I realized I probably could have done so much earlier without risking needed income. I soon became a regular on *Inside Washington*, the rival program that outdraws *McLaughlin* in Washington but has little national distribution. Gordon Peterson, the moderator, is a nice man whose ego, if any, is well hidden. The show is taped on Fridays in no more than and usually less than ninety minutes, arrival to departure, with never a harsh word. The producer, Tina Gulland, and the panelists, Charles Krauthammer, Evan Thomas, and Nina Totenberg, are all civil to one another, both on and off the air. I can go for weeks without getting angry at anyone except perhaps some jockey choking my horse on the backstretch.

Would I have preferred never to have done *McLaughlin*? Sure. I realized how grotesque it could become some weeks. I knew I was risking whatever reputation I had gained for being a serious reporter. But I didn't have the luxury of doing only the things that were above criticism, unless of course I chose to spend my career making a marginal living or becoming an editor. I didn't enjoy the option of writing two columns a week for the *Times* or *Post* for two hundred thousand a year. I needed that occasional gig at the annual meeting of the Smokeless Tobacco Council or the Mortgage Bankers Association.

A better question would be one that Tom Shales, television critic for the *Post,* once asked me at the end of a long interview about *The McLaughlin Group:* If you weren't on the show, would you watch it? I wouldn't answer then, but I can now: No.

CHAPTER 15

A CAST

OF THOUSANDS

Covering politics isn't just about covering presidential campaigns. The presidential story is, by any definition, the big one, but campaigns for the Senate and House of Representatives are often more interesting. And I've always enjoyed writing about governors and mayors because they have to make real decisions that have a direct meaning for their constituents. By contrast, faced with a problem, a senator or congressman will follow the first instinct to hold a public hearing and bury the issue in blather.

The early stages of presidential campaigns are the most rewarding for full-time political reporters. You can travel with a candidate and spend some time with him, take him out for dinner or even a few pops once in a while, before his campaign becomes a mob scene. You can learn a lot that cannot be learned when there is always an entourage of television crews. By the final weeks of, let's say, a New Hampshire primary campaign, the state is overrun with reporters and photographers who are covering primarily the spectacle they themselves create. Most of them don't know the candidate or his advisers, let alone the local activists who may be knowledgeable. They might as well be covering the World Series. They get in the way, and they change the nature of the event. When there are eight camera crews, including two from Europe and one from Japan, at a luncheon meeting of the Manchester Rotary Club at the Chateau Restaurant, it isn't the usual meeting.

And it's not just the electronic journalists. There is also a late invasion of print reporters from every newspaper and magazine that makes any pretense of covering politics, most of them with no sources beyond *The Boston Globe* and thus doing reporting that is largely derivative. Sometimes I think they all should be turned back at the Massachusetts state line, but what the hell, they have to make a living, too. And I know there have been times when my own reporting has been derived from someone else's spadework.

The rewarding times, however, are rarely, if ever, mob scenes. For me the golden moments covering politics have always been the times spent on stories that were especially satisfying either because I learned something interesting and perhaps even significant that I could pass on to readers before my competitors got onto it or—more often—just because I had a hell of a good time.

Some of the stories of which I have been the proudest didn't make any waves or even earn much attention, let alone praise, from my editors. In 1970, for example, I reported and wrote a series of articles forecasting the transformation of the South from solidly Democratic to solidly Republican. No one lauded me for a dazzling insight, although I allowed myself to enjoy the thought. In 1973 I did a series of pieces for Gannett on how the separation of the races had evolved and hardened in the five years after the Kerner Commission found, in its famous phrase, "two societies, separate but unequal." Again, only I knew how apprehensive, sometimes even frightened, I had been while reporting on life in the black ghettos of New York and Chicago and Cleveland and Detroit, so I could contrast it with white life in the suburbs. Thus, figuratively at least, I slapped myself on the back and told myself, Way to go, you've still got your fastball.

The truth was that I reported and wrote that series largely for that personal satisfaction. I had been sent up to Ithaca late in 1972 to help the Gannett paper there with a story. During the course of my visit I went to a bar one night with several of their young reporters, who wanted to know what it was like to cover Washington and the president and Congress and all that big stuff. I was happily name-dropping when one young punk suggested that my reporting life had become mostly covering official actions, reading reports, and attending press conferences. In other words, I inferred, he figured that at forty-five I no longer did reporting that might get my hands dirty. I don't know why that suggestion ticked me off—it may have been the leggy young woman reporter at the table whom I was trying to impress—and I didn't rise to the bait. But I remember thinking to myself, I'll show that little asshole some reporting.

On the face of it, I am guilty of gross immodesty in recalling great successes and failing to recall many gaffes. But the quality that makes a reporter spend his life at the trade is the ability to tell himself that he is giving the readers information and insight they otherwise would not have at their disposal, even if the editors are too dense to see the beauty of his work. More often, however, the desire to serve the reader well is secondary to the desire to cover "a good story" and beat the competition. Or, to cut to the heart of the matter, many times the attraction of a story is that the politicians involved are interesting and fun to cover. I like politicians who are willing to wear their hearts on their sleeves and are not embarrassed to admit they enjoy the game and feel some passion for the causes they advocate.

Robert Strauss was one of them. He never made any secret of the fact he enjoyed it when a president, even a Republican one, asked his advice or sent him off as an ambassador in some touchy situation. He relished his stature in all its facets. When he built a fancy new swimming pool at his home in Dallas and friends teased him about the fact that he didn't swim, Strauss explained it this way: "Every night I come home and make myself a drink and then I stand at the window and look out at the pool and I say to myself, 'Strauss, you're one rich sumbitch.'" When a bawdy old lady on the Democratic National Committee retired and asked for a picture with her old friend Strauss, he signed it: "To Ruth, still the best lay on the DNC."

Bob Strauss was simply consumed by the game. One autumn day while he was serving as Democratic national chairman in the mid-1970s, I ran into him on a Braniff flight to Dallas. We were both sitting in first class (which in my case means I must have been going

to Texas to give a speech, because first-class travel is one of the an-
cillary benefits of the lecture circuit but not of newspaper reporting), and we got into the martinis pretty forcefully. Then Strauss
told me how upset he was that John Connally, his close friend from
their undergraduate days at the University of Texas, had defected to
the Republican Party and was serving in Richard Nixon's cabinet as
secretary of the Treasury. It made things so awkward, Strauss said,
that he was planning to step aside as party chairman at the end of
the year. Under most circumstances this would have qualified as a
story for the *Washington Star,* and I had the story and, all the better,
the *Post* didn't. But I never wrote the story because I didn't believe
it. I knew that when it came down to it Strauss would never surren-
der the chairmanship until his term ran out. He liked to say that
being a party chairman was like making love to a gorilla, "You don't
quit when you get tired, you quit when the gorilla gets tired." He
was having too much fun. And he was good at it. His job as chairman in the aftermath of 1972 was to make the party whole enough
to be in contention in 1976, and it was.

At one point in the early 1980s, after his stint as Carter's trade
ambassador, Strauss began to think about running for president
himself. People were telling him he ought to do it, he told me when
we had breakfast at the Watergate Hotel one morning. It wasn't as
if there were all these great choices already out there, he went on. I
agreed with that point although I didn't say so. In fact, Bob Strauss
was more streetwise than anyone ever nominated for president by
either party in my time covering politics. And simply in terms of raw
intelligence, if it mattered, his only peer was probably Jimmy Carter.
But I didn't tell him any of that at breakfast because the last thing
he needed was reinforcement of his ego. Instead, I reminded him
that morning that he was also a Jew from Texas who had made a lot
of money in a lot of deals everybody would be poking into. And,
more to the point, he was a devout wiseass. If he became a candidate, he would be forever explaining his smart mouth. What he
should do, I told him, was go back upstairs to his apartment and
take a cold shower. Helen Strauss has been forever grateful. Bob
and I remained friends. And the country has had a succession of bad
presidents.

The purists in the newspaper business, those who think of themselves as journalists, will contend that it is a mistake and perhaps even a mortal sin for a reporter to become a friend of a news source, that a certain distance is needed to maintain the proper detachment. I can't argue with that, and I have tried to follow that policy throughout my working life. But sometimes it hasn't been possible. I couldn't help but go into the tank for Strauss; he was too good company.

Hubert Humphrey also was a man who wore his heart on his sleeve. And I spent one of the best days of my life with him late in August 1970, when, having lost the 1968 presidential election, he was starting a comeback by running for the Senate again. There was no serious doubt Humphrey would be elected, so it made sense to fly up to St. Paul, do the story early in the campaign, and get it into print before everyone did it.

As it happened, Humphrey was spending a Sunday flying around the outskirts of the Twin Cities, Minneapolis and St. Paul, in a helicopter, dropping down on a state plowing contest and then a series of street fairs and carnivals and church socials—anywhere, in short, there were a few hands to be shaken. It was one of those stunning days they sometimes get in Minnesota in late summer. The air was cool, the colors clear, the water in the lakes below us bright and inviting. But, most of all, there was Hubert Humphrey at his best, brimming over with fresh enthusiasm for a new campaign. It was a small chopper, carrying a pilot and the two of us, and we flew low from stop to stop so Humphrey could point out the features of the landscape—and his role in them over the years—to his visitor. "You see that," he said, pointing down to a stretch of the Minnesota River. "I got a nine-foot channel dredged in that river, opened it up." Or, a few minutes later, "See that schoolhouse, that's where we had some great teachers pushing their kids way ahead on math and science so we got 'em some extra money." Or, gesturing at a small industrial plant, "I was there for the dedication, gave them a short speech, or as short as I can manage."

In the late afternoon we began landing on the grounds of churches, mostly Catholic, where picnics were under way. Humphrey would shake hands for a few minutes, sample the potato salad, and say a few words. Then he might take a small drink of cheap whiskey in a paper cup "and one for my copilot here"—meaning me—to tide us over until the next stop. By the time we landed back at the airport shortly before sundown, I was relieved to find there was a driver to meet us. I was even happier to eat a large, sobering bowl of Muriel Humphrey's beef soup while Hubert told me more stories about what we had seen. I have no idea what kind of a president Humphrey would have been. But he loved the power of his position not just for itself but for the things it allowed him to do, which is the right reason to be in politics. And he was the perfect companion for a beautiful August day flying over the lakes.

There was, however, one occasion on which Humphrey's enthusiasm might have been overdone. He came to dinner with our political writers' background group in Washington one night not long after being treated for bladder cancer. While we were having drinks somebody made the mistake of asking him about his illness, whereupon Humphrey launched into an excruciatingly detailed and vivid description of how modern medicine treats bladder cancer in the adult male. By the time he finished several of us were sweating and pale, others flush from guzzling their whiskey. We diverted him from the grisly topic only by getting him to tell us about all the picayune things Lyndon Johnson had done to him while he was vice president—forbidding him to take reporters on his plane, for example.

Sometimes the good stories are just insights you gain into people you don't know very well. I spent a weekend on the road with Elliot Richardson a few months after he had been fired in the Saturday Night Massacre and while he was considering a run for the Republican presidential nomination in 1976. He knew that, given his role in Watergate, his chances were not good. But he developed what he called his "dill pickle theory" that he could be nominated only if the Republican Party developed a "strange craving" for him akin to those that afflict pregnant women. He had the reputation of being a patrician stiff and a heavy drinker. But I found him a fascinating man and heavy drinker. On one leg of the trip, flying from Chicago to Philadelphia, I asked him to explain why he had allowed Spiro Agnew to resign the vice presidency and get away with a nolo contendere plea when he should have gone to jail. Richardson talked for an hour, leading me through his thinking and that of his associates in the Justice Department as they considered the prospect of having the vice president on trial in a criminal court while the president was on trial in the Senate in an impeachment proceeding.

I wanted to find out if his reputation as a drinker was true. The second night of the trip we checked into an airport motel in Philadelphia after Richardson had given a speech in Atlantic City. It was about midnight, and as we were getting our keys, I asked the desk clerk if the bar was still open. He assured me they would be pouring for at least another hour or two. I told Richardson I was going to drop my bag, call my wife, and repair to the bar. If he'd like to join me, he would be welcome. Sure enough, a few minutes after I took a table, he arrived. He drank several black Russians—some terrible concoction of high-powered stuff—while I drank cognac and we both did some light flirting with a dynamite cocktail waitress. So I knew he was a drinker but still an interesting politician. After an hour or so of what I considered good conversation, we both went to our rooms to get a few hours' sleep before catching another plane.

Not all the good days involve potential presidential candidates. I once spent a special hour or two with Senator Claiborne Pell, drinking tea and eating cookies on the terrace of his home outside Newport overlooking Rhode Island Sound. I didn't know Pell very well. In the Senate he was chairman of the Foreign Relations Committee, which was off the subject for me, and heaven knows he was never considered a national player worth getting to know because he might be influential within the party or even on a national ticket someday. On the contrary, Pell was often a target of ridicule in Washington and had been almost from the moment he arrived after winning the seat in 1960. He was a patrician from a very old family he revered, and he behaved as such and thus was not combative enough to be considered a force in the Senate. He was sufficiently vague and absentminded to be widely known as Stillborne Pell.

But in 1990 Pell at seventy-one was facing a challenge from an attractive and popular Republican member of Congress, Claudine Schneider, who was considered a good bet to capture his seat in a year in which control of the Senate seemed in doubt. Pell had made his situation more perilous than it might otherwise have been by committing a political gaffe in a televised debate. Asked to name a bill he had passed to help his Rhode Island constituents, he confessed, "I couldn't give you a specific answer. My memory is not as good as it should be." Given his age, it was precisely the wrong thing to say. In American politics you are not allowed to admit to aging. The story line was obvious. So I went up to Providence to write a column about how Stillborne Pell was finally going down after thirty years of muddling through in the Senate. I spent a few hours with Schneider one afternoon, and when I called to arrange to see Pell the next morning, I was invited out to his house. His young press secretary would ride along and show me the way.

It was one of those glistening autumn days, and the air off the ocean was fresh. Pell was the quintessentially gracious host, showing me some of the family pictures that lined the walls of his seaside home and giving me a tour of his office before leading me to the terrace, where Mrs. Pell produced the tea and cookies and I produced my notebook. But the story wasn't what I expected. He was not apologetic or defensive about his gaffe. Nor was he vague and absentminded. Instead, he was entirely adult and civilized, qualities not always common in politics. Yes, he agreed, he was refusing to do any more debates with his forty-three-year-old rival because, he added cheerfully, "I'm perfectly capable of shooting myself in the foot."

His young press adviser tried not to choke on his cookies, which became increasingly difficult. When I suggested to Pell that Schneider was implying he was simply too old for the job and should be replaced, he replied, "I very much like and respect my adversary. She is saying I was more productive in earlier years, and she is absolutely correct." By this point I was the one trying to keep the straight face. And what about the memory question? Again, there was no apology. "My memory is not as sharp but my judgment is a lot better, and you get hired for your judgment, not to be a Quiz Kid."

By the time I left to drive back to Providence, I realized that I and many of us in Washington had undervalued and misunderstood Claiborne Pell all those years. He might have been vague and absentminded at seventy-one, but he'd had those same qualities when he arrived in Washington with John Kennedy at forty-one. We had been slow to look beyond those quirks and quick to categorize him. What we had missed was this totally disarming quality that allowed him to discuss and concede his own weaknesses without being defensive about them—perhaps a function of the confidence that comes from growing up in the aristocracy. Whatever it was, the voters of Rhode Island seemed to understand. As much as they admired Claudine Schneider, they elected Pell for another term.

During that same fall campaign I passed a memorable day with a very different kind of American politician, Mario Cuomo. He was running for governor again, and this time there was no serious doubt about his reelection. But because of the chance that he would run for president in 1992, I went up to Albany to spend a day with him. I met him early in the morning outside the old executive mansion on Eagle Street, from which we were going to the airport for a flight west to Buffalo for a series of ceremonies and campaign speeches. I had known Cuomo for almost twenty years, since his first public position as New York's secretary of state and his first unsuccessful campaign for mayor of New York City. I had interviewed him a dozen times and spent several days with him, and I always enjoyed the experience. He keeps you on your toes.

This time he greeted me by telling the two staff people making the trip that "Germond's here to write another dumb story" about how he was going to run for president, which of course was precisely why I was there. On the plane we sat across a table from each other, drinking coffee and eating bagels, and spent two hours jousting. Every question would be greeted by derision or at least a quibble. Either I didn't understand what he had been saying all along. Or I was trying to trick him. Or I was using faulty premises. So I would argue the point and he would argue back, finally answering the questions as he always did, eventually if obliquely. And, also as always, with much extravagant arm waving and eye rolling, in which I found myself joining to the point I began to wonder if I wasn't a little Italian myself.

I had the notion that day that running against the incumbent Republican president, George Bush, would be particularly attractive to Cuomo. The guy from St. John's against the preppy from Andover and Yale. The former minor-league outfielder against the Yale first baseman who couldn't hit. The Democratic son of immigrants against a Republican son of privilege. Cuomo had never forgotten that when he came out of St. John's Law School with the highest honors he couldn't even get an interview from the big Manhattan and Wall Street law firms. Now he could be the long-odds outsider against the overwhelming favorite for a second term. But Cuomo would have none of it. To think that way would be beneath him. The decision about running for president couldn't be based on your own ego. You had to know not only that you could do it better but that you were the best alternative available. What I was suggesting, he said with a show of indignation, "would be self-aggrandizing . . . the height of egoism and the height of selfishness."

The trip to Buffalo didn't produce a story of any consequence, although I did write another dumb column about whether Mario Cuomo was going to run for president in 1992, just as I and every other political reporter had written about whether he was going to run for president in 1988. The fascination with Cuomo on my part, and I suspect on the part of many colleagues, was based on several factors, not the least being that he was still an unreconstructed liberal who opposed the death penalty despite the polls showing his constituents wanted it. I also liked the fact that he soaked up knowledge and, as a result, knew what he was talking about on government matters. I never forgot a day in 1977 when he was running for mayor—in the end he lost to Ed Koch—and held a press conference on the reforms that were needed to deal with many abuses in ambulance service in New York City. He handed out a fact sheet and answered questions for twenty minutes or so before the television crews began packing their equipment and the reporters started putting away their notebooks. But one young radio reporter, a student from Columbia, asked him if she could pose a few more questions. Cuomo agreed and then realized from the questions that this young woman had studied the ambulance service problem and probably knew more about it than he did. So he sat there for another forty-five minutes answering her questions and learning. It didn't make a sound bite, but it told you something about this strange politician from Queens.

Most of all, however, what I saw in Cuomo was someone with the personal force to be a leader. It was not just that he could give a hell of a speech; Jesse Jackson could do that. It was that he could make people listen to rational arguments for the government's role in correcting some of the most glaring inequities in our society. He could capture and hold their attention.

But Cuomo played us like fish, letting out a little line, then pulling it tight. He wasn't going to run, he would say, but he wouldn't "take a Sherman" and declare himself totally out of the picture. "They would say," he would say, " 'He must have colon cancer, he must have a Mafia uncle.' " He was particularly sensitive to suggestions he was, as they say, "connected."

Although he wouldn't run, Cuomo seemed reluctant to yield center stage. In 1988, four years after he came to national attention with his speech at the San Francisco convention, he refused to compete with Michael Dukakis for the Democratic nomination although most professionals believed he could have taken it away from him. But from the sidelines Cuomo played a little dog in the manger with Dukakis during the New York primary that spring. He withheld his endorsement in a way that made me and others suspect he was hoping for the front-runner to falter and a cry to arise from his party for someone to save the day. By this stage of the process, it was clear Cuomo could not endorse either of the only rivals still standing against Dukakis, Jesse Jackson and Senator Albert Gore, Jr., of Tennessee, who was being led around by the nose by Ed Koch. But Cuomo still hesitated.

Then, through his son and political confidant Andrew, he offered the Dukakis campaign manager, Susan Estrich, two pieces of advice that could have blown Dukakis sky high in a New York primary in which the tension between Jews and blacks was manifest and being exacerbated by Jackson and Koch. To strengthen his hand with the more militant Jews, Cuomo suggested, Dukakis might want to soften his statement of support for a letter thirty senators had written backing Secretary of State George P. Shultz in a testy dispute with the Shamir government in Israel. Second, the Cuomos told Estrich, Dukakis would be wise to suggest publicly that he might put Jackson on his list of potential vice presidential choices.

Both of these were political grenades with the pins already pulled. If Dukakis had backed down on the Shultz issue, it would have been seen as the crudest kind of pandering to the most conservative Jewish leaders and would have cost him heavily among other voters, including many Jews. Then he would have outraged those same Jewish leaders—as well as many blue-collar conservative Democrats—by appearing to cave in to Jesse Jackson despite his policy of refusing to discuss the vice presidency. These ideas were, in short, a formula for political disaster, although both Cuomos insisted to me after the election that there was no such intent. Happily for his campaign, Dukakis was not inclined to accept either piece of advice, and Estrich recognized the perils.

The ultimate Cuomo tease came in the next presidential cycle, when he stalled until the very last minute before deciding in December 1991 not to fly to New Hampshire and qualify for the primary there by giving the secretary of state the filing fee of one thousand dollars. It was a Friday afternoon, and I had gone to the NBC studio in Washington to tape a *McLaughlin* show, but the taping was being delayed until we knew what Cuomo was doing. Joe Klein, then of *New York* magazine, was also in the studio to sit on the panel, and he and I spent the afternoon speculating about which course Cuomo would take. I thought that this time he would run, but Klein took a different view. The problem, he argued, is that Mario doesn't want to do all the running around the country that's involved. He's up there in Albany thinking that, you know, St. John's is going to have a great basketball team this year and if I run, I'm going to miss those games. In a way, it made sense. Cuomo was an extremely provincial politician, from the school that seemed to believe that if you leave New York, maybe even Queens, you're camping out. When he was forced to travel to some out-of-state conference, he always made a point of rushing back as quickly as possible. If he had any curiosity about the rest of the country, he kept it well hidden.

Klein was right. Although he could scarcely conceal his contempt for Bill Clinton, Cuomo passed on the 1992 campaign and, for all practical purposes, on any chance of becoming president of the United States. I've never fully understood why he wouldn't run. The common "explanation"—that he had a Mafia connection he was trying to hide—was garbage. There was never a shred of evidence connecting Cuomo or his family to organized crime. If there had been, it would have been discovered in the thorough and expensive investigation of him the Republicans financed during his first campaign for governor. But Cuomo's cover story for 1992—that he was conflicted about walking away from the state budget crisis at the time of the New Hampshire deadline—was also nonsense. And I didn't find his ruminating about the decision revealing when I interviewed him after the election.

"I have difficulty with the notion of wanting it badly," he said that day. "I'm not sure what that means. I'm afraid some people want the office too much, and I've always tried to guard against that. If you say, 'Did you have a great hunger for it?' I was always afraid of people who had too great a hunger for it. I thought they had the process backward. It shouldn't be that you desire the office and then you go out and get it. It should be that you are better than anybody else who's available. Otherwise, it's a very difficult thing to justify."

In the end, it seemed that you could conclude only that Mario Cuomo wanted to be president and probably for the right reasons. But he was unwilling to make the extraordinary effort it would have required. He didn't like the idea of all the travel and all the smiling and all the business of putting up with reporters picking at him and staff nagging him to raise money. It wasn't worth it to him. So he set up this artificial standard of being "better than anybody" and quickly decided he didn't meet it. And by so doing he left the country a choice of Bill Clinton, who had been hungering for the office his entire adult life, or four more years of George Bush, who already had proven once he got the office that he had no idea what to do with it.

There are many thoughtful people in politics who contend that Cuomo couldn't have been elected anyway. He was too liberal, too ugly, too Italian for all those white Protestant folks down south and out west. I was always convinced, however, that Cuomo could have cleared the hurdles to his candidacy just as Ronald Reagan managed to overcome the problem of his age and Jimmy Carter managed to overcome the problem of being a nobody from Georgia. Michael Dukakis didn't lose the 1988 election because he was a son of Greek immigrants.

I had also formed a theory that I still consider valid—that a politician with gravitas will convince the electorate of that quality if given enough exposure over time. The voters may tire of him eventually because of too much television exposure, as they did Cuomo when the Republicans defeated him in 1994. But they can get beyond surface appearances and come to appreciate true quality in a public official even if that official goes against public opinion from time to time.

There are many examples. Another New York politician, the Republican senator Jacob K. Javits, whose career overlapped Cuomo's for a few years, is one of them. Javits had been elected state attorney general as the Jewish candidate on the Republican "three-I league" ticket—Israel, Ireland, and Italy—and was serving in relative obscurity when a vacancy occurred in the United States Senate in 1956. Republican leaders called the party's state committee together in Albany to name Javits as their candidate, not because they particularly admired him but because they didn't want to create a potential rival for the governorship. For upstate county chairmen, however, it was a tough moment; they were being asked to cast a unanimous vote for this aggressive, bald-headed, acid-tongued, arrogant Jew from Manhattan. I was covering the meeting, and I saw at least a dozen of them slip out and make for the men's room. As one of them confessed to me, "I know it didn't make any difference, but I just didn't want to hold my hand up for that guy."

To everyone's surprise, Javits won the election, defeating Mayor Robert F. Wagner of New York by riding the coattails of President Dwight D. Eisenhower. And within two or three years those same upstate county Republican leaders were singing the praises of their "good friend Jack Javits." There was no mystery about what happened. Javits did not become any more charming or any less stereotypically the Jew from Manhattan. He was still almost terminally pompous. At one point he considered capping his career by running for mayor of New York City. But rather than talk about how he wanted to replace the Republican-turned-Democrat John Lindsay, he told me about becoming a latter-day Cincinnatus who would throw down his weapons and return to save the city of his birth. I kept a straight face; Jack Javits was not a man to enjoy a laugh at his own expense. But over the years he demonstrated to his constituents, as well as his colleagues in the Senate, that he was a brilliant public official who took his responsibilities seriously. He became an expert on a whole range of issues, some involving international economics and others domestic policy. He was a constant goad from the left of the Republican Party on civil rights questions. He never became a barrel of laughs, but he was enormously popular, holding the seat until 1980 when, at age seventy-six, he lost a primary after being crippled by Lou Gehrig's disease. He was replaced by a healthy Alfonse D'Amato, and the Senate was the poorer for it, a lot poorer.

Unlike Mario Cuomo, there have been many governors left to blush unseen in the back lots of American politics although they have the qualities that would be refreshing at the national level. Tom McCall, the Republican governor of Oregon in the 1960s and early 1970s, was one of them. McCall was a New England Yankee who never lost his down Maine accent while spending his adult life in Oregon, sometimes as a television commentator, more often as a public official. As governor he made a brilliant record for recognizing and meeting potential threats to his state's matchless environment. Among other things, he promulgated the first statewide ban on throwaway bottles.

With political reporters like me, however, Tom McCall was prized for his personality and, above all, his exquisite use of the language. An example: In 1968 he flew to New York to urge Nelson Rockefeller to run for the Republican presidential nomination after Rockefeller had declared himself susceptible to a draft. But despite the public urging of McCall and other moderate Republicans, Rockefeller announced he would not run. Of all those left out on a limb, no one suffered more than McCall, because while he had been all the way across the country in New York importuning Rockefeller a riot broke out in the Oregon state penitentiary. Not only that, McCall himself was holed up in a hotel, suffering from bronchitis. The complaints from the folks back home were long and loud. So when I passed through Oregon a few weeks later, I stopped in Salem and asked McCall if he felt he had been "manipulated" by his friend Nelson.

"Manipulated?" he roared. "I wasn't just manipulated. I was fondled."

Then he added: "There I was, ravaged by double pneumonia and my jail burned down."

McCall was not happy with Nixon's choice of Spiro T. Agnew for vice president or with the "southern strategy" by which Nixon and Agnew were taking his party. On one occasion the Oregon governor was quoted as having said privately that Agnew had delivered "a dirty rotten little speech" at a party meeting. Asked about it publicly, McCall explained, "I don't remember saying 'little.' " The controversy bubbled along for a time until a meeting of Republican governors in Sun Valley, at which the dismay of the moderates, meaning McCall and two or three others, ostensibly would be addressed and put to rest. As it turned out, however, Agnew was in no mood to be conciliatory. And when reporters caught up with McCall after the meeting, he described it this way: "It turned out that the vice president had a dagger in his shawl."

I went out to Oregon when McCall tried a comeback in 1978 after having been forced into private life by the state's limit of two consecutive terms for governors. I found him fighting what proved to be a losing primary battle against conservatives who had taken over the Republican Party and were depicting his environmentalism as a threat to the state's economy. He invited me to dinner at his home and, after several Bloody Marys, confessed in his characteristically vivid way that he was in some trouble. "They are trying to stake me out as some kind of Woody Weirdo," he said. "All I said was that you have to have some finesse. You don't throw yourself at every puking smokestack."

McCall lost that primary, but I continued to call him every time I went to Portland. My final dinner with him, in which Tom Pettit of NBC joined, came a couple of years later, when McCall had suffered a recurrence of an earlier cancer and was beyond therapy. It sounds like a formula for a grim evening, but it was anything but grim. McCall joined us at the London Grill of the Benson Hotel and, in high spirits, put away several martinis and a large slab of broiled salmon while regaling us with stories about all the wonderful things that were being said about him now that he was terminally ill. "Why couldn't they have written all these marvelous words when I needed them?" he kept asking. "I could have been elected in a landslide. Instead, I'm getting all these advance looks at my obituary."

Not all politicians are funny, of course. Some of them are just interesting. Jerry Brown was one of the latter when he was first elected governor of California as Ronald Reagan's successor in 1974. By the time he ran for president one last time in 1992, Brown had become a joke. He had reinvented himself so often that no one could tell if he was being serious or just putting you on by doing one of his numbers. But as a young governor, Brown was considered no worse than unorthodox until Mike Royko labeled him Governor Moonbeam. He was the guy who preached the age of limits and small is beautiful, the governor who rode around in the unmarked Plymouth and slept on a mattress on the floor rather than move into the governor's mansion in Sacramento. He was the son of a classic old pol, Pat Brown, the governor Reagan defeated, so maybe he had something to prove. In those early years he made many interesting appointments, reaching out to people usually not included in the ruling mix, and proposed many innovative approaches to long-standing problems.

And, for all the aberrant behavior, the early Brown was interesting. Shortly after his election he came to Washington for a National Governors' Conference winter meeting and chose to stay with Joe Allbritton, the publisher of the *Star* and a family friend from years past. So Allbritton invited several of us from the staff for dinner with Brown at his home—my partner and I; Mary McGrory; Jim Bellows; the national editor, Barbara Cohen; and the political reporter, Jim Dickenson.

At the dinner table we immediately fell into a discussion of whether a politician should claim he holds the moral high ground because of a position he has taken on an issue. Brown insisted there is no place for what he called "absolutes" in government and politics. To argue that you hold the moral position is to tell constituents who disagree with you that they are immoral themselves or at least defending immorality. It is better to deal in pragmatism. The function of the government official and politician is to solve the problem and make the trains run on time, not to provide moral leadership and spiritual solace. Several of us began to question his premises by posing hypothetical situations in which a governor or a president might feel obliged to claim a moral position as justification for his actions. But Brown kept countering with ways the same situation might be handled without those "absolutes" he detested. The argument was never resolved, of course, but what was so striking was the fact that the conversation remained centered on this topic for two full hours—as we posed one hypothetical case after another. It was impossible to think of another politician with whom such an evening would have been possible.

Brown always seemed ready for such conversation. I went to California two or three times a year in those days and often spent an evening with him eating Mexican food and drinking beer. And on each occasion he would have some new enthusiasm, a book he had read or an issue he had just stumbled into. One night we spent more than three hours in a restaurant in San Diego talking about how politicians should deal with citizens' uneasiness about the safety of nuclear power plants, particularly in areas with a history of earthquakes. Should their fears be calmed or exploited to force them to demand that the plants be built elsewhere? Was it an issue with the potential to elect someone governor? But Brown flitted from one issue to another so often that his reputation deteriorated to the point he was no longer electable except, of course, as mayor of Oakland. And even early in his career his zigs and zags made you suspect he was really involved in political positioning.

That suspicion cost him dearly with some Democrats. During his first term in Sacramento he had attracted favorable notice from some of the professionals of the United Auto Workers that translated into interest on the part of Douglas Fraser, the president of the UAW then and one of the most thoughtful public figures of our time. Fraser and his union had been critical elements of Jimmy Carter's success in 1976, first embracing him as the man to defeat George Wallace in the South and later giving him critical help in some industrial states. But the union activists were never totally comfortable with the former governor of Georgia. Brown seemed attractive as a possibility for the future both because he was conventionally liberal and because he was intellectually intriguing to Fraser. Moreover, he was the son of Pat Brown, who had always been a favored candidate with the liberal unions.

But the day after California approved the infamous Proposition 13 limit on taxation and state spending in 1978, Brown reversed his adamant opposition and became an enthusiastic proponent. I telephoned Fraser at Solidarity House in Detroit and asked him what he thought of this sudden conversion. There was a long pause, perhaps twenty seconds, before he replied: "I guess I would say he's not reliable." Politically, it was a critically damaging negative judgment, one in which many Democrats of the left joined. Jerry Brown continued to attract some UAW locals in his subsequent campaigns but never at the level he needed to make him a serious factor in national politics.

The stories about his distance from his father were legion but perhaps not totally accurate. One year I invited Pat Brown to the spring dinner of the Gridiron Club in Washington. During the evening I told him I had been out to California earlier in the month and had seen Jerry. Pat was all over me. How's he doing? Is he handling this controversy all right? Could he have avoided that other controversy? A few weeks later, interviewing Governor Brown in Sacramento, I mentioned that I had been seated next to his father at a dinner in Washington. Jerry was all over me. What did he say about me? What did he think of how I handled that situation? I was told later that the distance between father and son eventually narrowed a great deal. But by that time I had lost interest in Jerry Brown.

Family connections matter in politics. I learned that from, among others, Tim Hagan, a Democrat from Cleveland who served many years as a Cuyahoga County commissioner and Democratic county chairman. I got to know him back in 1976, when he was supporting Mo Udall against Jimmy Carter in the Ohio presidential primary, and then in 1980, when he went with Ted Kennedy against Carter. In any campaign Hagan was with the more liberal candidate. You could go to the bank on it. But he was also a perceptive judge of what was going on, meaning he was a good source as well as good company.

Once during Roger Mudd's heyday at CBS News, meaning before Dan Rather was chosen over him to succeed Walter Cronkite, he was going to Cleveland on a story, so Jules and I told him to look up Hagan. He would be a big help. Mudd called Hagan, whose secretary announced that Roger Mudd was on the line. Hagan thought it was one of his buddies playing some game, so he picked up the

phone and said, "Roger Mudd, big fucking deal." When Mudd finally convinced him, they went out to lunch and had a good conversation. Next time you come to Washington, Mudd told Hagan,
give me a call. Several months later Hagan went to Washington and
called Mudd, whose secretary told him Tim Hagan was on the line.
Without missing a beat, Mudd picked up the phone and said, "Tim
Hagan, big fucking deal."

In the 1980s Ohio had a Democratic governor, Richard Celeste,
who had ambitions to join the pack of candidates for the 1988 presidential nomination. So he was pleased when the party's state chairmen scheduled a meeting in Cleveland in the fall of 1987 that
would attract all the potential nominees and perhaps allow Celeste
to work himself into the mix in the views of the state chairmen and
the national press. And, to make his intentions clear to even the
dullest reporter, he scheduled a trip to Iowa, home of the Iowa caucuses, for the day after the meeting.

Hagan was a bitter critic of Celeste, however. That enmity became apparent the day the session opened when the Cleveland
Plain Dealer carried a front-page story about an opinion poll commissioned by, surprise, Tim Hagan. It said that 69 percent of Ohio
voters thought Celeste should stay home rather than run for president while only 21 percent thought he should run.

The embarrassment for Celeste was obvious, and James Ruvolo,
the state party chairman and a Celeste ally, called the poll "a cheap
shot." Pursued by reporters, Hagan didn't gild the lily. "The figures
speak for themselves," he said. But when he and I went to lunch together, I asked him what it was all about. I knew he and Celeste
didn't get along, but this was a real whack in the mush. As it turned
out it all went back to the Democratic National Convention in San
Francisco three years earlier. As governor, Celeste had control of all
the Ohio tickets to the convention, for spectators as well as delegates and alternates. And he had refused to give any tickets to
Hagan's three brothers.

"You leave my brothers standing out on the sidewalk," Hagan explained, "and I'm not going to forget about it." Of course not. Why
did I even bother to ask?

When it comes to family first, however, there is none more dedicated than the Kennedys of Massachusetts, as I discovered in 1977. I was working for the *Star* when I heard that young Joseph Kennedy, son of Robert, was planning to replace Robert Crane as state treasurer of Massachusetts by challenging him in a primary as a first step in his political career. Crane was an old pro who had held the job for years and, I knew, had carried water for the Kennedys for even longer.

I hurried up to Boston, and the story proved to be a beauty. Jim Bellows, my editor, told me to forget the usual seven-hundred-word limit on the column and write as much as it took. So the column started on Page One under a headline that read: RFK'S SON NEEDS A JOB AND A KENNEDY ALLY FEELS THE CHILL.

The piece began:

> By Jack W. Germond and Jules Witcover
> BOSTON—On the wall in Bobby Crane's office in the statehouse here there is a 19-year-old photograph of Crane and John F. Kennedy, then a senator seeking reelection as prelude to seeking the presidency. They are both all smiles.
>
> Bobby Crane remembers the occasion well—the first $1,000-a-throw fundraising breakfast ever held in Massachusetts and he was one of the arrangers. The pride of the moment is captured there in his toothy Irish smile.
>
> Bobby Crane has a lot of memories of Kennedys. He worked for John F. Kennedy in 1958 and 1960. He sided with Teddy Kennedy against Eddie McCormack in 1962. He worked for Robert F. Kennedy in New York in 1964 and in the California presidential primary in 1968. A few years later he took the Democratic Party chairmanship here at Ted Kennedy's request when no one else was willing.
>
> He has always "done for" the Kennedys and now the Kennedys are giving him his reward. They are threatening to take away the job as state treasurer he has held since 1964 because Joseph P. Kennedy, the 25-year-old son of Robert, wants "to get into politics" and it seems that state treasurer is just the job that would fill the bill. It is a lovely piece of work, just lovely.
>
> But Bob Crane won't go quietly. "This office," he says, "isn't that much to hold on to, but there's a certain amount of pride." He smiles that thick grin. "You know, foolish Irish pride."

There were other elements of the story. For one thing, Crane had just been the subject of a grand jury investigation of his taxes and campaign contributions and, although he had been cleared, he was politically vulnerable. "It's been a tough year," he said. "I'm not as strong as I was"—meaning even less able to fend off a Kennedy in a Democratic primary.

"They're like sharks," another Boston pol told me. "He's bleeding and they're sweeping down on him."

Moreover, it turned out that young Joe fixed his gaze on Bobby Crane only after, despite broad hints, two Democrats who held seats in the House of Representatives that he fancied had refused to step aside. Imagine their arrogance. Imagine their selfishness.

The move on Crane was a classic Kennedy power play. First, a mutual friend of Ted Kennedy and Crane suggested to Bobby that he might step aside. Then the word came indirectly from two others close to the Kennedys, including their brother-in-law Stephen Smith, which is about as close as it gets. So Crane called the senator and confirmed it from the horse's mouth. Ted Kennedy started talking about other things the fifty-one-year-old Crane might do. But Crane was tougher than they figured. At a wake the very next day he confronted the senator and reminded him that, after Chappaquiddick, Ted Kennedy had wanted to vindicate himself and he, Bob Crane, had helped. Now he was the one who wanted to vindicate himself after the grand jury investigation. Several Democrats privy to the conversation told me later that Teddy was outraged because Crane raised Chappaquiddick.

Young Joe would not talk to me about his ambitions. An assistant in Boston said he was not "granting interviews." That was fine with me. It was one of those cases in which the reporter is obliged to seek out the "other side" when he already knows the full story. If this kid didn't want to "grant" me an interview, it was no problem. The story would be better with it, but I didn't need it, so to hell with him. But the senator, whom I had known for years, wouldn't return my telephone calls or see me when I got back to Washington. It was clear they were on the defensive. After the column ran in the *Star* and then in *The Boston Globe,* Joe Kennedy put his ambitions on hold until a House seat opened up that he could win without cutting the throat of a longtime ally of the family. Bobby Crane got himself reelected and always believed I had saved his job.

The senator was angry. When he ran into my partner in the Senate lobby, he began upbraiding Jules in loud tones, although he knew full well I was the one who had written the column because I was the one who had been trying to reach him. And from that point on I always felt a little chill when our paths crossed. Family was family, and I had intruded.

Ted Kennedy was always a complex personality. He was widely blamed for treating his first wife, Joan, badly. And he was widely chastised for drinking too much in public. But he could be remarkably considerate. There are dozens of stories about how thoughtful he can be, and I saw a couple of occasions myself.

Once on a small-plane flight up to Atlantic City, he overheard a conversation between me and John Lindsay of *Newsweek*. We were riding along with him to cover a speech he would deliver that night. We were talking about Lindsay's son having a serious problem with asthma. Real John, as we called Lindsay to distinguish him from the New York mayor of the same name, was even thinking of transferring to the magazine's bureau in the Far West, where the air would be better. The senator, who had been reading documents from his briefcase, suddenly joined in and asked Real John about his son. He wrote a card to the little boy, but it didn't end with a gesture, Real John told me later. The trip to Atlantic City was made on a Saturday, and at nine Monday morning an asthma specialist called Lindsay at home and asked him to bring his son in for a look.

(Lindsay had a special distinction among political reporters. He was probably the first to fully understand how those of us in the print media were being supplanted in influence by our competitors from television. And, to make the point, he would often adopt the persona of "Larry Largelung of Action Central News." One day in Oregon he jumped off a campaign bus as Larry and walked along the crowd behind the rope line, conducting interviews with voters while using a chocolate cupcake as his microphone. "Talk into the cupcake," he would say, and the voters would lean down and do just that.)

Similarly, when he discovered that my daughter Mandy had leukemia, the senator called me and offered to help arrange for her treatment. His own son Teddy, he pointed out, was also a cancer patient at the time, so he knew how difficult it could be. And, although he didn't mention it, I knew he was a high-ranking member of the critical health care subcommittee in the Senate. As it happened I didn't need the help because Mandy already was being treated in the National Institutes of Health pediatric oncology program. But I prized the offer. Over the next five years there were several times when I was able to draw some solace from talking to Kennedy about our two children and the strain put on our families by their illnesses. I found him to be an extraordinarily kind and considerate man—so long, of course, as you didn't screw around with his family.

Kennedys aside, Boston is a gold mine for a political columnist who must produce several times a week. I've always been convinced that I could fly into Logan Airport at noon on Christmas Eve, head for the statehouse or city hall, and come away that night with an interesting piece about some elaborate political intrigue under way in the Bay State. Even as politicians have become terminally bland clones of one another elsewhere, Boston has enjoyed a wealth of genuine characters totally consumed by politics. Walk into the Parker House or Doyle's and they're talking either the Red Sox or politics.

One of the most interesting was Kevin H. White, who was mayor of Boston for four terms, beginning in 1968. White was a remarkable politician who combined the conventional liberalism of the Democrat from the Northeast with many of the qualities of the old-fashioned machine boss and more than a dash of the Irish rogue. Although he had been educated in private schools and at preppy Williams College, White had an easy rapport with the Irish and Italian blue-collar voters who outnumbered his core of liberal supporters several times over. They seemed to understand that he relished the job and thus was committed to the city, which was clearly the case. When I went to Boston he would sometimes invite me to have an early-evening drink at Parkman House, a Beacon Hill mansion owned by the city where the third- and fourth-floor windows look out over Boston Common and the Public Garden. White loved to sit there at sundown, gazing over his empire and pointing out its special qualities to the heathen from Washington. He was a consummate full-time political player who loved the game, enjoyed the power, and relished the gossip. Mike Barnicle, the great local columnist of the *Globe,* once wrote that when White was born and the doctor gave him the slap of life, his first words were "What do you hear?"

White came to power as the liberal darling in 1967 by defeating a woman named Louise Day Hicks, a member of the city council and leader of the opposition to racial integration of the public schools in the city. After a federal district judge, W. Arthur Garrity, Jr., ordered desegregation in 1974, White found himself obliged to enforce a busing plan that had torn the city apart. It was not a responsibility any politician would prefer; politicians like for people to like them. But White did it, although it was hard for him to accept the hostility from South Boston, where the plan called for black children to be bused in from Roxbury and local white children to be bused back out to Roxbury. In South Boston he was now Mayor Black. I have a vivid memory of going with him to a supper meeting in Southie that ended with his constituents throwing rolls at their mayor. Back in the car, speeding away somewhat ingloriously, White was shaken. "Politics is supposed to be fun," he said. "You have your generals and your sergeants and your privates, and it's supposed to be fun, but they're using live ammunition."

The controversy over busing had reached a fever pitch when I passed through Boston in May 1975. I was on my way to New Hampshire but decided to stop to see White and Michael Dukakis, then a newly elected governor. But, with a morning to kill, I went over to South Boston, where I encountered a clutch of white kids who would have been the first in their families ever to finish high school but had been forced by the pressures of their extended families to drop out. One pimply young man named Denny explained the whole thing: "My old man didn't want me going to school with the niggers over in Roxbury so he said, 'Get a job, who needs it.' " The sad thing, I discovered when I checked with their teachers, was that Denny and two of the three other punks standing on a street corner that morning were making better-than-average grades and might even have been able to go on to college.

I abandoned my plan to go to New Hampshire and the next morning went to Roxbury, where black mothers were putting their kids on school buses that would transport them to white areas. When I tried to interview two of them, they asked me to wait until the buses left and then took me into a neighbor's kitchen. There four mothers had developed a routine of having their morning coffee while watching the live television coverage of angry mobs throwing rocks at the buses of black children. They relaxed only when they could see that their kids had weathered another gauntlet safely. This was the story of race relations in the Athens of America.

White was politically lucky in his campaign for reelection in 1975. His identification with the hated busing plan had reached the point at which he was clearly vulnerable to a challenger with reasonable credentials who was also against busing—in other words, someone more broadly acceptable than such stalwarts of the antibusing movement as Elvira Pixie Palladino, the leader of Restore Our Alienated Rights (ROAR), and Louise Day Hicks. White's principal opponent was Joe Timilty, a young state legislator with anchorman good looks and solid political credentials. But Timilty, to his everlasting credit, would not play the race card despite intense pressure from his political advisers.

"If you use the busing thing, you can beat him, can't you?" I asked him over a beer one night.

"I can't do that," he replied. "I've got my own kids in the public schools."

White won reelection thanks to Timilty's responsible restraint, then returned the favor when they opposed each other a second time in 1979 by running a series of extraordinarily harsh television commercials depicting Timilty as someone who turned in the wind. By this time White's support among the liberal do-gooders was wearing a little thin. There had been too many stories in the *Globe* about how his fund-raising skirted the edges of propriety or how he was using his machine to perpetuate his power or how he was brooding at the Parkman House. But his media consultant that year, David Sawyer, produced some masterly commercials that played off his eccentricities—the most memorable being a television spot about "A loner in love with his city." And White's police commissioner let it be known late in the campaign that if Timilty were elected he would have to step down, the obvious implication being that Joe Timilty was mobbed up. For whatever reason, the mayor won again.

Kevin White is also one of the many what-might-have-been stories of American politics. In 1972 George McGovern had decided, tentatively at least, to choose the Boston mayor as his running mate for vice president. Shortly before the Democratic convention at Miami Beach, McGovern called White and told him of his decision, subject only to clearing it with the proper people. That group obviously would include the senator from Massachusetts, Ted Kennedy, and White made the mistake of telephoning Kennedy to let him know what was in the works.

Kennedy was not entranced by the idea. As a close friend once said in another context, "Teddy likes to be the only rooster in the barnyard." So he called two prominent liberals, Robert Drinan, the priest then serving in the House of Representatives, and John Kenneth Galbraith, the Harvard professor who served as a sort of all-purpose intellectual for the Massachusetts Democrats. They, in turn, called McGovern and warned him off Kevin White. The mayor, they pointed out, had been a supporter of Ed Muskie in the spring. If he was nominated now, there would be a riot in the Massachusetts delegation. So McGovern made the fatal mistake of choosing Tom Eagleton.

It would be a stretch to contend that White on the ticket would have saved George McGovern and defeated Richard Nixon. But Kevin White was a politician of extraordinary charm who could have been the one person to emerge from that campaign with burnished political credentials.

As a group mayors have been my favorite politicians. They are under even more extreme and direct pressure than governors in being forced to respond quickly and decisively to situations often beyond their control. And because they receive such constant scrutiny, the successful ones seem to play politics with the utmost attention at all times.

One day in the mid-1960s I went to see Jerry Cavanaugh, the young mayor of Detroit who had become a favorite of the Kennedys a few years earlier and appeared to have a limitless future. He was a chunky, red-faced man who seemed to exude energy. When I was ushered into his office, I found him and his press secretary studying two newspaper clippings on his desk.

Cavanaugh turned them around and pushed them across the desk at me. What do you see? he wanted to know. Both were pictures of the Democratic mayor and Michigan's Republican governor, George W. Romney, at public events the previous week. In each case at the moment the picture was taken Romney appeared to be talking and gesturing emphatically, his right hand chopping into his left palm. The obvious inference was that the older governor was lecturing the young mayor, and that's what I told Cavanaugh.

"That's right," the mayor said, nodding vigorously, "and it's not going to happen again."

He handed the clippings back to his press secretary and began answering my questions about presiding over a city with many problems in those days. But the next morning I was amused to see in the *Free Press* a picture of Romney and Cavanaugh at another public function. This time when the camera went off both men were talking and chopping the left palm with the right hand. The lesson was that Jerry Cavanaugh was a politician who paid attention to detail and wasn't going to be jerked around by some governor. As things turned out Cavanaugh's career ended with his stint as mayor, short-circuited by, among other things, a messy divorce.

For all of their quality, mayors have a difficult time advancing politically. In many cases their attempts to run for governor or the Senate are forestalled by the prejudice in the electorate against the biggest city in the state. Even mayors of great personal force and popularity in their cities—such as, in my time, Ray Flynn of Boston and Ed Rendell of Philadelphia—run into resistance in Springfield or Allentown or even smaller communities. Beyond that, however, they are identified with and inevitably somewhat preoccupied with issues that most voters would rather ignore, such as crime, poverty, and racial tension. So they rarely come as close as Kevin White to a place on a national ticket, and none of them has been a serious presidential candidate in my years.

John Vliet Lindsay of New York seemed to be an exception at one point. After a decade in the House of Representatives as a liberal Republican representing the Silk Stocking District of Manhattan,

Lindsay won a three-way race for mayor in 1965. He was a tall, classically handsome man who combined a patrician manner with an acerbic tongue and plebeian street smarts. It became fashionable after he left office to write him off as a failure at city hall, but that judgment was never entirely or even preponderantly fair. As mayor he did manage a few marked advances in difficult times. He succeeded, for example, in getting the concept of productivity measures into a couple of municipal union contracts. The provisions were not stringent enough that anyone noticed, for example, that the sanitation men were picking up more trash per shift, but that would be asking a lot. Suffice it to say the changes were considered a breakthrough at the time.

More important, Lindsay largely succeeded in keeping a political dialogue going with enough black leaders to help his city get through some difficult times without going up in flames. His display of nerve and self-assurance in dealing with racial tension was vivid enough so that his switch to the Democratic Party made him almost instantly a figure of some national influence. Unsurprisingly, he decided to seek the Democratic presidential nomination in 1972 and, contrary to his intention, quickly showed why a big-city mayor couldn't do it. His day job was simply too consuming to allow him to run a national campaign with any chance of success.

During the Florida primary campaign, for example, there were two occasions when he was forced to cut short his campaign schedule—once almost in mid-speech—because he received news from home: in one case a policeman had been killed, and in the other there was a report of police corruption serious enough to require a prompt response on the scene.

On another occasion Lindsay was attending a Democratic state gathering in Indianapolis when he was notified that there was a racial confrontation between police and some kids in Harlem that was threatening to get out of hand. He was quickly shuttled to his plane and flown back to La Guardia. But the special logistical problem this time was that his main appearance at the meeting was to be a breakfast speech the following morning. The upshot was that he flew back to Indianapolis and appeared in the hotel pressroom, where a poker game was in progress, shortly after two. "I really need a martini," he announced. As it happened we had the makings, so we suspended the game to share an odd cocktail hour with an exhausted politician trying to get down enough gin to sleep two or three hours before the breakfast. He was not at his best that morning, but he hadn't lost his perspective. When I asked him how he was feeling after so little rest, he replied, "You guys drink really cheap gin." Lindsay limped through a few primaries, but his candidacy never shook off the image of the big, wicked city. And Americans reelected Richard Nixon and Spiro Agnew. Terrific.

Many of the stories I enjoyed were about campaigns involving total unknowns who became interesting players later. In 1974, for example, the word filtered up from Arkansas that some hayseed governor named Dale Bumpers was showing the temerity to challenge Senator J. William Fulbright, chairman of the Committee on Foreign Relations and a Washington icon, for the Democratic nomination. I made the first of what proved to be many trips to Little Rock and discovered that Bumpers not only was going after Fulbright's seat but was likely to win it. Indeed, Bumpers was the best stump campaigner I had ever seen. He had the ability to give the same speech, using exactly the same words, to a group of farmers gathered in a town square and to a bar association luncheon in Little Rock and make it sound entirely different. I also liked him because he had just enough acid in his tongue to make him distinctive.

Senator Fulbright was, nonetheless, Senator Fulbright, so it was not easy to imagine him being cast aside by an ungrateful electorate. I began to see it was obviously possible when he showed up at a sale barn about fifty miles from Little Rock one morning wearing a linen jacket with a folded copy of *The Wall Street Journal* sticking out of his pocket. I didn't expect him in blue jeans and flannel, but his dress and manner both suggested he had grown somewhat out of touch with those who buy and sell cattle for a living. And a long night of dinner and drinking with his principal political consultant, Mark Shields, and his local campaign chairman, a liberal hero from the Central High days named Brownie Ledbetter, confirmed my suspicions. They were already talking in the past tense and explaining away the mistakes of the campaign. Bumpers won and went on to a long career in the Senate, where he managed the considerable

feat of avoiding the smarminess that infects most senators. Ironically, he ended his public career as a defense attorney for Bill Clinton in his impeachment trial, although it was no secret that
Bumpers held Clinton in minimum high regard at best. I always
thought he should have run for president himself.

Not all of the candidates you meet in odd campaigns around the
country prove to be as promising as Dale Bumpers, however. There
is the case, for example, of Jerry Springer, the same Jerry Springer
who became the king of sleaze television. In 1982 Springer was a
city council member and former mayor of Cincinnati who decided
to seek the Democratic nomination for governor against the heavily
favored Richard Celeste. What made Springer interesting was the
fact that he quickly raised $1.5 million for his campaign, an im-
pressive sum in those days. It turned out he had a whole list of novel
approaches. One that had yielded handsome dividends had been to
copy the tail numbers off the private planes at Ohio airports, get the
lists of owners, and write to them. Springer reasoned, correctly, that
many of those planes would belong to young entrepreneurs who had
never been involved in the political process even to the point of giving money.

But Springer, I found, had a problem that money wouldn't solve.
One night while serving as mayor he had crossed over the Kentucky
border, patronized a whorehouse—and paid with a check. In his
home city he had survived this bolt of gross stupidity and even been
reelected to the city council. But, of course, most of the voters of
Ohio didn't know about the episode. Nor did they have any store of
more positive information that apparently led Cincinnati voters to
forgive him. So I was skeptical when he told me over lunch in
Columbus one day that "everyone already knows about Kentucky."
They didn't until, with a little help from the Celeste campaign, the
incident came to light statewide late in the primary campaign. To no
one's surprise, Springer lost and moved on to provide a different sort
of public service.

On too many occasions when I have gone into states cold on a
story I have ended up mistaking the situation and writing some story
I still find humiliating years—hell, decades—later. In 1969 I spent
a few days covering the Los Angeles mayoral campaign between the
longtime nutcake incumbent, one Sam Yorty, and the black police

chief, Tom Bradley. Ten days before the election I wrote a short piece for *The New Republic* that appeared a week later under the headline LOS ANGELES IS ABOUT TO SAY SO LONG, SAM. When Yorty was reelected easily, I discovered how many people read *The New Republic* in those days. I also discovered that I had allowed my political judgment to be skewed by my personal distaste for Yorty and hopes for a black man to succeed. It was the kind of mistake reporters must fight repeatedly if they are to play in a fast league.

On another occasion, a decade later, I went to South Carolina to write about a gubernatorial campaign and convinced myself that a lawyer named Tom Turnipseed had a good chance to win a multi-candidate Democratic primary because he was exploiting consumer anger at the power company, often a factor in southern campaigns in those days. As it turned out, his campaign collapsed, he didn't even make the runoff, and I once again had egg on my face.

My failure this time was that I was beguiled by the Turnipseed persona. He had been a supporter of George Wallace in the 1960s, then renounced racism and become a populist, a conversion I was convinced was genuine. He was an articulate, colorful, and charming man by my criteria but not by those of the good citizens of South Carolina, who elected Richard W. Riley, later the secretary of education in the Clinton administration.

In this case I did make a recovery of sorts. Riley was twenty to thirty points behind the favored candidate in the primary, Lieutenant Governor Brantley Harvey, one of those last-name-for-a-first-name people so common in southern politics then. But when Harvey would not release his income tax returns just four years after Watergate, I figured he had made himself vulnerable to a candidate making a lot of sense on the issues and open about his finances. I was right that time, and one of the great things about newspaper reporting is the quick opportunity for redemption you are offered. But for years every time I thought about South Carolina I thought about Tom Turnipseed and how I had screwed that one up.

I rarely get emotionally involved in political stories I cover. People outside the business have a hard time believing this, but most political reporters don't care who wins most of the elections they cover. We are selfish people who care most about getting the story right and, if we are lucky, first. There are, however, exceptional cases, and one of them for me was the 1986 contest for a seat in the House of Representatives between John Lewis and Julian Bond in Georgia's Fifth District. I had known both men since they were kids of nineteen or twenty running the Student Nonviolent Coordinating Committee in the early 1960s, Lewis as the chairman and Bond as the communications director. I knew them to have been personal and family friends in Atlanta for a quarter century, close enough even to share family vacations. After leaving SNCC, Lewis worked as an organizer for the Southern Regional Council, then replaced Vernon Jordan as director of the Voter Education Project (VEP) before serving in the Carter administration running Volunteers in Service to America (VISTA)—known as the domestic Peace Corps—and then winning a seat on the Atlanta City Council. Bond served in the Georgia Senate long enough to become a committee chairman and made speeches for honoraria that often were used to help finance the VEP rather than the Bond family.

Now, I discovered, they were competing against each other in a remarkably tense contest you could not help but hope both could win. It was a wrenching story to cover because of the deterioration in the relationship between the men who had been such an effective team at SNCC. Bond, the celebrity of the two, was heavily favored, but he won the first twelve-candidate primary by defeating Lewis by only twelve points, with 47 percent to 35 for Lewis, forcing a runoff. Then Lewis did something that seemed totally out of character for a man widely known as Saint John because of his personal probity. In a showdown debate shortly before the runoff, he challenged Bond to join him in taking a drug test. The tactic injected into the campaign debate and the news media the gossip that Bond had been using drugs. It was not the kind of thing anyone expected from John Lewis, and in his autobiography Lewis himself seemed self-conscious about it, depicting the raising of the drug question as a reaction to a suggestion from Bond that Lewis might have been guilty of a conflict of interest while on the city council.

Bond, it seemed to me, had shown extraordinary restraint in attacking Lewis. He was being urged by Eugene Duffy, his closest political adviser, and others to make the argument that he, the bona fide celebrity, was the one who would make the most effective and articulate case for black Americans if he were in Congress. The implication would have been that Lewis was less articulate than he should have been to carry out that mission successfully. I remember sitting in the lobby bar of the Colony Square Hotel one night and listening to Duffy press his case while Bond resisted and watched the women go by. It may have been that he was so confident of success that he didn't think it necessary to undermine the John Lewis image. But it was also clear that he was far from comfortable denigrating his friend of twenty-five years.

In the end, it cost him. Although Bond carried about 60 percent of the black vote, Lewis beat him overwhelmingly among whites, captured the seat, and went on to a career in the House of Representatives in which—to the surprise of no one who knew him—he earned widespread respect in the world of politics. But just for that one moment in that debate, John Lewis behaved like any politician. Even saints don't have to be flawless.

The only hero I ever had in politics was a largely forgotten Democratic senator from Alaska named Ernest Gruening, whom I came to know not by covering his campaigns but by the accident of living next door to him when I first moved to Washington in the early 1960s. He was already in his late seventies, a small man, potbellied, slightly stooped, and appearing myopic. He had been sent to the Senate by the voters of Alaska in 1958 as the final stop of a long career in public service that had included a significant role in achieving statehood.

He had a remarkable history. The son of a Jewish physician, he graduated from Harvard Medical School in 1911 but decided he didn't want to practice medicine after all. He had too many other interests, he once told me, and he needed more time to pursue them than a career in medicine would allow. So he went into journalism, starting out as a reporter in Boston and eventually serving at different times as editor of several of the many newspapers then published in Boston and New York. He was twice editor of *The Nation*, once running it by himself and at another time as a member of a board of editors. And he wrote what for years was considered the definitive archaeological history of Mexico.

But he turned from writing to public service when President Franklin D. Roosevelt chose him in 1934 to be director of territories, a post that put him into continuing conflict with the notori-

ously testy Secretary of the Interior Harold Ickes. One of Gruening's claims to fame, or at least notoriety, was his policy of preaching birth control to Puerto Ricans as a first step in helping
themselves out of poverty. That initiative evoked such a stern reaction from the Roman Catholic hierarchy that Jim Farley, the Democratic national chairman, asked FDR to call off Gruening or risk
losing the Catholic vote in 1936. Ernest's commitment to birth control continued throughout his public career, producing one memorable press photo of him holding up a birth control coil during a
Senate hearing in an era when the topic was rarely discussed in
public.

When I came to know him Ernest's distinction was as one of the
two maverick liberals in the Senate—the other was Wayne Morse of
Oregon—who were the first to oppose President Lyndon B. Johnson
on the war in Vietnam. Because the president wanted unanimity behind the Gulf of Tonkin resolution, the pressure on Gruening was
intense, but he seemed to accept it with the equanimity that comes
from genuine self-confidence. I would be cutting the grass on a hot
day in the summer of 1964 when Ernest would appear in his backyard, in shorts and sandals, balancing precariously on his stringy
legs. "That looks like hot work," he would call out. "Time to take a
break." So I would abandon the mower and accept a cold beer, then
listen for an hour while Gruening brought me up to date on LBJ's
attempt to change his mind on Vietnam. What we are doing is
worthwhile, Ernest would say, because as long as there are even a
few dissenters, he will feel some restraints on his freedom of action.
I like Lyndon, he would say, but he tends to get stubborn about
things like this. Eventually, he would say, the whole country will realize this war is a mistake.

Ernest Gruening was, in short, a serious politician acting on his
convictions, not only on Vietnam but on a whole list of issues on
which he became a leading spokesman for the left. He didn't last
long in the Senate, however. In 1968, after ten years, he was defeated in a Democratic primary by a younger, slicker candidate who
ran clever commercials and once elected was never heard from
again. It might have been the beginning of a trend.

Gruening was not silenced by defeat. He continued to take a

prominent role on liberal issues. And he was particularly outraged by Richard Nixon, campaigning for George McGovern in 1972 when he was eighty-five years old and assailing Nixon on matters as diverse as his Supreme Court appointments and his attempts to intimidate the press. What made him special was that he cared about getting something done, not just getting elected. There isn't enough of that going around.

CHAPTER 16

HITTING BOTTOM

There is something out of whack when a newspaperman and confessed liberal looks back with something like nostalgia to the good old days when Ronald Reagan was president of the United States. It is not inexplicable, however. I haven't decided in my dotage that Reagan was right about very much, and I still feel small tremors of unease at the notion of him as Leader of the Free World. But next to George Bush and Bill Clinton, Ronald Reagan looks ten feet tall. So do all but one of the presidents I have covered—John F. Kennedy, Lyndon B. Johnson, Gerald R. Ford, and Jimmy Carter. The only exception is Richard M. Nixon, whose felonious conduct puts him in a category beyond comparison.

George Bush didn't commit any felonies in the Oval Office so far as we know, although I never bought his story that he was out of the loop in the Iran-Contra affair when he was vice president. I was always impressed, if puzzled, by the fact that so many people who professed to know him well liked him so much. Many of those who worked with him in Congress, including heavyweights like Barber Conable, were quick to tell me with great emphasis what a decent man he was. The same was true of those who worked for him in his various appointive posts (although I always wonder a little about a director of Central Intelligence ostensibly admired by a bunch of people who usually resist and resent their civilian bosses). Everybody has heard all the stories about how kind he was to his grandchildren.

I also heard all the stories about what a wonderful kid he had been, so obliging one of his family nicknames was Willing Feet. He was a favorite of his teachers and classmates. One day in Quincy Market in Boston I ran into an elderly and very tweedy man who told me he had seen me criticizing Bush on television. He wanted to give me a different perspective he had gained as the basketball coach at Andover when "Poppy" was a student. The young Bush was, in fact, serving as manager of the team, meaning the nonplaying volunteer who did the scut work of bringing the balls and towels to practice. Then one afternoon, Mr. Chips told me, he had seen Bush idly shooting baskets and realized that he was probably a better player than some of the starters on the team. So he suggested to Bush that he become a player. He might even be a starter, said the coach. But Poppy would have none of it. He already had the chance to play on the first team in baseball, he explained, so it wouldn't be fair to take it away from somebody else in basketball, too. I didn't doubt the story was true. I had heard too many like it.

But I had a hard time reconciling another account of George Bush's saintly behavior with the politician I saw boasting to a blue-collar worker about how he "tried to kick a little ass" in his debate with Geraldine Ferraro in 1984.

My principal complaint with Bush, however, was that I thought he was the most vacuous man to occupy the Oval Office in my time in Washington. He seemed to want the presidency so he could cap off his stunning résumé. Once he got there, however, it became clear that the signals from his campaign were all correct—that is, that he had no idea of what he might do in the office to improve the condition of the society he governed other than, of course, prevent any tax increases. Read his lips. Indeed, he took his responsibilities to the American people so lightly that he chose Dan Quayle for vice president, twice. He had so little respect for the institutions of our democracy that he handed a lifetime appointment to the Supreme Court to Clarence Thomas just to make a point about race. Nyah, nyah, liberals.

Bill Clinton, by contrast, displayed all the right instincts. He had an extraordinary grasp of the most complex issues, as thorough and insightful as that of Carter. He offered intelligent and usually practical solutions to long-standing problems. He understood what needed to be done politically so that he could accomplish his aims governmentally. But he is the most selfish and egocentric politician I have ever seen in decades of close association with so many leaders who are egocentric and selfish. And those characteristics ultimately compromised his leadership and the presidency itself. There were never a lot of people telling anyone Bill Clinton was really a nice guy when you got to know him.

I first came to know Bush, although not well, when he was serving as chairman of the Republican National Committee during the height of the Watergate scandal in 1973. He was trying to persuade everyone that it wasn't a Republican Party scandal. No sir, by golly, the party was separate and pristine. No one took him seriously, but he didn't seem to be a bad guy. He was just another white-shoe Republican going from one appointive job to another and probably dreaming of a place on the national ticket. Most of all, he seemed to be a nice man. When my daughter died in 1977, he wrote a very kind letter recalling his own experience with the death of a child from leukemia.

But our relationship went from equable to wretched when Bush began to run for president in 1979. It was not entirely my fault, although I caused it. On the day that Bush announced his candidacy in May 1979, after months of testing the waters, I wrote a column for the *Star* that ran on the front page right next to the story about the declaration of his candidacy. The column began this way:

> After several months of stumping the country, George Bush has declared his candidacy for the Republican presidential nomination at a time when many professionals in his party suspect his campaign already has peaked.
>
> This is a harsh judgment, obviously, but it is one that you hear among Republicans who are unaligned and might be expected to be sympathetic toward, even supportive of, George Bush.
>
> There is, of course, no suggestion that Bush is a hopeless case. That kind of reading cannot be made about any candidate who has

at least enough money to see him through the early presidential primaries next year. And George Bush has that.

The column went on to discuss Bush's strengths and weaknesses as a candidate and to compare him with his rivals. It concluded:

> George Bush still has ample opportunity, obviously, to dissolve the doubts about his candidacy. If his stock begins to rise demonstrably in the polls, other Republicans will find virtues there they never suspected in the past. And if he wins a primary or two, all the reservations about him will be forgotten.
>
> But, for the moment, it is plain that he becomes an official candidate at a moment when his stock seems to be declining. That is not the usual way.

I compounded the problem a few months later by being incautious with a reporter. *The Wall Street Journal* was doing a piece in the fall of 1979 about how "the pack" of political reporters decided who were the serious contenders for president and who were not. So Robert Merry, then one of their many excellent reporters, came up to New Hampshire to spend a few days with me while I made my reporting rounds. I decided from the outset that there would be no going off the record, no tailoring of my routine, no nights early to bed when my habit was a few jars at dinner and a few more after dinner. At one point Merry asked me what I thought about Bush, and I replied, "If you hold him up to the light, he doesn't throw a shadow." When the story about "the leader of the pack" appeared on the front page of the *Journal* in December 1979, the quote was included. George was pissed, I was told by a friend in the Bush camp, but Barbara was really pissed. Steer clear.

The column about Bush peaking in May proved to be dead wrong when he won the Iowa precinct caucuses in January 1980, defeating Ronald Reagan in a shocking upset. I was sorry I had written it, or at least had written it so baldly, but my partner never complained, to his everlasting credit. He knew, although Bush did not, that at the time I wrote it the piece was the product of substantial and careful reporting. Among the unnamed sources who thought his campaign might have peaked too soon were two of Bush's most senior advisers. They were worried with good reason, because their candidate was not finding a message with the kind of substance to sustain it. He was, they told me in separate interviews conducted "on background," too preoccupied with the political game, not interested enough in giving voters a rationale for supporting him.

In Iowa, however, Bush was carried forward by his own determined efforts to reach as many Republicans as possible and by the cleverness of Rich Bond, the young professional who ran the Iowa operation and years later served as Republican national chairman. I was impressed enough two weeks before the caucuses to write a column saying Bush had "at least an outside chance" of defeating Reagan although Reagan was leading him better than three to one in opinion polls. The way columnists keep score, that counts as a three-run homer.

Bond understood that the caucus process might be intimidating to some people. It required them to go to a school or fire station or perhaps someone's home and then band together with other like-minded Republicans to express their presidential preference. The theory of the caucus-convention process is that at each step—the precinct caucus, then the county convention, then the congressional district convention, and finally the state convention—the people chosen to move up reflect the share of support for each candidate. If there were fifty people at the precinct caucus, and twenty of them were for Bush, he would be entitled to two of the five delegates representing the precinct at the county convention.

The Democrats had held precinct caucuses that attracted national attention in both 1972 and 1976, but for the Republicans this attention was a new experience, and Bond recognized some of them would be shy. So the campaign sent a postcard to everyone identified as a Bush supporter telling that supporter the time and place for the caucus and, more to the point, the names of neighbors also supporting Bush. In addition he established an elaborate telephone canvass of volunteers calling their neighbors. In Mason City, the community that was River City in *The Music Man*, Bush chairman Diane Ruebling arranged 2,000 calls in a population of 30,000. The plan worked even better than Bond expected. He sent out 8,000 cards, and Bush got 33,530 votes at the caucuses. It was the kind of tactic that became routine in subsequent campaigns, but Bond was a step ahead. It helped, too, that Reagan's manager, the usually brilliant John Sears, made a miscalculation and kept his candidate out of the state, above the fray, because he thought he was sitting on an unassailable lead.

Jules Witcover, Tom Ottenad, and I had dinner with Sears the Saturday night before the Monday caucuses, and we kept asking him if he was sure Reagan was going to make it. No problem, Sears kept saying, they had identified 30,000 Republicans they could rely upon and that would be enough even if the turnout reached something as outlandish as 60,000, which would be three times what it had been in 1976. But the next morning, Sears told me later, he went to church and there was the priest urging everyone to take part in the caucuses—and, not incidentally, causing Sears to wonder if his assumptions about how many votes he would need were correct. They were not. The turnout ran over 110,000, and Reagan's 31,148 votes were good for second place.

The morning after the caucuses I went over to the Fort Des Moines hotel to appear with Dave Broder, Tom Pettit, and Tom Brokaw on the *Today* show. When we went down to the coffee shop after doing our number, there was the entire Bush family eating the celebratory breakfast. I might as well get this over with, I said to myself, so I went over to the table and said, "Congratulations, George, I guess I'm going to have to write you a new peak." It was an invitation to take his best shot so we could put this behind us. Bush, trying to be gracious but failing, grudgingly muttered something about how mistakes happen once in a while. I thought he was a wimp. Barbara Bush gave me an unforgiving glare. I didn't think she was a wimp.

The fears of Bush's advisers were well founded. Bush kept talking about how he had "the big Mo"—for political momentum—but he didn't use his new celebrity to tell the voters what he wanted to do as president now that he had their attention. The result was that in the four weeks between the caucuses and the New Hampshire primary that year, Reagan rolled right over him and, for all practical purposes, won the nomination.

As a candidate Bush was the quintessential empty suit. In his speeches he would list all the problems he intended to deal with as president, but he wouldn't say how he intended to deal with them

because he didn't know and wasn't very interested. The only thing
that mattered seemed to be winning the damned thing. The same
was true of his campaign for the presidency in 1988, when he had
the good fortune to be opposed by a candidate, Michael S. Dukakis,
who didn't understand how to fight back. And it was true of Bush's
1992 campaign for reelection against Bill Clinton, who did know
how to fight back and then some. When an incumbent president
who has successfully promulgated a war against a Saddam Hussein,
meaning the George Bush of 1992, can get only 38 percent of the
vote against two people as politically flawed as Bill Clinton (43 percent) and, for heaven's sake, Ross Perot (19 percent), he is a paper
tiger. Or, as they used to say in New York, he's so light he could walk
on a charlotte russe.

Bush had a special problem figuring out how to deal with Jules
and me when we wrote our books chronicling his campaigns and
asked to interview him. He resisted in 1980 out of hostility, which
was understandable. But then he found out Reagan had spent an
hour with us in the Oval Office. So Bush not only invited us to interview him but gave us a couple of tapes of a diary he had dictated
most days during the primary campaign in New Hampshire. We
used one brief quotation from it in our 1980 book but decided
against using any more excerpts. He was such a whiner it was too
embarrassing. We even returned the tapes without copying them, a
bit of preppy good form of a kind neither Jules nor I have often been
accused. We must have had a dizzy spell.

After the 1984 election the same pattern was followed. Reagan
gave us a long interview so Bush felt obliged to follow suit, although
we were informed by an intermediary he wasn't happy about the
whole thing. After the 1988 campaign the new president would
agree only to answer a few written questions. And after his loss in
1992 he sent back a succinct message: "Tell those guys to go fuck
themselves." I felt better about that one.

My problem with Bush went beyond what I saw as his shallow-
ness, however. I think he demonstrated repeatedly that, as he once
said himself in an interview with David Frost, he would do whatever
it took to win an election. He might have been a sweetheart at Andover and Yale, but he was a totally amoral campaigner.

Preparing for his 1988 campaign, Bush was taking special pains to counter the image of "the wimp" that he had acquired in eight years as a yes-man vice president for Reagan. Given his history as an athlete at Yale and a Navy fighter pilot in World War II, it shouldn't have been necessary. But he had become an object of derision because he made such a determined effort to accommodate himself not just to the president but to the most conservative elements of his party by tailoring his views on, for instance, abortion rights. Then, when a dinner was held to honor the memory of the late William Loeb, the viciously conservative publisher of *The Union Leader* in Manchester, New Hampshire, the vice president showed up and spoke despite the fact that Loeb had disparaged him repeatedly in print, labeling him at one point as "unfit to be the Republican nominee." Bush described Loeb as "part of a great newspaper tradition of outspoken publishers." But everyone in politics knew that Bill Loeb was one of a kind, a man who wrote about Henry Kissinger as "Kissinger the Kike" and President Dwight D. Eisenhower as "Dopey Dwight" and Senator Edmund S. Muskie as "Moscow Muskie." Loeb wasn't just "outspoken," he was venal. So what we saw was Bush kowtowing both to Nackey Loeb, the publisher's widow and successor as publisher, because she was the one now writing the vicious editorials, and to the extremists of the right who were the only people imaginable who might have wanted to honor the memory of William Loeb. Then a few weeks later it was Bush praising Jerry Falwell and meeting with Jim Bakker. At one point the preppy from Connecticut even described himself as a born-again Christian.

So it was no surprise when the columnist George Will, the high priest of the right, called Bush a "lap dog." And it was no secret that he was not a favorite of Nancy Reagan or of others close to Reagan. Indeed, Paul Laxalt, the senator from Nevada who had been Reagan's closest political ally since the days when both were governors, considered running for the 1988 nomination himself for a few weeks, largely because he was appalled by the notion of a Bush presidency. Laxalt, a politician of quality, knew an empty suit when he saw one.

Bush's frenzy to rid himself of the wimp image reached a noxious level, however. In a *60 Minutes* interview with Diane Sawyer, then of CBS News, he cited his history as a father who had endured the

246 • JACK W. GERMOND

death of a daughter from leukemia as evidence of how tough he was. Asked if he had a response to Will, Bush replied: "Just that he'll never play linebacker for the Chicago Bears. Have you ever seen him? I'll put my record out there with anybody. You know that I was shot down two months after my twentieth birthday fighting for my country. I didn't detect any wimp factor there. Did you know that we had to sit, my wife and I, and watch a child wrenched from our hearts in six months of cancer, knowing she was going to die? A little strength comes from that."

I don't expect much of politicians, but that was clearly going beyond the bounds. Experiencing the death of a child doesn't make you tough; it is just something you are obliged to go through. I obviously had the firsthand experience to know as much, as I was reminded in a dozen telephone calls from friends the day after Bush appeared.

In the campaign against Dukakis, Bush displayed other facets of his willingness to do whatever it took to win the White House. It was a campaign based on two premises. The first was that Dukakis could be depicted as unpatriotic because he had refused, on the advice of his state attorney general, to order the Pledge of Allegiance recited in every public school classroom in the commonwealth. The second was that he could be depicted as soft on crime because a black man serving a sentence for murder, Willie Horton, was allowed to go on a weekend furlough from prison during which he committed another violent crime. These were the linchpins of the Bush campaign, and they worked because Dukakis was so naïve he thought the voters would see through them. When I asked him in June 1988 how he was going to "deal with the patriotism question" Bush was raising, Dukakis replied, "I'm not going to deal with it anymore. People are too smart to listen to that."

That was the problem with Dukakis throughout that year. He thought the campaign was some kind of an educational exercise in which the voters would sort out the serious stuff rather than being beguiled by things such as Bush's television commercials accusing Dukakis of polluting Boston Harbor and unleashing black murderers on innocent women and children. He had a strong cadre of street-smart advisers—Nick Mitropoulos, John Sasso, Charlie Baker, Jack Corrigan among them—who understood how the campaign needed to react, but Dukakis was simply unwilling. He didn't understand that television's influence on American politics had reached the point at which the image on the screen was all that mattered, whether it was a picture of Willie Horton in a commercial or one of Michael Dukakis looking totally out of place driving a tank on the evening news.

I had known Dukakis since his first campaign for governor in 1974, and although I thought well of him as a public official, I would never have been considered a fan. He was too controlled, too dry for my taste. But one night during the New York primary I saw a different Dukakis, and I have wondered ever since what might have happened if the American people had gotten even a glimpse of this other side.

It was the night of the Academy Awards, and Dukakis's cousin Olympia Dukakis was the favorite to win the Oscar for best supporting actress. The candidate was scheduled to make a speech at a catering hall in Staten Island, then drive back to watch the Oscars on television with some campaign workers and friends at a bar and grill in Greenwich Village. I followed him to Staten Island because I wanted some time for an interview and Mitropoulos had arranged for me to ride back into Manhattan with the candidate, which would give me at least forty minutes. But the event ran late, so we ended up watching the program in the office of the caterer—several members of the campaign staff, a few local pols, the candidate, and me, all sitting in chairs arranged in a semicircle in front of a television set. Dukakis was sitting in an executive armchair on my immediate left, staring intently as the envelope was opened and the announcement came that the winner was—Olympia Dukakis, for *Moonstruck*.

The caterer's office exploded in cheers from everyone but Dukakis. He was gripping the arms of the chair so tightly I could see the whites of his knuckles and the cords of muscle running up his forearms. Tears were streaming down both cheeks. A few moments later Olympia accepted the Oscar, waved it toward the screen, and shouted, "Let's go, Michael." Again the office rang with cheers, and again Dukakis was riveted by his emotions, gripping the chair, knuckles white, his face wet with tears. A few minutes later, settling into the back of the car for the ride into Manhattan, he was still overcome with the moment. All the way to Manhattan he poured out the story of how hard his cousin had worked for so many years, all the time she and her husband spent in backwater theaters in New Jersey learning their craft and trying to build their careers. You have to understand how hard she worked, Jack, that's what nobody understands, how hard she worked. And now she had succeeded. The lesson was clear. I had long since forgotten whatever it was I wanted to interview him about, but I had seen a side of Michael Dukakis rarely shown. Every time I read about or hear someone on television talking about the colorless automaton whom George Bush defeated in 1988 I think of that night.

In my eyes, Bush hit his absolute low point one day in October at Christ the King High School in Queens, where he had gone to accept once again the endorsement of the Police Benevolent Association. It was a classic photo opportunity. Behind Bush on the stage were several dozen cops in uniform standing at attention. In front of him in the audience were several hundred Catholic kids waving little American flags and screaming their approval of the death penalty. All in all, it was an inspiring picture. There's nothing quite like young kids showing how bloodthirsty they can be.

The drama of the occasion, however, was provided by a man named Matthew Byrne, whose patrolman son had recently been shot and killed by a drug dealer he was trying to arrest. The grieving father presented his son's shield to Bush and told him that he had established a foundation in his son's name. To which Bush replied: "If the liberal governor of Massachusetts doesn't understand it when a Matt Byrne stands up and creates a foundation for his son, I do and so do the American people." Riotous applause from the kids with the flags.

What struck me later as I repeated this story to my friends was that the reporters of my generation, the older hacks, were the only ones appalled by the willingness of a presidential candidate to stoop so low. Many in the next generation, equally capable reporters, seemed to shrug it off, suggesting this was the kind of thing they had come to expect. Or, more to the point, they had seen nothing different.

In interviews after the campaign, Lee Atwater and Roger Ailes, Bush's two principal strategists in that campaign, kept telling Jules and me how difficult it was to get Bush to do the tough things that were necessary to win the election. But the important thing is that in the end he *always* did whatever they asked, whatever it took.

The passage of time hasn't warmed my relationship with George Bush. Two or three years after he left office, I ran into him at the Portland, Maine, airport. It was seven o'clock in the morning, and I was seated on a Boston-bound commuter plane drinking coffee and reading a newspaper when two Secret Service agents came up the aisle followed by the former president. He spotted me, nodded curtly, said, "Hello, Jack," and passed on to the rear of the plane.

"Good morning, Mr. President," I replied, and that was the end of it. There was no small talk about old times and how the hell are you, old buddy. I didn't notice if he cast a shadow.

I should note here that I might appear to be guilty of a conflict of interest in defending Dukakis against Bush. In 1987 I had fallen in love with Alice Travis, a political activist and campaign operative from California. At the time she was working in Denver for the Gary Hart campaign with the responsibility for seeking support among the so-called superdelegates to the Democratic convention. After the Hart candidacy self-immolated, Alice moved to the Dukakis campaign for the rest of the 1988 cycle. But it should be clear that I formed my impressions of both George Bush and Michael Dukakis long before Alice and I met in 1984. The same applies to my sour views on Bill Clinton, for whom Alice worked in the 1992 campaign as political director for California. So much for disclosure statements.

My history with Bill Clinton was quite different from that with Bush. I met him in the spring of 1978. I had gone to Arkansas to write a piece for the *Star* about a Senate campaign when I was told by several local politicians that I should meet this kid who was the attorney general and now running for governor. He was, I was told, a piece of work. He was indeed. In fact, he was impressive enough that after listening to him for an hour or so I ended up writing a column about him for the *Star* that ran under the headline ANOTHER POLITICAL WUNDERKIND—CAN HE HIT THE CURVE BALL?

It began this way:

LITTLE ROCK, ARK.—One of them comes along every once in a while—some young politician so precocious that there seems to be a limitless future for him—and the word buzzes through the political community.

A decade or so ago, for example, professionals used to talk about a young lieutenant governor of Colorado, Mark Hogan. Then there was the rising star of Democratic politics in Texas, Ben Barnes. Then it was the Republican governor of Missouri, Christopher Bond. There have been at least a dozen others in that same period.

It usually doesn't work out. Something happens so that the promise is not fulfilled. Their timing is bad or they get caught in a scandal or they lack the final drive of ambition. Sometimes they just aren't up to the big league of politics—like the legendary baseball rookie who hits .400 all through spring training, then runs into real pitching and wires home: "Don't rent out my room, Mom. They started throwing curve balls today."

This year the political "phenom" is Bill Clinton, who at 31 is about to become governor of Arkansas after only two years as state attorney general. He is engaged in a five-way contest for the Democratic nomination in the primary next week and is considered likely to win with such a landslide that he will avoid a runoff. And already politicians here and, more important, elsewhere are talking about Bill Clinton's future. A Little Rock columnist noted in print, for example, that Clinton will be only 46 years old at the time of the 1992 presidential election campaign.

The column continued with a summary of his credentials and some quotations from an interview about his good intentions toward the people of Arkansas. It was, by any measure, an outrageous puff piece, and Clinton clearly loved it. He had faked me out of my shoes. He had learned he could con the national press just like the locals.

I kept in touch and went by to see him again when I passed through Little Rock while reporting on the Carter-Reagan presidential campaign in 1980. I had been told by Paul Manafort, a professional I had learned to trust, that Reagan had a good chance of carrying Arkansas, so I went to see for myself. If it was true, I figured, Carter was definitely down the drain.

Clinton invited me to the governor's mansion for a late-afternoon drink and told me that both he and Carter were going to be all right in their campaigns for reelection. He had seen some troubling polling figures, but he wasn't taking them seriously. The poll taker wasn't very good, and he had replaced him. That sounded an alarm bell for me simply because a candidate who fires a poll taker because of the numbers is usually a candidate kidding himself. In this case, nonetheless, it was hard to imagine him losing to Frank White, the Republican challenger who was so culturally conservative he seemed out of place in Democratic Arkansas. But Clinton's and Carter's managers in Arkansas missed a late rush of voter registrations in the northwest part of the state that had been stimulated by the Moral Majority. The result was that both Reagan and Frank White won Arkansas.

Two years later I was back down there watching Clinton's comeback. It turned out that White had made himself a figure of fun early in his term by supporting the notion of teaching creationism as well as Darwinism in the public schools. A cartoonist for the *Arkansas Gazette,* George Fisher, had drawn White holding a half-eaten banana, the peels curled back over his fist, as he made the case for creationism. It was such a hit that he had continued to draw White holding a half-eaten banana, whatever the topic. The image was devastating.

But Clinton was campaigning hard and taking no chances he would seem too uptown for his constituents, an image that had contributed to his defeat in 1980, according to postelection polling. His wife was now calling herself Hillary Rodham Clinton, not just Hillary Rodham, as she had done during his first term. She was only moderately amused when I told her in Jonesboro one night that I was pleased to see she and Bill had been married. I inferred that I was not the first to have made that lame wisecrack.

In any case, Clinton was returned to office—and almost immediately to the future books of those handicapping politicians for national office. I made a point of keeping up with him, stopping in Little Rock or calling him or Betsy Wright, the longtime professional who was running his political operation. Occasionally Clinton would call to tell me about something he was pushing on education or economic development or whatever. I was by no means the only national political reporter he was staying in touch with, so

I managed to avoid getting too giddy about his calls. But I gave him credit in my head for keeping himself in the picture while getting himself reelected.

Like so many of them, he didn't like rivals for attention. I went down to Arkansas one weekend in 1987 to spend a day flying around the state with Dale Bumpers. I had the notion he was going to run for president in 1988, and I wanted to see if he still had his fastball as a campaigner. When I arrived at the Little Rock airport general aviation terminal early on a Saturday morning, however, I found Clinton as well as Bumpers. The governor and senator were sharing a small campaign plane for a day of hopping around northwest Arkansas. At each stop they would hold a joint press conference, then separate for a couple of hours of solo campaigning before flying on. The day would end with a joint appearance at a party dinner in Harrison, a town of 10,000 or so. Clinton was surprised to see me and, I suspected, a little miffed when I told him I was there to cover Bumpers and when I went off with Bumpers at each stop. He was accustomed to being the Alpha Dog in this relationship.

All this was brought home to me almost seven years later, when Clinton, now the president, invited me and a couple of other reporters for an early-evening drink as part of one of those stroke-the-press campaigns that their flacks tell them will help. We were ushered into the Oval Office, and Clinton began showing us the various artifacts displayed on the credenza behind his desk. When he found one from Harrison, he turned to me and said, "You remember Harrison, Jack, we were there with Dale a while back." This was the same Bill Clinton who couldn't remember whether he had ever been alone with Monica Lewinsky.

Throughout his time as governor, I always thought Clinton was a little too cute to be a totally effective self-promoter. He called me a few weeks after his reelection in 1990 to talk about whether he would be able to run for president in 1992 considering the promise he had made to Arkansas voters to serve out the four-year term for which he was running. I wondered why he had made such a pledge in a state that seemed to take pride in the national figures it had sent to Washington. But Clinton insisted he had to do it, the pressure from the opposition was too intense. They were saying he wanted to use the governorship as a stepping-stone, if you can imagine that. What was clear, of course, was that he never had any intention of keeping the pledge and was only concerned with how to get around it with the least damage in national terms. I was not in the advice business, but I thought he had been a damned fool to make the promise. He could have finessed the question if he had been willing to take a little heat for a while, which he was not. No wonder they called him Slick Willie.

He was also, however, a politician who connected with people and, equally important, who had a genuine understanding of how government could work for them. I brushed off the stories about his womanizing on the totally mistaken theory that if they were true they would have been exposed by the Arkansas press or his political enemies or both. It became more difficult to keep my head in the sand as I heard more stories about Clinton making a move on the daughter of a prominent political ally or holding on a little too long in an embrace with the sexy wife of a candidate. And when the Gennifer Flowers story surfaced, I didn't doubt it for a minute. Clinton's cautiously parsed denials were so much like the stories gradually pulled out of him about whether he smoked marijuana and how he dodged the draft. But I shared what I took to be the popular consensus that his private behavior was relevant only if it intruded on his public performance. And, I figured, now that he was becoming president of the United States, he would have enough sense not to be playing slap and tickle with some bimbo. Wrong again.

My dismay at Clinton because of the Monica Lewinsky episode wasn't based on moralistic disapproval of his conduct. My own personal conduct has not always been unblemished, and I dislike judgmental people. But a president and political leader is not free to act as his glands dictate. Quite aside from whatever obligation he feels to his wife, he has a responsibility to the people who got him there, to his political party, to those who serve on his staff or in his administration, and, finally, to his constituents. With Clinton, however, loyalty ran only one way, from the bottom up. So he lied to those who deserved the truth, and he made it impossible for himself to fulfill his commitments to his constituents to deal with tasks as daunting as finding a formula to protect the Social Security and Medicare programs for generations to come.

Clinton's conduct was particularly egregious because he had

every reason to know he couldn't get away with it, beginning with the experience of Gary Hart in 1987.

Hart had emerged from the Democratic wreckage of 1984 as a strong favorite for the nomination he had lost to Walter Mondale by a whisker. But he had a long-established reputation as a man who pursued and often caught women dating back to his days as George McGovern's campaign manager in 1972—a reputation public enough that reporters raised it on his campaign plane the day after he announced his candidacy in April 1987. Hart rebuffed the questions, replying in effect that whatever he might have done in the past, he was clean as a whistle now. Follow me around, he told an interviewer for *The New York Times Magazine*.

I was one of the simple tools who believed him. I thought Hart was so well positioned to win the presidency that he would never be foolish enough to jeopardize the ultimate prize of American politics. When I accompanied him on a weekend of campaigning in Alabama and Georgia later the same month, I became even more convinced of his dominant position. His new stature as the front-runner seemed to have given him a greater self-confidence, which in turn had made him a more outgoing candidate. Those of us who had known him over the years knew he could be extraordinarily charming, and now that quality was less often hidden under a brooding reticence.

And as for messing around with women, I had it right from the horse's mouth. I had gone to dinner with Hart on the first night of that campaign weekend, along with his wife, Lee; two of his close advisers, Billy Shore and John Emerson; and his friend Bill Broadhurst. Seated at one end of the table with Hart and Broadhurst, I asked Gary about the womanizing issue being raised on his campaign plane. He replied by telling me how it happened, then added with table-thumping emphasis: "I don't have to worry about that stuff because there's nothing there."

It wasn't said for Lee's benefit. She was at the other end of the table in a separate conversation with Shore and Emerson. So I took it to mean there's nothing there now even if, as we both know, there was something there in the past, because this is too damned important. And, besides, would he lie to his old friend Jack? As it turned out, he would, shocking as that may seem. It turned out, in fact, that the very next day, during a campaign stop at a National Guard armory in Columbus, Georgia, Hart telephoned Donna Rice to make arrangements for her visit to Washington the following weekend—the visit that ended, of course, in blowing up into a political scandal that destroyed Hart's candidacy.

Clinton had followed that closely enough so that he put his own tentative plans for 1988 on ice for a while. If a little cruise on the *Monkey Business* was going to cause such a gigantic stink for Gary Hart, he decided, it would not be a good year for some newcomer from Arkansas to be vetted for the first time. The lesson he apparently did not learn from the Hart episode is that political leaders— and certainly presidential candidates and presidents—have a responsibility to many people they dare not forget every time they fancy a break in life's routine.

Presidents tend to be self-centered, of course. They are surrounded by people telling them how wonderful they are, and it is hard not to inhale. But Clinton was more egocentric than most. He grew up, after all, as the fair-haired "good kid" who always did the right thing and enjoyed the fawning attention of the adults around him. He was the one who won the Rhodes Scholarship and went off to Oxford, and he was the one who got special treatment from the draft board. Then he went into politics, and, except for a couple of years as a lawyer and teacher, he was once again the center of attention, the sun around whom the planets rotated. He was the principal surrounded by members of his staff who would clean up after him when he made a mess.

It was clear that his mother, Virginia Kelley, doted on him. I met her the weekend before his inauguration after someone called Alice from the White House, saying the new president's mother wanted to go to the racetrack, and they wanted somebody who knew the trainers and jockeys at Laurel to help her with handicapping. So Bob Woodward of the *Post*, his wife, Elsa Walsh, and Alice and I joined Virginia and her husband, Richard Kelley, a charming man who had retired from business and shared his wife's enthusiasm for the track. It was a splendid afternoon. Virginia Kelley turned out to be the presidential relative least affected by her status that I had ever met and, more to the point, an excellent handicapper who studied the *Daily Racing Form* at length. We both cashed some handsome exactas. When we returned to the track the following year, she was suffering from cancer and only a few weeks from death. But she could place her own bets, she said, because she had been given a blood transfusion, and "I'm having one of my good days." We didn't pick as many winners that day, but Virginia Kelley shared the universal view of the dedicated horseplayer: The next best thing to a winning day at the track is a losing day at the track. Her son Bill, however, disapproved of her addiction to the racetrack. He had other hobbies.

Most of all, Bill Clinton is a politician who thinks he can charm his way through any situation. He could, as they say in Pine Bluff, talk a dog out of a pork chop. It is a skill that sometimes has led him into trouble and perhaps a false sense of security. If he can schmooze long enough, he seems to think, he can bring anyone around. Most of all, he wants to please everyone. After the Republicans took control of Congress in 1994 and began to promote their social agenda, Clinton suddenly said at a press conference that he might find it possible after all to support a constitutional amendment to permit prayer in the public schools. The very notion was a betrayal of one of the most loyal constituencies of his party, Jewish voters, who had just cast more than 80 percent of their ballots for Democrats in the House and Senate elections. So the next day Clinton backed off with a White House "clarification" of his remarks. What was clear, nonetheless, was that he was so anxious to please the newly ascendant Newt Gingrich he forgot that not everyone looks benignly on the idea of prayer in public schools.

The quintessential example of Clinton trying to please was something he said off the cuff during the Pennsylvania primary campaign of 1992. It was Earth Day, and Candidate Clinton was at Drexel Institute in Philadelphia delivering a speech on the environment. He ran through every issue, showing where he stood and where he disagreed with the Republicans. I was following along on the printed text desultorily when I realized he was adding a few things. He had been surprised, he said, when he moved "into town"—meaning Hot Springs—to discover that there were just as many snakes, spiders, and tarantulas on the ground as there had been in Hope. Then he said, "So we had to figure out how to make them our friends rather than our enemies."

I wrote the quotation down in the margin of the speech text, although I noticed most of the reporters who traveled with him regularly paid no attention. They apparently had become inured to this kind of world-class bullshit. At dinner that night I pulled out my notes and read what Clinton had said to Curtis Wilkie of *The Boston Globe,* a Mississippian with a thick accent and a fine sense of the ridiculous. "Shoot," Wilkie said, "in Mississippi we used to take a shovel to them."

In Bill Clinton's world, however, everyone has to be a friend.

CHAPTER 17

CAN I TAKE A
MULLIGAN?

It turns out that I have not made
the world safe for democracy. But I have always argued that newspapers should not have any civic purpose beyond telling readers
what is happening. If the political system is rotting away, as seems
to be the case, it is our job to report it but not to make the repairs—
except perhaps on the editorial pages, where they seem to think all
things are possible. Stuffy as it sounds, it has always seemed to me
that reporters have a certain purity of purpose that would be under-
mined if we found some cause to espouse.

I've also been a leading advocate and practitioner of what the political scientists disparage as horse race journalism, which means
putting the emphasis on winners and losers rather than the Issues.
I would agree that voters need to be told where candidates stand, or
pretend to stand, on their concerns. But a reporter who doesn't
quickly tell the readers what they most want to know—the score—
won't last long on the beat. Better he should teach political science.

The longer I have covered politics, the more dubious I have become about electing people on the basis of some checklist of issues.
In presidential elections, other things being equal, I prefer candidates who support abortion rights and don't feel some macho need

to spend huge amounts of money on the Pentagon. In other words, I am sort of a garden-variety liberal inclined toward Democrats. But "other things being equal" is one of those caveats that leave a lot of room. My experience has been that other things never are equal. The fatal flaw in the sorting of candidates by issues is that it is almost impossible to anticipate which issues will confront a president during his four years in office. No one was thinking about Saddam Hussein when George Bush was elected or about Monica Lewinsky when Bill Clinton was elected.

The hard truth is that after all these campaigns I don't know what qualities make a good president. I used to think it was just intelligence, but there has been no one more intelligent than Jimmy Carter, and we know how that turned out. The one quality I believe to be essential is the ability to understand that political opponents are adversaries, not enemies. But that alone is probably not enough. Ronald Reagan had that quality, and look at some of the bizarre things he did.

In any case, the joy of covering politics has not been diminished by the lack of great purpose on my part or by my inability to find any final answers. It is the joy of knowing America and of telling the readers how things work, to the extent you can find out. It is the people you meet and the places you go and the tales they tell you about who did what to whom and why. In the last forty years I have covered stories in forty-nine of the fifty states—the only time I made it to Hawaii was to pick up a handsome fee for making a speech— and I have come to know the country intimately. It isn't all rewarding. One year, for reasons lost in the mists, I was obliged to make five trips to Utah in the days when you had to go to some trouble just to get a drink before dinner. Except for Charleston's special ambience, even a few days in South Carolina can be a long sentence at times, and I have never found much redeeming social value in Indianapolis outside of the St. Elmo steak house. But there have been good political stories almost everywhere at one time or another. In our days at the *Star*, with its limitless appetite for politics, Jules or I frequently set out on prospecting trips when we didn't have particular stories in mind but knew there would be plenty of them out there. Neither of us ever came back empty-handed. With the *Sun*, where the appetite for politics is understandably less voracious, we no longer write about obscure regional governors' conferences.

The country is less diverse than it was a generation ago. The airports tend to look the same, and the same fast-food restaurants line the road from downtown to the interstate. More to the point for me, everyone sees the same television programs and the same network news, meaning that most people gain their basic understanding of politics from the same superficial sources. There are, nonetheless, still differences in the way they play politics in Boston and Austin, Tallahassee and Sacramento. And most of the time I have looked forward to the travel because of the people—politicians and other reporters, usually—I would be seeing again.

Going up to Boston I could share a meal or a few pops with Ed Jesser, a consultant who is not unknown at Doyle's, or Dave Nyhan of the *Globe*, who seems to be known everywhere. If I was continuing on up to New Hampshire, I could have dinner with Joe Keefe to find out about the Democrats or Tom Rath to catch up on the Republicans. Or I could have a talk with Hugh Gregg, a onetime governor who has run Republican primary campaigns there going back to the 1960s and Nelson Rockefeller. I wouldn't go to Miami without calling Ron Silver, a state legislator who took his politics seriously. In Maine the first call would be to Harold Pachios, who once worked in Lyndon Johnson's White House and practiced law and Democratic politics in Portland and Augusta ever after. A trip to Los Angeles would be a chance to have dinner with John Emerson or Bill Carrick or Joe Cerrell, all of whom know different things. In Austin my first call would be to Saralee Tiede, the best political reporter in the state for many years, and the second to Jack Martin, a professional who cut his teeth in politics as Lloyd Bentsen's main man in the state. In Chicago the wise man for years has been Bill Daley, even if his wisdom was called into question by his decision to join Bill Clinton's cabinet. In Des Moines the imperative has always been dinner with David Yepsen of *The Des Moines Register*, one of the premier political writers in the country, and before him Jim Flansburg. If you were looking for a reading on North Carolina, Ferrell Guillory was the name that came first to mind. If you were going to Alabama, you wanted to call Al Lapierre and Natalie Davis. And so on.

The trick is knowing who is contemporarily relevant. The danger for any political reporter is relying on people who may be great company and even old friends but who are no longer good sources because they are out of touch. In some places I have developed separate generations of sources—those I have relied upon for years and those I am learning to rely upon now so I can avoid being beaten by younger reporters. In every state, as the demographics change, the culture and politics change as well.

There are, of course, some politicians who are just fun to cover because they are smart and interesting people from whom you learn something or so outrageous they are intriguing. Spending a day with Ed Rendell when he was mayor of Philadelphia or a night with Ray Flynn when he was mayor of Boston was a cram course in the problems of the big cities. Spending a day with Edwin Edwards when he was governor of Louisiana was a chance to see that politicians don't have to be hypocrites. Spending a day with David Duke in north Louisiana or the New Orleans suburbs told you how thinly concealed is the racial resentment felt by people who would never join a lynch mob. Touring North Carolina's Fifth District with Richard Burr, the Republican congressman there, showed me how great the distance really was between Washington and Winston-Salem. Walking down the main drag in Peoria with Robert Michel showed me how a quintessential Midwest Republican kept in touch with the thinking back home.

The easiest part of the job is covering anything that qualifies as an event—a debate or a convention or a candidate's trip. The story unfolds before your eyes, and there are always a lot of people around who know what it means, if anything, and why it happened that way. There are always many precedents against which the story can be weighed. And it's pleasant because there are both sources and your reporter friends with whom to have dinner and maybe sit around the saloon for an hour or two telling stories and comparing notes. I cannot even estimate how many hundreds of dinners I have eaten over the years with, to name the most obvious suspects, Tom Ottenad, John Mashek, Walter Mears, Bob Healy, Curtis Wilkie, and Loye Miller. There are rules for this sort of thing. Dave Broder is good company and welcome if he doesn't insist on bringing a political scientist along. Mears, who eats only steak, has not been allowed to choose a restaurant since he took us to a place called Fazio's in Milwaukee in 1972. My partner, Jules Witcover, isn't allowed to choose the wine since he ordered a bottle that came without a label in 1967. The "Germond rule"—now observed only by the senior set—says the check is whacked up by the number of people at the table, which encourages heavy drinking and dessert.

Poker games used to be a staple of covering campaigns, as did gin rummy. Warren Weaver of *The New York Times* and I had a running gin score, paid off to the closest five dollars, that I kept in my wallet for twenty-five years. I loved to play with Bob Novak because he hated to lose. We had a rule that if we were playing on a plane, the hands were thrown in the moment the wheels touched down for landing. Flying into Pittsburgh on a Jimmy Carter charter one day in 1976, Novak was about eight dollars ahead of me and crowing about it. Suddenly, however, the ceiling dipped below acceptable levels and the pilot had to circle for a half hour or so. I used the time to nail Novak with a triple schneider and ended up winning a few bucks. He whined about it for days. I enjoyed it immensely and will probably forget about it when I am ninety.

Some of us, myself included, regularly drank too much, but we insulated ourselves from criticism, or so we thought, by drinking hard stuff only after we had filed our copy for the day. As long as you got up in the morning for that seven-thirty breakfast interview or seven o'clock plane, you were all right. Or at least that was my rationalization. There was always some sex happening on presidential campaigns, but I wasn't a regular participant. It wasn't that I disapproved. But there were relatively few women on campaign buses in those days, and not many who seemed more interesting than another evening swapping stories with the boys.

As a columnist I rarely ride the campaign planes anymore. But on those occasions when I have dropped in for a day or two, I have seen much less poker and drinking, and the womanizing, if any, has been reasonably well concealed. The next generation of leading political reporters—people like Paul West, my colleague with the *Sun*, Dan Balz and Tom Edsall of the *Post*, Robin Toner and Rick Berke of the *Times*—are every bit as good as we were as reporters, but their lifestyles are more disciplined. They tend to drink white wine or beer rather than Irish whiskey, and they carry cell phones so they can talk to their offices more than the once or twice a day I considered adequate. They go out running early in the morning, and a lot of them eat salads from room service, believe it or not. Some of the best—and often the most intensely motivated—are women. Many of the men seem to view covering politics as just another assignment, a place to get your ticket punched on the way to becoming managing editor or something equally Rotarian. For me and many of my contemporaries, covering politics was the ultimate assignment, an end in itself that you cherished and defended for the rest of your career. That isn't the case very often with the reporters of this generation, and I cannot say they're wrong.

The joy of the assignment has been tempered by the way politics has evolved over the last twenty years, at least at the national level. It has become too often a mindless contest between competing media consultants and fund-raisers working for candidates programmed by their poll takers. And those of us who cover politics, whether for newspapers or for television, have rarely given our readers and viewers an accurate, multidimensional, nuanced picture of either the people or the events we have covered. Instead, we have allowed the standards of the political managers to be the critical criteria in assessing candidates. The ones who are "serious" are those who can raise enough money and avoid taking unpopular positions on volatile issues.

Or they are the ones who do not commit a gaffe. Perhaps the most egregious weakness of those of us who cover politics is our lack of any sense of proportion. If a candidate misspeaks, God help him. Corrections and explanations are not allowed, lest we be accused of being "soft" on one candidate or the other. There are, of course, cases in which a minor episode may indeed reveal a basic inadequacy in a candidate. But there are too many in which candidates are doomed by a single sentence.

A classic case of a trivial matter blown far out of proportion may have been decisive, for example, in the contest for the Democratic presidential nomination in 1984. All through the primary season Walter Mondale and Gary Hart had competed intensively for the privilege of challenging President Ronald Reagan. The lead had swung back and forth until it seemed to come down to the final two primaries in California and New Jersey on the first Tuesday in June.

The Mondale strategy was to concentrate on winning New Jersey, where his union backing would be most effective, and settling for a decent share of the delegates in California, where the former vice president's protectionist message and stiff personal style contrasted poorly with the image of Hart as the candidate of the new generation and international economic expansion. With New Jersey in hand, all Mondale would need would be enough delegates from California to claim the morning after the primary that he had a majority to assure his nomination.

But ten days out I had dinner in New Brunswick one night with Bob Beckel, Mondale's campaign chief in New Jersey, and the late Paul Tully, a consultant I considered one of the most insightful analysts in the business. These were also men high on my list of those who, political qualifications aside, were good company. On this particular night, however, over several drinks and some barbecue better than you should expect in New Jersey, they were clearly in a funk. They never said we're going to lose here; they were too professional to say that to any reporter.

Nonetheless, from their account of which issues were cutting with whom among Jersey primary voters, I could infer that they thought they were going down the drain. The Hart managers had discovered New Jersey also had a yearning for the internationalist trade policies Hart was describing in his speeches. More important, Ray Strother, his media consultant and another certified star of the business, had designed a series of television spots showing Hart, with the then new Meadowlands sports complex as a backdrop, appealing to the pride of New Jersey voters in the economic success the state was suddenly enjoying after being maligned for so long. Tully and Beckel were watching those spots on New York and Philadelphia stations and feeling the ground breaking up under them.

Suddenly the prospect for the whole campaign was quite different. If Hart could win New Jersey as well as California, Mondale might not be able to hold the nomination even with his vastly greater support among party regulars and union leaders.

All that changed over the weekend ten days before the primary when Hart flew out to California to join his wife, Lee, in Los Angeles for a little live campaigning. One of the first stops was a cocktail party fund-raiser at the Bel Air home of a wealthy real estate developer where many of the beautiful people had gathered. He and Lee had been dividing the campaign duties, Hart told them. "The deal is we campaign separately," he said, "That's the bad news. The good news for her is she campaigns in California and I campaign in New Jersey." When Lee interjected that she had been given a chance to hold a koala bear, Hart dug himself in a little deeper. "I won't tell you what I got to hold," he said, "samples from a toxic dump."

It was the kind of wisecrack anyone could make while enjoying a balmy evening with the beautiful people in Bel Air looking out over the Pacific. But presidential candidates are not allowed even a wisecrack. In New Jersey, where the sensitivity to jokes about toxic wastes was high, Gary Hart was suddenly cooked. When I stopped by the Mondale headquarters on Monday I found Beckel and Tully displaying their customary ebullience. The infamous "Jersey joke" had been on the top of the front page of the Newark *Star-Ledger* and Mondale and his supporters were being allowed to cry crocodile tears all over radio, television, and the newspapers. Mondale himself was insisting, tut, tut, that Hart owed New Jersey an apology. He should join in a debate and explain himself, tut, tut.

More to the point, the Hart commercials that had seemed so effective in appealing to Jersey pride now seemed like apologies and probably should have been pulled. When Rudy Abramson of the *Los Angeles Times* and I had dinner that night with Sue Casey, the young professional from New Hampshire who had become Hart's national campaign scheduler, she was distraught. I can't believe this is so important, she kept saying. It was just a wisecrack, it can't be taken seriously. But it was. Although Hart won easily in California, Mondale captured all the New Jersey delegates and claimed the nomination.

Sue Casey was right, of course. The campaign should not have turned on a single wisecrack. But those of us in the press treated it as something approaching a mortal sin, a political gaffe of an order candidates are not permitted. And, more to the point, we aided and abetted Mondale and his managers in their display of hand-wringing. Those who argued that the real question for Jersey voters should be trade policy were drowned out by the hooting at Hart's clumsiness.

In the long run, of course, this episode probably didn't change the course of the Republic. Mondale lost to Reagan but Hart probably would have done so as well. And, as we have seen, Hart was given another chance four years later that he frittered away with a blonde. There are, however, cases where the fascination of the press with the picayune does make a critical difference.

At the presidential level we never seem to elect or even nominate the right candidate—or, at least, the candidate I would have preferred. On the contrary, the press is often responsible for sinking some of the best. One prime example is Howard H. Baker, Jr., of Tennessee, the longtime Republican leader of the Senate who ended his public career lending his credibility to Ronald Reagan as White House chief of staff in Reagan's final two years in office.

During the late 1970s Baker was the answer to the Washington dinner party parlor game question If you could just appoint someone president of the United States, who would it be? It wasn't unanimous, of course, but H'ard Henry, as some of his Tennessee friends liked to call him, probably would have been the man named most often. He had a reputation for being intelligent, decent, self-effacing, and sophisticated in the ways of the world of power. He was the Republican most feared by the Democrats in the White House, Carter and Mondale, as they looked ahead to the 1980 election.

But Baker stumbled as a candidate, and that was, for all practical purposes, the end of his hopes for the White House. It happened in November 1979, when he decided that he would follow up his declaration of candidacy with an appearance at a Republican state convention in Maine at which, his advisers assured those of us in the press, he would win a straw vote on presidential preference. I was one of the reporters who crowded onto his chartered plane to Portland for the grand occasion. Baker had the support of Senator William Cohen, the most popular politician in the state at the time, and of Hattie Bickmore, the Republican state chairman. Although George Bush had a summer home in the state, everyone said Baker was a far better fit with the kind of moderately progressive people who were Republican activists there.

Baker, however, went to bed without spending enough time in his hospitality suite the night before the vote, setting off some grousing among delegates about being taken for granted. At breakfast the following morning I began to hear some muttering about Bill Cohen trying to "dictate" the outcome of the straw vote. Sitting in the bleachers along one wall of the convention hall, Carolyn Stewart, a Baker volunteer from Boston and a political veteran, told me she was growing uneasy. Then Baker, a politician with a reputation for being both thoughtful and articulate, delivered a bum speech. The result was he lost the straw vote to Bush, 466 to 446. The instant judgment of press and politicians alike was that he had suffered a "stunning" setback—a judgment Baker shared. I had been scheduled to talk to him on the flight back to Washington that night, but when we got to the plane, he begged off. "I can't do it," he told me. "I don't know what to make of this thing, but I know it's bad. Call me next week." So instead I rode with Ron McMahan, perhaps his closest adviser, who swilled down six Jack Daniel's on the flight while he tried out various "explanations" that might be less damaging than the truth. Back in Washington, Baker told his wife, Joy, and McMahan that he knew the campaign might never recover, and he was right.

In the political press we buried him, writing at length about his humiliation and about what this political misjudgment said of his ability to be a successful candidate. We didn't write about what should have been the central question: Why in the world should a public official of the quality of Howard Baker be eliminated as a presidential candidate on the basis of this one episode? That would have required us to deal with the trivial nature of what we were all covering. We would have had to say to the readers and viewers, in effect, we have assigned all this high-powered journalistic manpower to cover what is essentially a meaningless story.

The Republic did not collapse because Howard Baker never became president. We also survived without other potential presidents in whom I saw special qualities—Nelson Rockefeller, Mo Udall, John Connally, Paul Laxalt, Dale Bumpers. But it would be hard to argue the case that we were better off with Reagan, Bush, and Clinton than we would have been with Howard Baker.

Given the people we have elected, it is not surprising that my interest in who's president has been flagging. The message seems to be that anyone can do the job well enough to muddle through four or eight years. There are enough people who make up a sort of permanent establishment to keep the White House on a relatively stable course. I've become more interested in campaigns at lower levels, which may be at least marginally less sophisticated and may have something to do with voters as well as commercials. In a presidential campaign that seems to be true only in those early precinct caucuses in Iowa and that first primary in New Hampshire. The images conveyed on television are important even in those contests, but they are not the entire campaign. Once the competition moves on to Florida and New York and California, the whole story is what happens on the home screen every night. Whether some candidate drew a crowd to a rally or failed to do so is largely irrelevant as anything other than an indicator of his organization's effectiveness. Who cares whether he can give a coherent speech if he has the money to buy saturation television advertising?

My attitude also has been affected, I suspect, by the facets of my life that have nothing to do with being out covering a campaign. My marriage to Barbara ended in a bitter divorce that grew out of circumstances I instigated. Alice and I were married, and we live in West Virginia on a bend of the Shenandoah River seventy-five minutes from our offices in Washington, where we keep an apartment for use two or three nights a week. More important, we are ten minutes from the Charles Town racetrack, where the thoroughbreds are extremely cheap but don't know it. My daughter Jessica Moreland, a pediatrician who does both clinical work and research, comes to visit occasionally and is in danger of becoming a serious person although she hides it well. Alice's son and daughter, David and Abigail Travis, and David's wife, Yukari, also come for visits. And many friends join us for weekends to eat the vegetables Alice grows when not working on a campaign. Sitting on my deck watching the river flow by while I study the racing form, I don't feel driven to spend every weekend traveling with some presidential candidate who has no real chance of being nominated but has either inherited or raised enough money so he can command some attention.

I have not given up on politics, however. I still nourish the notion that one of these years they will get it right and we will elect someone to the presidency who will bring out the best in the country. We might even find a leader willing to take an unpopular position occasionally because it is the right one to take, then set out to persuade Americans of that fact. That has been known to happen, but not lately.

EPILOGUE

They didn't get it right in the 2000 campaign, either. On the contrary, they got it so wrong I decided to quit writing a political column once the election was over.

I had been thinking about giving up the column for a year or so, but the decision crystallized when I realized I wasn't enjoying it. Nobody writes for newspapers for the money, so if there's no pleasure in it, there is no reason to do it. There were some bright spots, of course. The New Hampshire primary campaign was intriguing and revealing. And during the general election campaign I spent a few days every month reporting from Pennsylvania, the most intensely contested of the swing states with large prizes of electoral votes.

But the story was the presidential contest, and it was a bummer. The candidates were an obvious problem—two guys who had never once been forced to worry about the rent money. Both made me think of Jim Hightower's description of the elder George Bush— "born on third base and thought he hit a triple." I realized, of course, that it was not reasonable to write off someone simply because he or she has enjoyed a life of privilege and position. We have had many presidents with such backgrounds. But these were not impressive candidates, even by the cheapened standards of the time.

Although I didn't want to say so out loud, I had grown stuffy enough to question whether my work might be beneath whatever was left of my professional dignity. I couldn't convince myself that parsing the rhetoric of George W. Bush was serious work for a political reporter. The same could be said of trying to fathom which Al

Gore persona was the real one, if any. I thought it was totally appropriate that the campaign ended in the equivalent of a scoreless tie and that the loser became the winner by virtue of a Supreme Court finally revealing its partisanship for all to see.

All the factors that seemed to have been tainting American politics came together in the 2000 campaign. Both sides raised and spent such grotesque amounts—even more than in 1996—that money alone changed the nature of the campaign. When candidates have essentially unlimited budgets, they will hire more and more consultants to do more and more sophisticated manipulation of the process. If you want to know what issues to use on red-haired, left-handed Roman Catholic women between thirty-five and fifty, they can tell you. And neither Gore nor Bush was the kind of candidate who would tell the consultants to take a hike. So the campaign was a contest of contrived events and the careful projection of images. There was nothing that might have passed for political debate, although there were clear differences between Bush and Gore on many issues.

The candidates followed timetables that were intended to produce a single result, a "hit" on the television network news programs each evening. Success in achieving that goal was the measuring stick of the campaign. Even with the proliferation of cable outlets and other sources of what passed for information, the political strategists understood that the first priority was always the broadcast networks. We in the print press understood it as well.

Because the candidates were so controlled—heaven forbid they should act like fallible human beings even for a moment—the campaign was remarkably sterile. Much of the contest seemed to be exchanges of charges and countercharges by the flacks for the two candidates, dutifully reported by even the best mainstream newspapers in the absence of any revealing rhetoric from the principals. I never understood why it was news when a hired hand working for Bush attacked Gore or vice versa. That seemed to me to be dog biting man, not the reverse, and thus not news. But the voters seemed easily manipulated. Most of them weren't paying much attention anyway, and there was a conspicuous lack of enthusiasm in both parties. This was apparent in the development of a seesaw pattern in the daily polling during the general election campaign. If Bush ran clearly ahead for a few days, the numbers would suddenly re- verse themselves, as if the voters were saying, "Wait a minute, we can't have this dumb cluck for president." But when Gore moved ahead, there was a similar correction, as if voters were saying, "Wait a minute, we can't have four years of this stiff."

My nose was also out of joint about what had happened to my business. Anyone could claim to be a political reporter without re- gard to whether they knew any of the principals or the history or the demographics or the political dynamics. When a candidate traveled with two busloads of reporters and a dozen television camera crews, foreign and domestic, they became a spectacle that was grist for their own mills. During the primaries and nominating conventions, we were covering a phenomenon we had created.

Every news organization of even the most modest pretensions seemed to require its own correspondent reporting from the scene, as if he or she knew something. Shortly before the primary a friend from the State Department asked me to participate in a briefing for foreign reporters in New Hampshire. It turned out there were fifty or more of them, few of whom had even the foggiest idea what was going on. But even among American news operations, there was no premium on either knowledge or sources. I recall a night late in the New Hampshire primary campaign when I was having dinner with Bill Daley, then the secretary of commerce, and Charles Campion, a professional with the Dewey Square Group in Boston. We were at Richard's Bistro in Manchester, the restaurant of choice in the last two presidential campaign cycles, and there were two or three tables of other reporters in the room. During dinner several of them sidled up to the table to speak to Daley, perhaps hoping for a quote to lend verisimilitude to their stories or expense accounts. But it was clear that none of them recognized Chuck Campion, one of the Demo- crats who knew the most about New Hampshire primaries dating back to his service as Walter Mondale's campaign coordinator there in 1984. I don't mean to judge these reporters harshly. I have been just as clueless when tossed into covering stories about foreign af- fairs and environmental issues, to cite just two areas of my igno- rance. But many of these people were covering the campaign by reading *The Boston Globe* and watching Channel 9 in Manchester. You could find them standing in the back of the room at rallies, peering intently at the audience and candidates and stroking their chins thoughtfully. In some cases, these were instant experts serving as television pundits or columnists for some obscure magazine or website while observing their first primary campaign, and I wondered what basis they had for comparisons and judgments about how a candidate was "doing" this time. Their reporting inevitably was derivative.

There was, nonetheless, a brief period early in the campaign when I and many of my colleagues and competitors became entranced by the notion that 2000 could be a different year in which the candidates anointed by money and establishment support would be defeated by maverick challengers: Bill Bradley in the Democratic competition, and John McCain on the Republican side. I felt like a journalistic Charlie Brown, racing up once more to kick the football and hoping Lucy wouldn't pull it away again.

I found Bradley particularly intriguing during the early 1999 stages of the campaign for the Iowa precinct caucuses and New Hampshire primary, which would initiate the convention delegate selection early in 2000. At this point, Gore had not shown his limits as a campaigner and Bradley was taking a fresh approach by, among other things, giving a prominent priority to race relations. In a sense, this was counterintuitive for Democrats of the Bill Clinton era. In the aftermath of the defeats suffered by the devoutly liberal Mondale in 1984 and Michael Dukakis in 1988, the smart strategy for Democrats had become one of muting their identification with blacks while strengthening their rapport with conservative working-class whites. That was precisely the strategy Bill Clinton had used in 1992 when he emphasized welfare reform and deliberately affronted Jesse Jackson. And Democratic politicians, both black and white, had taken approving notice. As Adlai Stevenson put it, the first duty of any politician is to win the election.

But Bradley wanted to confront the racial divide. Like several other politicians who had been professional athletes—Jack Kemp is one obvious Republican example—"Dollar Bill" Bradley, late of the New York Knicks, had the kind of rapport with blacks developed through common undertakings. And, he told me one day in Iowa, he could not believe most Democrats wouldn't welcome what he was saying on the race question. I found his confidence naïve but nonetheless beguiling.

The former senator from New Jersey had other problems as a candidate, however. He was sometimes aloof and withdrawn. He did not always suffer fools gladly, a quality I admired but not one often found in successful politicians. Bradley also made a politically fatal strategic error in deciding to compete against Gore in Iowa, where the vice president's support from unions and other party interest groups gave him a formidable advantage in the kind of organization politics that makes the difference in caucuses. In their one debate in Iowa, Bradley allowed Gore to whack him without snapping back. He seemed to believe the campaign was an educational experience, and I began to think of him as a tall Dukakis. Even after losing badly in Iowa, however, Bradley ran a strong race against Gore in New Hampshire, which the Democrats should have recognized as an early indicator of the vice president's weakness. Instead, the party elders and power brokers rallied around Gore and drove Bradley out of the campaign.

The most intriguing phenomenon of the 2000 campaign was, however, Senator John S. McCain of Arizona. He proved in the New Hampshire primary campaign that a candidate could prosper politically by saying precisely what was on his mind day after day—indeed, in his case, hour after hour—without filtering everything to fit some consultant's prescription. When McCain, racing around the state in his "Straight Talk Express" bus, said something politically stupid, he didn't hesitate to correct it a few miles down the road. He wasn't perfect by any means, but he was authentic, and he didn't have to be cosseted or hidden. Real people make mistakes and the voters understand that much.

Many Bush operatives and supporters, and a few Democrats, attacked the press for its love affair with McCain. He was playing to us by being so constantly available and, our critics said, we were all being led down the garden path. But they missed the point. We were not causing the McCain phenomenon; we were reflecting it and reporting it, even if we were also enjoying it.

The New Hampshire primary campaign was ideal for a candidate such as McCain trying to compensate for less money with his unorthodox approach. The significant thing is that the campaign went on for long enough—through most of 1999 as well as January of 2000—that McCain had the time to become known as something more than a heroic naval officer who had spent five years in North Vietnamese prison camps. It was a campaign in which the small indicators of his independence and authenticity could send ripples to reach an ever-widening circle of Republicans and independents eligible to vote in the primary. He also was appealing to a surprising number of Democrats despite his conservative positions on such issues as abortion rights. With McCain, the specific issues seemed less important than the persona.

I had a chance to watch this ripple effect in Milford, New Hampshire, a town I had chosen early in 1999 to visit every month to monitor how the primary was playing out in one community. When I made my first visits in May and June, there was the predictable evidence of support for George W. Bush, whom the opinion polls at the time showed holding more than 50 percent of the likely primary vote. McCain was just another of the also-rans with Elizabeth Dole, Pat Buchanan, Lamar Alexander, and John Kasich. But a man named Jack Spanos, a Republican town chairman, surprised me by not joining in the establishment support for Bush. He knew the son of the former president was the candidate of Senator Judd Gregg and almost everyone else of any stature in the Republican hierarchy other than Senator Bob Smith, who was off on some bizarre presidential campaign of his own. But Spanos said he had noticed that when the Kosovo issue arose in Washington, McCain had spoken out rather than joining most Republicans in ducking the question. And he had heard of McCain's maverick sponsorship of a campaign-finance reform bill. As the year passed I heard similar things from a growing number of Republicans in Milford. John McCain was still a minor player in the polls, but people were talking about his independence and candor.

In the end, McCain became one of those rare candidates who, in the favored phrase of politics, "catch fire." As he went from one town meeting to another, the crowds grew more substantial and more enthusiastic and his position in the polls improved dramatically. He won the Republican primary by 19 percent, a staggering margin considering the advantages of money and alliances enjoyed by George W. Bush. Many voters had come to see what Jack Spanos saw seven or eight months earlier.

As it turned out, however, it didn't matter. Bush returned to Austin for a weekend of meetings with his strategists, then stepped out of a telephone booth Monday morning to announce he was "a reformer with results," the implication obviously being that McCain was an ineffectual reformer. Bush's description of himself was ludicrous, given his record as governor of Texas. So far as anyone knew, the only thing he had ever reformed was his drinking habit. But he was a disciplined candidate with a disciplined campaign behind him. For a week or ten days, both the candidate and his surrogates kept repeating that line about "reformer with results," and every time the candidate faced the television cameras there was a blue curtain backdrop with shiny silver letters carrying the same message. It worked. Voters are lazy and not very interested, so they will fall for anything if they hear it often enough. Ten days after Bush started using the phrase, polls showed that Republican primary voters considered him and McCain both to be "reformers" in about equal measure.

McCain made some mistakes of his own, and the post–New Hampshire primaries didn't offer him such hospitable ground. In some of them, independents were not allowed to vote. In others, the alarmed party hierarchy rallied their forces against this maverick from Arizona who seemed so determined to interfere with the regular order of things Republican. In none of them did McCain have the opportunity for prolonged exposure to the voters. So, once again, we learned that you can't fight city hall.

There also was an important lesson about the press in the ability of Bush to come back so quickly with a combination of his new message of reform and some extremely nasty attacks on McCain. It demonstrated that the so-called mainstream press was essentially powerless in debunking or rebutting big lies and negative attacks. At one point in South Carolina, for example, the Bush campaign produced some codger who headed an obscure veterans organization —or at least had a letterhead claiming as much—who accused McCain of failing to stand up for veterans during his years in the House of Representatives and Senate. Given McCain's history in Vietnam, it was an outrageous accusation. But Americans are so uninterested and the news media so ineffectual that there is no penalty for bad behavior in American politics.

The demise of both Bradley and McCain left slim pickings for a political reporter or, for that matter, the voters. We were treated to a campaign of Bush trying to demonstrate gravitas and Gore trying to settle on a personality that would appeal to voters. Neither succeeded. And neither did Ralph Nader, who frittered away the thirty years of credibility he had earned for good causes by indulging his ego. His premise that there was no difference between the two major parties and their candidates was ridiculous, as Bush demonstrated as soon as he took office. (Does anyone really believe Gore would have chosen a John Ashcroft for attorney general?) But the fact that so many voters were put off by Bush and Gore made it inevitable that some would grasp at straws.

And, once again, the press fell short in teaching the politics of the Real World. We simply failed to reach too many Americans with an accurate picture of the choice they were being offered. Bush kept making moderate gestures that we were too ready to appreciate because he was so much more amiable than the Newt Gingrichs or Tom DeLays or Dick Armeys of the Republican Party. And when he managed to make it through the first televised debate without making some outrageous gaffe, we were quick to assure everyone he had crossed the threshold to at least acceptable gravitas. This might not have happened if Al Gore had been a more persuasive alternative, but the picture of Bush was never sharply projected.

The clearest proof of our failure as reporters is that we never managed to convey a picture of the candidates perceptive enough to tell us which one might be best equipped to confront a crisis such as the one visited on America by terrorists on September 11, 2001, only ten months after the election.

For me, the saving grace in the general election campaign was Pennsylvania, the largest of the five industrial swing states that usually decide presidential elections (the others are Illinois, Ohio, Michigan, and New Jersey). I used it as a political barometer as Milford had been during the New Hampshire primary, visiting every three or four weeks to try to measure the way the campaign was playing out with different groups of voters. Along the way I met a lot of local politicians and ordinary Americans who were puzzled by the choice they were being offered. And I spent some time with two Pennsylvania politicians—Governor Tom Ridge, a Republican, and former Mayor Ed Rendell of Philadelphia, a Democrat—who made me wonder about our political values. It seemed to me, for one thing, that Ridge, a self-made political success, would have been a far more formidable and impressive presidential candidate than George W. Bush. Ridge made no secret of his ambitions for higher office. If he could have raised the money that is the first essential, he might have been a strong presidential candidate. That being impossible, he was still a logical choice, in terms of both background and skills, for the vice presidency. But in the Republican Party of the era, his support for abortion rights, albeit with some restrictions, made him essentially ineligible for the ticket.

The tail also seemed to be wagging the dog on the Democratic side. Al Gore was clearly qualified by experience and intellect to be president. As we have seen, it doesn't take much. But Gore lacked the personal force and perhaps the self-assurance to capture and hold the attention of the electorate. By contrast, Rendell, serving as the party's national chairman in the final days of the Clinton presidency, made the case for Gore and the eight-year Clinton-Gore record on the economy in far more vivid terms than the vice president himself ever managed.

But, for a reporter, watching Tom Ridge and Ed Rendell show how it should be done was not enough to compensate for the national embarrassment of the 2000 campaign. Maybe we'll get it right next time, but I wouldn't bet on it.

INDEX

ABOUT THE TYPE

This book was set in Fairfield, the first typeface from the hand of the distinguished American artist and engraver Rudolph Ruzicka (1883–1978). Rudolph Ruzicka was born in Bohemia and came to America in 1894. He set up his own shop, devoted to wood engraving and printing, in New York in 1913 after a varied career working as a wood engraver, in photo-engraving and banknote printing plants, and as an art director and freelance artist. He designed and illustrated many books, and was the creator of a considerable list of individual prints—wood engravings, line engravings on copper, and aquatints.